Forensic Language
and the Day of the Lord Motif
in Second Thessalonians 1
and the Effects on the Meaning of the Text

WEST Theological Monograph Series

Wales Evangelical School of Theology (WEST) has produced a stream of successful PhD candidates over the years, whose work has consistently challenged the boundaries of traditional understanding in both systematic and biblical theology. Now, for the first time, this series makes significant examples of this ground-breaking research accessible to a wider readership.

Forensic Language and the Day of the Lord Motif in Second Thessalonians 1 and the Effects on the Meaning of the Text

Matthew D. Aernie

WEST Theological Monograph Series

WIPF & STOCK · Eugene, Oregon

FORENSIC LANGUAGE AND THE DAY OF THE LORD MOTIF IN SECOND
THESSALONIANS 1 AND THE EFFECTS ON THE MEANING OF THE TEXT

Copyright © 2011 Matthew D. Aernie. All rights reserved. Except for brief quotations in critical publications or reviews, no part of this book may be reproduced in any manner without prior written permission from the publisher. Write: Permissions, Wipf and Stock Publishers, 199 W. 8th Ave., Suite 3, Eugene, OR 97401.

Wipf & Stock
An Imprint of Wipf and Stock Publishers
199 W. 8th Ave., Suite 3
Eugene, OR 97401
www.wipfandstock.com

ISBN 13: 978-1-61097-486-8
Manufactured in the U.S.A.

All scripture quotations, unless otherwise indicated, are taken from the Holy Bible, New International Version®, NIV®. Copyright ©1973, 1978, 1984 by Biblica, Inc.™ Used by permission of Zondervan. All rights reserved worldwide.

Contents

List of Abbreviations / vii
Acknowledgments / xv
Introduction / xvii

1 Preliminary Issues Surrounding Second Thessalonians / 1

2 Paul's Heritage and Theological Background / 22

3 Acts 17:1–9 and the Conflict at Thessalonica / 45

4 The Judicial Language of 2 Thess 1 / 69

5 The Theological Significance of Judicial Language in 2 Thess 1:1–12 / 116

6 The Theological Significance of the Judicial Language in 2 Thess 1 in Relation to the Entire Epistle / 148

7 Conclusion / 175

Bibliography / 183
Author Index / 213
Scripture Index / 222

List of Abbreviations

AB	*Anchor Bible*
ABD	*Anchor Bible Dictionary.* Edited by D. N. Freedman. 6 vols. New York: Doubleday, 1992.
Aeg	*Aegyptus*
AJT	*American Journal of Theology*
AnBib	*Analecta biblica*
AOAT	*Alter Orient und Altes Testament*
AsTJ	*Asbury Theological Journal*
ATD	*Das Alte Testament Deutsch*
AThR	*Anglican Theological Review*
AUSS	*Andrews University Seminary Studies*
BBR	*Bulletin for Biblical Research*
BDAG	Bauer, W., F. W. Danker, W. F. Arndt, and F. W. Gingrich, eds. *Greek-English Lexicon of the New Testament and Other Early Christian Literature.* 3rd ed. Chicago: University of Chicago Press, 2000.
BDB	Brown, F., S. R. Driver, and C. A. Briggs, eds. *The Brown-Driver-Briggs Hebrew and English Lexicon: With an Appendix Containing the Biblical Aramaic; Coded with the Numbering System from Strong's Exhaustive Concordance of the Bible.* Peabody, MA: Hendrickson, 1996. Reprint, 2004.
BDF	Blass, F., A. Debrunner, and R. W. Funk, eds. *A Greek Grammar of the New Testament and Other Early Christian Literature.* Chicago: University of Chicago Press, 1961.

BECNT	Baker Exegetical Commentary on the New Testament
BETL	Bibliotheca ephemeridum theologicarum lovaniensium
BGU	Aegyptische Urkunden aus den Königlichen Staatlichen Museen zu Berlin: Griechische Urkunden. 15 vols. Brussels: Weidmannsche Buchhandlung, 1977.
Bib	Biblica
BIS	Biblical Interpretation Series
BJRL	Bulletin of the John Rylands University Library of Manchester
BN	Biblische Notizen
BNTC	Black's New Testament Commentaries
BR	Biblical Research
BSac	Bibliotheca sacra
BZNW	Beihefte zur Zeitschrift für die neutestamentliche Wissenschaft
CBQ	Catholic Biblical Quarterly
CGTC	Cambridge Greek Testament Commentary
CIG	Corpus inscriptionum graecarum. Edited by A. Boeckh, J. Franz, E. Curtius, A. Kirchhoff, and H. Roehl. 4 vols. Berlin: Ex Officina Academica, Vendit G. Reimeri Libraria, 1828–77.
ConBNT	Coniectanea biblica: New Testament Series
CP	Classical Philology
CTJ	Calvin Theological Journal
CurTM	Currents in Theology and Mission
DNTB	Dictionary of New Testament Background. Edited by Craig A. Evans and Stanley E. Porter. Downers Grove, IL: InterVarsity Press, 2000.
DOTP	Dictionary of the Old Testament: Pentateuch. Edited by Desmond T. Alexander and David W. Baker. Downers Grove, IL: InterVarsity Press, 2003.
DPL	Dictionary of Paul and His Letters. Edited by Gerald F. Hawthorne, Ralph P. Martin, and Daniel G. Reid. Downers Grove, IL: InterVarsity Press, 1993.

EBib	*Etudes bibliques*
EDNT	*Exegetical Dictionary of the New Testament.* Edited by H. Balz and G. Schneider. 3 vols. Grand Rapids, MI: Eerdmans, 1990–93.
EKKNT	*Evangelisch-katholischer Kommentar zum Neuen Testament*
EstBib	*Estudios bíblicos*
ETL	*Ephemerides theologicae lovanienses*
EvQ	*Evangelical Quarterly*
ExpTim	*Expository Times*
FAT	*Forschungen zum Alten Testament*
FOTL	*Forms of the Old Testament Literature*
GNS	*Good News Studies*
GTJ	*Grace Theological Journal*
HDB	*A Dictionary of the Bible.* Edited by James H. Hastings. 5 vols. New York: Charles Scribner's Sons, 1906–1911.
HNT	*Handbuch zum Neuen Testament*
HTKNT	*Herders theologischer Kommentar zum Neuen Testament*
HTR	*Harvard Theological Review*
ICC	*International Critical Commentary*
IEJ	*Israel Exploration Journal*
IG	*Inscriptiones graecae.* Edited by W. Dittenberger, K. Otto, H. von Gaertringen, and F. Freiherr. Editio minor. Berlin: apud G. Reimerum, 1897–1908.
Int	*Interpretation*
ITS	*International Theological Studies*
JBL	*Journal of Biblical Literature*
JETS	*Journal of the Evangelical Theological Society*
JJS	*Journal of Jewish Studies*
JLR	*Journal of Law and Religion*
JRS	*Journal of Roman Studies*
JSJSup	*Journal for the Study of Judaism: Supplement Series*

JSNT	Journal for the Study of the New Testament
JSNTSup	Journal for the Study of the New Testament: Supplement Series
JSOT	Journal for the Study of the Old Testament
JSOTSup	Journal for the Study of the Old Testament: Supplement Series
JTS	Journal of Theological Studies
L&N	Greek-English Lexicon of the New Testament: Based on Semantic Domains. Edited by J. P. Louw and E. A. Nida. 2nd ed. New York: United Bible Societies, 1989.
LNTS	Library of New Testament Studies
LSJ	Liddell, Henry George, Robert Scott, Henry Stuart Jones, and Roderick McKenzie, eds. A Greek-English Lexicon. 9th ed. With revised supplement. Oxford: Clarendon, 1996.
LTQ	Lexington Theological Quarterly
LXX	Septuagint
MDAI	Mitteilungen des Deutschen archäologischen Instituts
MM	Moulton, James H., and George Milligan, eds. The Vocabulary of the Greek Testament. London: Hoddern and Stoughton, 1930. Reprint, Peabody, MA, 1997.
MNTC	Moffatt New Testament Commentary
NAC	New American Commentary
NCBC	New Century Bible Commentary
NewDocs	New Documents Illustrating Early Christianity. Edited by G. H. R. Horsley, S. Llewelyn, R. A. Kearsley, and M. Harding. North Ryde, NSW: Ancient History Documentary Research Centre, Macquarie University, 1981–.
NIBCNT	New International Biblical Commentary on the New Testament
NICNT	New International Commentary on the New Testament
NIDNTT	New International Dictionary of New Testament Theology. Edited by Colin Brown. 4 vols. Grand Rapids, MI: Regency Reference Library, 1975–78.

NIDOTTE	*New International Dictionary of Old Testament Theology and Exegesis*. Edited by Willem VanGemeren. 5 vols. Carlisle: Paternoster Press, 1997.
NIGTC	New International Greek Testament Commentary
NovT	*Novum Testamentum*
NovTSup	Novum Testamentum Supplements
NTG	New Testament Guides
NTS	*New Testament Studies*
NTTS	New Testament Tools and Studies
OCD	*Oxford Classical Dictionary*. Edited by S. Hornblower and A. Spawforth. 3rd ed. Oxford: Oxford University Press, 1996.
OGIS	*Orientis graeci inscriptiones selectae*. Edited by W. Dittenberger. 2 vols. Hildesheim: G. Olms, 1960.
OTL	Old Testament Library
OtSt	*Oudtestamentische Studiën*
P.Cair.	*Zenon Papyri: Catalogue général des antiquités Zen égyptiennes du Musée du Caire*. Edited by C. C. Edgar. 5 vols. Le Caire: Imprimerie de l'Institut Francais d'Archeologie Orientale, 1925-40.
P.Gen	*Les Papyrus de Genève*. Edited by J. Nicole, P.Schubert, I. Jornot, and C. Wehrli. 3 vols. Amsterdam: Hakkert, 1967-96.
PGM	*Papyri graecae magicae: Die griechischen Zauberpapyri*. Edited by K. Preisendanz. Stuttgart: Teubner, 1973-74.
P.Hib.	*The Hibeh Papyri*. Edited by B. P. Grenfell, A. S. Hunt, G. Turner, and M. T. Lenger. 2 vols. London: Egypt Exploration Fund, 1906-1955.
P.Lips.	*Griechische Urkunden der Papyrussammlung zu Leipzig*. Edited by C. Wessely, L. Mitteis, and R. Duttenhöfer. Leipzig: Teubner, 1885-2002.
PNTC	Pillar New Testament Commentary

P.Oxy.	Oxyrhynchus Papyri. Various editors. 68 vols. London: Egypt Exploration Society in Graeco-Roman Memoirs, 1898–2003.
P.Ryl.	Catalogue of the Greek and Latin Papyri in the John Rylands Library, Manchester. Edited by A. S. Hunt, J. de M. Johnson, V. Martin, C. H. Roberts, and E. G. Turner. 4 vols. Manchester: Manchester University Press, 1911–1952.
P.Tebt.	The Tebtunis Papyri. Various editors. 5 vols. London: Oxford University Press, 1902–2005.
PWSup	Supplement to A. F. Pauly. Paulys Realencyclopädie der classischen Altertumswissenschaft. New edition G. Wissowa. 49 vols. Chicago: Ares, 1980.
RB	Revue biblique
REJ	Revue des études juives
ResQ	Restoration Quarterly
RevExp	Review and Expositor
RSCT	Rutherford Studies in Contemporary Theology
RTR	Reformed Theological Review
SBJT	Southern Baptist Journal of Theology
SBLDS	Society of Biblical Literature Dissertation Series
SBLMS	Society of Biblical Literature Monograph Series
SBLSP	Society of Biblical Literature Seminar Papers
SCS	Septuagint Commentary Series
SEG	Supplementum epigraphicum graecum
SEÅ	Svensk exegetisk årsbok
SIG	Sylloge inscriptionum graecarum. Edited by W. Dittenberger. 3rd ed. 4 vols. Leipzig: S. Hirzel, 1915–1924.
SNTSMS	Society for New Testament Studies Monograph Series
SocAn	Sociological Analysis
SP	Sacra pagina
StudTheol	Studia Theologica

TDNT	*Theological Dictionary of the New Testament.* Edited by G. Kittel and G. Friedrich. Translated by G. W. Bromiley. 12 vols. Grand Rapids, MI: Eerdmans, 1964–76.
TDOT	*Theological Dictionary of the Old Testament.* Edited by G. J. Botterweck and H. Ringgren. Translated by J. Willis. 15 vols. Grand Rapids, MI: Eerdmans, 1974–2006.
Them	*Themelios*
TLNT	*Theological Lexicon of the New Testament.* Edited by Ceslas Spicq. Translated and edited by J. D. Ernest. 3 vols. Peabody, MA: Hendrickson, 1994.
TLOT	*Theological Lexicon of the Old Testament.* Edited by Ernst Jenni and Claus Westermann. Translated by M. E. Biddle. 3 vols. Peabody, MA: Hendrickson, 1997.
TWOT	*Theological Workbook of the Old Testament.* Edited by R. L. Harris and G. L. Archer. 2 vols. Chicago: Moody Press, 1980.
TynBul	*Tyndale Bulletin*
TZ	*Theologische Zeitschrift*
VT	*Vetus Testamentum*
VTSup	*Vetus Testamentum Supplements*
WBC	*Word Biblical Commentary*
WEC	*Wycliffe Exegetical Commentary*
WLQ	*Wisconsin Lutheran Quarterly*
WMANT	*Wissenschaftliche Monographien zum Alten und Neuen Testament*
WTJ	*Westminster Theological Journal*
WUNT	*Wissenschaftliche Untersuchungen zum NeuenTestament*
ZNW	*Zeitschrift für die neutestamentliche Wissenschaft und die Kunde der älteren Kirche*
ZTK	*Zeitschrift für Theologie und Kirche*

Acknowledgments

WORDS CANNOT EXPRESS HOW truly grateful I am for the privilege the Lord has afforded me to publish this monograph. It is my prayer that this work would bring Him glory and encourage Christians to remain steadfast in advancing the gospel of the Lord Jesus Christ.

This monograph initially appeared as a doctoral dissertation presented to and accepted by the University of Wales Lampeter (now University of Wales Trinity St. David) under the supervision of Drs. Tom Holland and Kathy Ehrensperger. I am thankful to Dr. Ehrensperger who offered significant criticisms that enhanced the overall argument of this work. I owe a special debt of gratitude to my direct supervisor Dr. Holland for his scholarly insights and suggestions, which have proven invaluable for this work. His passion for seeing Old Testament motifs fulfilled in the New Testament has cultivated in me a greater appreciation for the scriptures. It truly was a privilege to sit under his tutelage. Further thanks must be extended to Dr. Alan Tomlinson who initially discussed the forensic nature of 2 Thessalonians and encouraged further inquiry into the subject. Furthermore, I extend thanks to Kenzie Grubitz for her superb editing skills, Tina Campbell Owens for typesetting the material, and to Wipf and Stock for accepting this work for publication.

I would also like to extend my appreciation to Southeastern Bible College for their generous donation to the project. In addition, I would like to thank my extended family for their support in this endeavor. To my parents Debra Hansen and Robert Aernie as well as Gerry Hansen and Teri Aernie for their encouragement. To my brothers and their families Michael, Nicole, Haley Aernie and Dr. Jeffrey, Allison, Abigail and Chloe Aernie for their support. To my father and mother-in-law Paul and Harriet Lawrence for their tremendous interest in this project. Finally, I want to express my love and appreciation for my precious wife Bonnie. Her encouragement and support for her husband and this work was more than extraordinary. I thank the Lord for blessing me with you.

Introduction

For centuries, Christians have experienced persecutions for their faith in Christ and the message of the gospel. News of Christians around the world experiencing horrific and often deadly persecution is on the rise. Even today, many who follow Christ believe that the time is rapidly approaching when Christians can expect to be imprisoned for proclaiming the message of salvation in Christ alone in a culture that values diversity and tolerance. However, Christians should not be surprised to hear of persecution; their Lord, in fact, predicted it (Matt 24:9). Thus, for a Christian striving to bring a message of hope to those who follow Jesus Christ in a culture that denies absolute truth and for those who suffer or face death for the cause of Christ, the book of Second Thessalonians delivers a message that is starkly real and encouraging. Therefore, the message of the Thessalonian correspondence is as relevant today as it was for first-century Christians who undoubtedly experienced times of discouragement and wondered if their Lord would ever return and vindicate them for their steadfast perseverance in the midst of intense persecution.

The original contribution of the following work aims to demonstrate that an intentional forensic word grouping is not only evident throughout 2 Thess 1 but was derived from the theology of the Day of the Lord motif found throughout the Old Testament, rather than first-century Hellenistic culture. It will be argued that the apostle understood the Day of the Lord concept as a court day, which would be consummated at Christ's parousia. Furthermore, it is proposed that the legal language incorporated in 2 Thess 1 not only accentuates Paul's hermeneutic that the Old Testament understood the Day of the Lord as an appointed judicial day but that such judicial idioms were used to encourage the Thessalonian Christians to persevere, for they had not missed their day at court, where their vindication awaited.

This study is warranted since scholars are often too eclectic in their efforts to understand the theological background of Second Thessalonians and categorize Paul's theology as a Jewish/Hellenistic dichotomy. In fact, Hyam Maccoby has even suggested that "the central elements of Paul's thought are derived from Hellenistic religion."[1] Moreover, some have contended that Paul likely borrowed the forensic terms found throughout 2 Thess 1 from the Hellenistic political and legal arenas by comparing the coming of the emperor to the coming of Christ.[2] In other words, the judicial terminology was seemingly "Hellenized" by the apostle to communicate Christ's return to a predominately Gentile congregation. However, when considering Paul's intricate knowledge and familiarity with the Old Testament coupled with his devout Jewish heritage, it seems unlikely that he was dependent upon Hellenism for his theological instruction regarding Christ's return. Rather, it is more reasonable to conclude that the apostle intentionally utilized the numerous forensic idioms in 2 Thess 1 to emphasize that the Old Testament's theology regarding the Day of the Lord corresponds to the final eschatological court that will convene at Christ's return.

Therefore, the originality in this study is to demonstrate that the author of Second Thessalonians deliberately used forensic language, allusions, and idioms, specifically in chapter 1, in order to encourage the persecuted church to remain steadfast, for their vindication would come at the final assize. To support this thesis, it is suggested that such judicial language and allusions are an intertextual parallel originating primarily from the Day of Lord motif found throughout the Old Testament. Thus, it is maintained that the Day of the Lord concept was likely understood by the author of Second Thessalonians as referring to an appointed court day when the Lord would render righteous verdicts upon those who had both obeyed and disobeyed him. It is proposed, then, that the author of Second Thessalonians likely understood the Day of the Lord to be accomplished at the parousia of Christ, when the final court would convene. Therefore, borrowing from the judicial concept apparent in the Day of the Lord motif, it is suggested that the author intentionally utilized a forensic word grouping throughout 2 Thess 1 to encourage the church to remain faithful amidst great opposition as they awaited their

---

1. Maccoby, *Paul and Hellenism*, 182–83. See also Schnelle, *Apostle Paul*, 75–81.

2. See, for example, G. Green, *Thessalonians*, 291 n. 19; H. Koester, *Paul and His World*, 59–66.

ultimate justification at God's eschatological tribunal. It is proposed that analysis of such language is important for discovering the author's original intent, which, as is argued here, was to bring a message of hope that God would vindicate the persecuted Christians in Thessalonica. Such a message is seemingly relevant to Christians of any age who are experiencing the sufferings that come with standing for Christ in a culture that wants to silence both the message and the messenger.

1

Preliminary Issues Surrounding Second Thessalonians

THE SCHOLARLY DEBATE REGARDING Second Thessalonians mostly centers upon the issue of the "man of lawlessness" in chapter 2. Much has been written on the identity of this individual as well as the extent of his authority on the earth. Many authors often seem too enamored with this issue, to the extent that they may have misunderstood the purpose for the letter. The importance of this study, therefore, is to explore exegetically how the author used legal language and imagery in order to encourage the persecuted church at Thessalonica to continue in their perseverance, by reminding them that the Lord would return as the righteous Judge at the final assize. Consequently, the Thessalonian Christians would be found innocent and vindicated at God's court while their persecutors would be sentenced to eternal punishment.

Before delving into the text and the pending subject matter, a discussion of two preliminary issues is warranted. The aim of this present chapter seeks briefly to discuss the historical setting of Thessalonica and the question of the epistle's authenticity. It will be suggested that a proper understanding of these introductory issues ultimately advances the argument that the author deliberately incorporated legal language and allusions to encourage the Thessalonian church in the midst of persecution. The result from the ensuing discussion seeks to promote a more exact analysis of the contextual setting surrounding the Thessalonian epistles as well as the theological background of the author.

1.1 HISTORICAL BACKGROUND OF THESSALONICA

A brief explanation of the historical significance of Thessalonica to Rome may enable a better understanding as to why the Thessalonian Christians experienced persecution from their fellow residents and why Paul's ministry in that city was interrupted.

Thessalonica was founded in 315–16 BC by Cassander, a general in the military regime of Alexander the Great.[1] He chose Thessalonica because of her prime location at the head of the Gulf of Therme in the Aegean Sea. This enabled him to have access to the major ports of Syria, Palestine, and Egypt. In addition, Thessalonica was situated along the Egnatian Way, which served as the main east–west and north–south trade route. Such a favorable location not only allowed for easy and faster travel but also provided the city with an ample amount of commerce. As a result of the city's premier locality near the sea and along the Egnatian Way, Thessalonica enjoyed financial prosperity and was considered the most prominent port in Macedonia.

After the death of Cassander, Macedonia experienced arduous times. His successor, Philip V, found himself in conflict with Rome because of his allegiance to Hannibal of Carthage, a known enemy of the emerging empire. Consequently, Rome considered Macedonia an enemy, which resulted in four Macedonian wars.[2] Rome's ultimate victory in the wars put an end to the Macedonian kingdom and made it a Roman province.[3]

The victory of Rome destroyed the economic structure of Macedonia. The Romans captured about one hundred and fifty thousand Macedonian slaves and exiled important Macedonian officials. The kingdom, now economically and politically ineffective, posed no threat to Rome. Nevertheless, Rome wanted her citizens to know that she was not interested in enslaving free people, but rather freeing enslaved people. Thus, the Roman Senate decided to give Macedonia her independence,

---

1. See Brocke, *Thessaloniki*, 12–20; Dionysius *Roman Antiquities* 1.49.4; Edson, "Cults of Thessalonica," 153; Strabo *Geography* 7.21; J. Hill, "Establishing the Church," 18–70; S. E. Johnson, "Apostle Paul in Macedonia," 75–83; McRay, "Thessalonica," 1231–33; Meeks, *First Urban Christians*, 46–47; Simpson, "Thessalonians," 932–39.

2. For further information regarding the Macedonian Wars, see Appian *Roman History* 2.9; Bruce, "Macedonia," 454–55; Hammond, "Macedonia," 904–5.

3. See Appian *Roman History* 2.9; Bruce, "Macedonia," 454–55; Hammond, "Macedonia," 904–5.

a limited freedom full of conditions instituted by Rome. Although this new "freedom" allowed the Macedonians to create their own laws and elect their own government officials, they were still required to pay a tribute to Rome. Furthermore, Macedonia was divided into four districts in order to prevent the province from becoming a unified kingdom with the ability to attack Rome.[4] Livy writes, "Their country seemed mangled as an animal disjointed into parts."[5] Such measures were taken in order to ensure complete Roman dominance over Macedonia.

By 149 BC, many of the Macedonian citizens became tired of Roman rule. In an attempt to overthrow Rome, many rebellions spawned but were quickly extinguished. Such insurrections caused Rome to tighten control over Macedonia, and as a result, in 148 BC, Rome decided to make Macedonia a province. Rebellions continued to follow, but they were quickly stifled as Rome held absolute control over Macedonia.

Thessalonica, however, supported Rome. It is believed that during the rebellion of Andriscus, Thessalonica paid tribute to Metellus, the Roman praetor, honoring him for his defeat of Andriscus and his rebels. For that reason, Rome favored Thessalonica because of her unwavering allegiance.[6]

When civil war broke out in 49 BC between Julius Caesar and Pompey, Thessalonica proved a vital city. During the war, Thessalonica became the capital of the Roman administration and was considered a "second Rome." With the assassination of Julius Caesar in 44 BC, Rome's leadership was disputed. Brutus and Cassius, who were responsible for murdering Caesar, began their quest for the supreme authority over Rome. As a result, Thessalonica found itself under the reign of Brutus until the battle of Philippi, where he and Cassius were defeated by Antony and Octavian in 42 BC.[7]

---

4. Being divided into four districts meant four different capital cities. The capital of the first district was Amphipolis, the capital of the second district was Thessalonica, the capital of the third district was Pella, and the capital of the fourth district was Pelagonia. See Strabo *Geography* 7 frag. 47 (48); Livy 45.29.9.

5. Livy 45.18, 29–30.

6. See Hendrix, "Thessalonicans Honor Romans," 20–21. Hendrix reproduces an inscription that reveals the Thessalonians' tribute to Metellus. The inscription does not specify the exact honors the Thessalonians afforded Metellus. However, Hendrix argues that it is possible that the inscription appeared at the base of a statue of Metellus. See also Mordtmann, "Funde," 164–65.

7. See Appian *Roman History* 4.15.113–14; 4.17.131–32; Hendrix, "Thessalonica,"

Consequently, Thessalonica found herself under the regime of Antony. The city fervently supported Antony and Octavian, bestowing upon them many great honors, which resulted in Thessalonica gaining the status of a free city in 42 BC.[8] In fact, Simpson has noted that Thessalonica "remained the most important and populous city of Macedonia into the third and fourth century A.D."[9] By 32 BC, tension between Octavian and Antony had increased as to who would be the sole ruler of Rome. The two forces clashed at the battle of Actium, where Octavian was victorious and subsequently assumed sole authority of the Roman Empire.[10] Again, Thessalonica pledged complete allegiance to Octavian, bestowing the same honor upon him as the city had upon Antony.

In 27 BC, Octavian, ruler over the empire, took the name Augustus, which as Ferguson notes "was an ancient word suggesting that he was numinous and something more than human . . . this was not a normal Roman name and was indicative of the unique position he held."[11] It was during this time that Augustus placed Thessalonica under the authority of the Roman Senate. The Senate "was below the Emperor and served as his Council of State and increasingly as the organ whereby he caused law to be made."[12] Thessalonica remained an ally of Rome and enjoyed political autonomy as a prominent city in Macedonia. There was, however, another change on the horizon.

The death of Augustus ushered in the Roman imperial period, which signified the end of the republic.[13] In fact, Shelton has noted that "in the first two centuries of the Imperial Period, the common people

---

524; Papazoglou, "Macedonia under the Romans," 195; Simpson, "City of Thessalonica," 933–34; Vacalopoulos, *History of Thessaloniki*, 13.

8. See, for example, Hendrix, "Thessalonica," 31–37; Simpson, "City of Thessalonica," 933.

9. Ibid.

10. See, for example, E. Ferguson, *Backgrounds of Early Christianity*, 25; Suetonius 1.20.

11. E. Ferguson, *Backgrounds of Early Christianity*, 25–30. See also Jewett, *Thessalonian Correspondence*, 126; Shelton, *As the Romans Did*, 386–87.

12. Wells, "Roman Empire," 803. See also Papazoglou, "Macedonia under the Romans," 196; Wiedemann, *Tiberius to Nero*, 198.

13. For a detailed timeline of the Roman imperial period, see Shelton, *As the Romans Did*, 455–56.

of Rome, Italy, and the provinces enjoyed remarkable prosperity and security."[14]

In AD 15, Tiberius, son of Livia, Octavian's second wife, succeeded his step-father as the second emperor of the Roman Empire and become the first monarch of the imperial period at the age of fifty-five.[15] During his reign, Tiberius decided to combine the Senate-governed Macedonia with Achaia and Moesia, at the request of Macedonia and Achaia. Their motive for this amalgamation was tax relief, since, according to Tacitus, these regions believed the tribute they were paying Rome was too high.[16] For Thessalonica, being governed by the Senate was advantageous, for it further demonstrated the city's loyalty to Rome:

> Imperial provinces were problematic and usually located along the frontiers of the Empire. They were under the direct control of the Emperor and required one or more legions to maintain security. Senatorial provinces were under the control of the senate. These were peaceful and did not need such a strong military presence.[17]

Although Emperor Claudius, Tiberius's nephew, dismantled this large province in AD 44, Thessalonica continued under the authority of the Roman Senate.[18]

The foregoing brief survey of Roman history pertaining to Thessalonica reveals the importance of its loyalty to Rome, in order to remain at peace with the empire and continue enjoying various privileges. Thus, Thessalonica's commitment to Rome may provide a more comprehensive understanding regarding why many residents adamantly opposed the author of the Thessalonian epistles during his stay, which will be further explored in chapter 3.

1.2 THE ISSUE OF AUTHENTICITY

Regarding the message of Second Thessalonians, it seems important to understand the theological background of the author. The issue of

---

14. Ibid.

15. See E. Ferguson, *Backgrounds of Early Christianity*, 30–31; Suetonius 3.24; Wiedemann, *Tiberius to Nero*, 201–221.

16. Tacitus *Histories* 1.76.4, 1.180.1.

17. G. Green, *Thessalonians*, 19; See also Vacalopoulos, *History of Thessaloniki*, 11–16; Tacitus *Histories* 1.76.4; Dio Cassius *Roman History* 60.24.

18. Dio Cassius *Roman History* 60.24.

Pauline authorship of Second Thessalonians is highly debated, and the following discussion seeks to explore whether Pauline authorship can be considered valid. In other words, if Paul did not write Second Thessalonians, it may be difficult to ascertain the author's theological background and motivations for incorporating legal language in the letter. However, if Second Thessalonians can be considered authentic, then it would seem reasonable to conclude that Paul likely used judicial language, metaphors, and allusions, drawn primarily from the Old Testament to encourage the Thessalonian congregation to remain steadfast until the parousia of the Lord.

Regarding *First Thessalonians*, the external evidence supporting Pauline authorship is significant.[19] Eusebius understood the letter to have been genuinely Pauline,[20] as did Tertullian[21] and Irenaeus.[22] Even Marcion believed the epistle to have been authentic.[23] Until World War II, the issue of Pauline authorship of First Thessalonians was virtually undisputed.[24] Today the majority of scholars maintain that First Thessalonians clearly portrays Paul as the author (1 Thess 1:1). As a result, Wanamaker claims that "no contemporary scholars of repute seem to doubt the authentic Pauline character of the letter."[25] Furthermore, Jewett comments that "a widely shared consensus emerged in twentieth-century scholarship that 1 Thessalonians is an indisputably authentic letter, reflecting the earliest phase of Pauline writing."[26]

The authenticity of Second Thessalonians, however, is a more complicated matter. Prior to World War II, the majority of scholars did not question Pauline authorship of Second Thessalonians. Indeed, Green writes that:

---

19. For a more detailed description of the external evidence, see Rigaux, *Saint Paul*, 112–20.

20. Eusebius *Ecclesiastical History* 3.3.5.

21. Tertullian *On the Resurrection of the Flesh* 24.

22. Irenaeus *Against Heresies* 5.6.1.

23. Tertullian *Against Marcion* 5.15. See also Bornemann, *Die Thessalonicherbriefe*, 319–20, cited in Malherbe, *Letters to the Thessalonians*, 349–50.

24. It was questioned by Baur, *Paulus*, 275–79. However, his arguments had no effect on the consensus of scholarship that First Thessalonians was Pauline.

25. Wanamaker, *Epistles to the Thessalonians*, 17.

26. Jewett, *Thessalonian Correspondence*, 3.

The ancient church was unanimous in its acceptance of this book as an authentic work of the apostle Paul. In fact, the external evidence in favor of its authenticity is even stronger than that of 1 Thessalonians.[27]

The external evidence attesting the authenticity of Second Thessalonians is also extensive.[28] Ancient writers, such as Polycarp,[29] Irenaeus,[30] Clement of Alexandria,[31] and Tertullian,[32] have affirmed the genuineness of the epistle. Coupled with the vast external evidence there is also the internal evidence that would seemingly put to rest any doubt of the letter's authenticity since the apostle apparently wrote, "I, Paul, write this greeting with my own hand, and this is a distinguishing mark in every letter; this is the way I write" (2 Thess 3:17). It would seem, then, from this verse, that the issue of authorship was settled. However, subsequent to World War II, many scholars have questioned the authenticity of the epistle and have postulated various conjectures regarding the authorship of Second Thessalonians.[33]

It was William Wrede's work in 1903 that brought the issue of authorship to the forefront.[34] He argued that with the vast similarities of both letters, Paul would not have needed to write a second letter, and therefore, according to Wrede, Second Thessalonians is a forgery.[35] Moreover, scholars such as Rudolf Bultmann[36] and Willi Marxsen[37] popularized the theory of an inauthentic Second Thessalonians. By and large, modern scholarship has continued to adhere to the inauthenticity of Second

---

27. G. Green, *Thessalonians*, 59. See also Blomberg, *From Pentecost to Patmos*, 151–52.

28. For a more detailed description, see Milligan, *St. Paul's Epistles*, lxxvi–xcii; Rigaux, *Saint Paul*, 112–20.

29. Polycarp *Letter to the Philippians* 11.3, 11.4.

30. Irenaeus *Against Heresies* 3.7.2.

31. Clement *The Stromata* 5.3.

32. Tertullian *The Soul* 57; *Against Marcion* 5.16.

33. For thorough chronological surveys regarding the authenticity of Second Thessalonians see McDonald and Porter, *Early Christianity*, 422–27; Wanamaker, *Epistles to the Thessalonians*, 17–28; Wikenhauser, *New Testament Introduction*, 368–72; Witherington, *1 and 2 Thessalonians*, 9–16.

34. Wrede, *Die Echtheit*, 32–36. See also Jewett, *Thessalonian Correspondence*, 5.

35. See, for example, Wrede, *Die Echtheit*, 32–36.

36. Bultmann, *Theology of the New Testament*, 131.

37. Marxsen, *Introduction*, 37–44.

Thessalonians, being indebted primarily to the arguments proposed by Wolfgang Trilling.[38] In his monograph, Trilling presents three reasons why he believes that "dieser Verfasser mit hoher Wahrscheinlichkeit nicht Apostel Paulus ist."[39]

Scholars who advocate the pseudonymity of Second Thessalonians generally follow a threefold argument. First, proponents contend that the similar style and vocabulary between First and Second Thessalonians demonstrates inauthenticity. Second, since the form of Second Thessalonians is identical to First Thessalonians, Paul would not have needed to repeat himself. Third, while Paul's theology is evident within the epistle, it is deficient in common Pauline themes.[40] All of these will be summarized, followed by an assessment of each.

According to the first argument, the great amount of similarity between First and Second Thessalonians, with regard to their style and vocabulary, proves inauthenticity.[41] In other words, it would seem that Paul wrote the same letter twice. Proponents of this view contend that Paul would not have needed to repeat what he previously wrote in First Thessalonians. I. Howard Marshall clarifies the essence of this argument with the following statement: "How can one explain why Paul should so slavishly have followed his earlier letter, particularly when one bears in mind that there is no other example in Paul's writings of such parallelism?"[42] Because it is uncharacteristic of Paul to use such repetition in his writings, those who advocate pseudonymity believe that First Thessalonians was copied in Second Thessalonians in a non-Pauline manner.[43] For example, J. Bailey has argued that the phrase "God our Father and the Lord Jesus Christ," which appears once in the salutation

---

38. Trilling, *Untersuchungen*. Recent scholars include Bailey, "Who Wrote II Thessalonians?" 131–45; Beker, *Heirs of Paul*, 73; R. Collins, *Letters*, 222–23; Gaventa, *First and Second Thessalonians*, 93–97; Richard, *First and Second Thessalonians*, 23–24; Robinson and Koester, *Trajectories through Early Christianity*, 153–54; B. Thurston, *Reading Colossians, Ephesians*, 160–61.

39. Trilling, *Untersuchungen*, 108.

40. See Wanamaker, *Epistles to the Thessalonians*, 22–26; Jewett, *Thessalonian Correspondence*, 10–16; Malherbe, *Letters to the Thessalonians*, 364–70.

41. While Trilling agrees that this first argument is not as strong as the others, he does contend that "Die von zusammengetragenen Merkmale gestatten allein kein Urteil über die Echtheit oder Unechtheit von II, sprechen aber mehr zugunsten der Unechtheit" (*Untersuchungen*, 57).

42. Marshall, *1 and 2 Thessalonians*, 29.

43. Bailey, "Who Wrote II Thessalonians?" 135.

of First Thessalonians but is then repeated in the salutation of Second Thessalonians, proves inauthenticity. He concludes that "such repetition occurs in the prescript of no other Pauline letter, and can best be explained as due to 1 Thessalonians being copied in 2 Thessalonians in an un-Pauline manner."[44]

Another example provided by Bailey, related to this first argument regarding similar style and vocabulary is the phrase ἔργου τῆς πίστεως (1 Thess 1:3; 2 Thess 1:2). He argues that the phrase "work of faith" in First Thessalonians means "a man's manner of life determined by his faith," but in Second Thessalonians it means "a work of God," which, he believes, proves that the author of Second Thessalonians (not Paul) utilized the apostle's vocabulary in order to pick up on an element found in First Thessalonians.[45]

A further characteristic of this first argument, which has been brought forward by such recent scholars as R. Collins and B. Thurston, is that while much of the vocabulary in Second Thessalonians is similar to First Thessalonians, the former epistle demonstrates a less personal tone than the latter.[46] Advocates of pseudonymity contend that First Thessalonians is much more amiable in comparison to Second Thessalonians. Collins offers an example that he believes proves the validity of this first argument. He maintains that the phrase εὐχαριστοῦμεν τῷ θεῷ πάντοτε περὶ πάντων ὑμῶν (1 Thess 1:2, 2:13) compared to the Second Thessalonians rendition, which adds the term ὀφείλομεν (2 Thess 1:3, 2:13), sounds less affectionate and proves that Paul is not the author. Collins assumes that:

> this difference in tone points to a different quality of relationship between the respective authors of 1 and 2 Thessalonians and the community at Thessalonica. Were the two letters to have been written by the apostle himself, he would have had to change his attitude toward the Thessalonian Christians rather radically in a very short space of time—a few months at most.[47]

In short, this first argument promoted by advocates for inauthenticity presumes that due to the similar style and vocabulary throughout

44. Ibid.
45. Ibid.
46. See, for example, R. Collins, *Letters*, 222–23; B. Thurston, *Reading Colossians, Ephesians*, 160.
47. R. Collins, *Letters*, 222–23.

both epistles, coupled with an apparent disengaged tone, the writer of Second Thessalonians copied part of First Thessalonians, thus proving pseudonymity.

However, two possible weaknesses must be explored regarding this first argument. First, the argument that Paul would not have duplicated his style and vocabulary in Second Thessalonians may neglect to consider the length of his stay at Thessalonica. The apostle was forced to leave the city abruptly, which caused his tenure there to be extremely short.[48] The brevity of his stay likely prevented him from fulfilling the necessary teaching ministry he normally performed among the newly established churches. Since Paul did not stay long in Thessalonica, it is probable that he would have communicated with these new believers using vocabulary that they had become familiar with during his ministry among them. Second, while proponents such as Trilling agree that the vocabulary of Second Thessalonians is Pauline,[49] they also contend that the usage of over forty unusual expressions found throughout the letter confirms inauthenticity.[50] In fact, Trilling argues that it is the distinct *apocalyptic* expressions of Second Thessalonians that prove it was not written by the apostle.[51] But unique apocalyptic expressions hardly establish that Second Thessalonians is pseudonymous, and thus, caution must be observed when placing limitations on how Paul expressed eschatological events. Even Maarten J. J. Menken, a proponent for the inauthenticity of Second Thessalonians, recognizes this when he writes:

> In general, Paul is able to express his ideas in various ways, dependent upon the situation of his audiences and of himself . . . and when it comes to a description of what will happen at God's final intervention in human history, it is only to be expected that a variety of ideas and images will be used.[52]

---

48. See chapter 3 for a discussion on the length of Paul's stay in Thessalonica.

49. See Jewett, *Thessalonian Correspondence*, 10–11 n. 44. He comments that "the proportion of words peculiar to 2 Thessalonians is no higher than in 1 Thessalonians, and is proportionately lower than in the other Pauline letters." See also Morgenthaler, *Statistik*, 38.

50. See Trilling, *Untersuchungen*, 48–51. This list of expressions is borrowed from Rigaux, *Saint Paul*, 85–94 but was originally produced by Frame, *St. Paul to the Thessalonians*, 32–34.

51. Trilling, *Untersuchungen*, 57.

52. Menken, *2 Thessalonians*, 29–30.

Yet many argue that the different eschatological emphases found in Second Thessalonians are inconsistent with those of First Thessalonians and therefore prove the pseudonymity of the former. But such "inconsistencies" do not demand the inauthenticity of Second Thessalonians. John M. G. Barclay comments:

> Apocalypticists are notoriously slippery characters. Many apocalyptic works present conflicting scenarios of the end and inconsistent theses concerning signs of its imminence. That Paul should write both of these apocalyptic passages [1 Thess 4:13–5:13 and 2 Thess 2:1–12], and do so within a short space of time, is by no means impossible; why should his apocalyptic statements be any more consistent than his varied remarks about the law?[53]

Furthermore, if unusual expressions prove pseudonymity, it could be concluded that 1 Cor 15 must also be pseudonymous since that chapter is full of unique expressions.[54] But the vast majority of scholars overwhelmingly accept First Corinthians as authentic.

Consequently, it is reasonable to say that the first argument of similar vocabulary and unusual apocalyptic expressions as proof for the pseudonymity of Second Thessalonians may be unfounded. Paul had to address specific situations in particular contexts, and he did so in a variety of manners for the purpose of advancing the gospel and educating those to whom he ministered. The apostle was an exceptional communicator and therefore must not be limited in how he chose to convey his message. Moreover, the many Pauline similarities in the epistles may provide stronger evidence for the authenticity of Second Thessalonians rather than the inauthenticity.

Also noted above in this first argument was the issue of tone. It is believed that Paul could not have written Second Thessalonians because it lacks the personal tone that is so prevalent throughout First Thessalonians. But this fails to convince for two reasons. First, the context of the situation surrounding the Thessalonian church must be kept in mind. This newly formed church was experiencing severe persecution from their neighbors. They needed to be encouraged that God would vindicate them for their faithfulness and perseverance. Aware of their circumstances, the author exhorted the Thessalonian believers not to be led astray but to "stand firm and hold to the traditions which [they] were

---

53. Barclay, "Conflict in Thessalonica," 525.
54. See Wanamaker, *Epistles to the Thessalonians*, 21.

taught" (2 Thess 2:15). Thus, it seems that Paul is by no means impersonal, but rather he is encouraging the church to remain steadfast. Even Bailey recognizes that 2 Thess 1:7 and 3:1 contain personal warmth. Furthermore, the apostle informed the church that he and his companions "speak proudly of you among the churches of God" (2 Thess 1:4), which certainly does not reveal a cold tone.

The second reason this argument may be flawed is due to a misunderstanding of the phrase εὐχαριστεῖν ὀφείλομεν. Advocates for pseudonymity contend that the phrase εὐχαριστεῖν ὀφείλομεν, when compared to the phrase εὐχαριστοῦμεν τῷ θεῷ πάντοτε περὶ πάντων ὑμῶν, found in 1 Thess 1:2 and 2:13, sounds less affectionate, making it appear that Paul and his companions gave thanks for the Thessalonians out of sheer duty. Because such a formal attitude is uncommon in First Thessalonians, it therefore proves that Paul is not the author of Second Thessalonians. However, the phrase εὐχαριστεῖν ὀφείλομεν is often found in Jewish writings as an introductory prayer formula.[55] Evidence of such usage is found in Josephus, Philo, and the apostolic fathers regarding a person's thankfulness to God.[56] In such contexts, the attitude expressed is not one of "having to" give thanks, but rather it is an attitude of "wanting to" give thanks. This indication seems obvious from the syntax of the clause. The author wrote that he and his companions ought to give thanks τῷ θεῷ, making God the indirect object of their thanks. Grammatically this makes sense since indirect objects can only occur with *transitive* verbs that are in the *active* voice.[57] Furthermore, Paul added that it was ἄξιός for them to thank God for the Thessalonians' increasing faith and growing love. It was God who created faith and love among the Thessalonians, and it was with immense gratitude that Paul and his companions wanted to express their thanks to him. Furthermore, Malherbe contends that:

> had Paul wished to express an impersonal obligation, . . . he would have used a form of δεῖ ("to be necessary"). What he goes on to say further shows that he is anything but impersonal or cold.[58]

---

55. See Aus, "Liturgical Background," 432–38.

56. See, for example, Josephus *Antiquities* 8.2, 7; Philo *On the Special Laws* 1.224; 1 Clement 38.4; *Epistle of Barnabas* 5:3, 7:1.

57. See Wallace, *Greek Grammar*, 140–41; Porter, *Idioms*, 97–100. Wallace points out that occasionally indirect objects occur with transitive verbs in the middle voice.

58. Malherbe, *Letters to the Thessalonians*, 382.

Understanding ὀφείλομεν in this way demonstrates an expression of gratitude that God alone deserved thanks for what he had accomplished in Thessalonica, which arguably was precisely what Paul intended. Consequently, the apostle's use of the phrase εὐχαριστεῖν ὀφείλομεν may actually *strengthen* the notion for personal warmth and affection and, therefore, authenticity. Thus, Marshall has commented that "it is surely time that the myth of the cold tone of the letter was exploded."[59]

In conclusion, the assertions that similar style and vocabulary coupled with an apparent informal tone proves Second Thessalonians to be pseudonymous may be unconvincing. The many Pauline similarities in the epistles may actually provide stronger evidence for the authenticity of Second Thessalonians. As a result, Wannamaker has concluded that this line of reasoning is simply "a series of weak arguments based on marginal evidence [and] does not add up to a strong case."[60]

The second argument against the authenticity of Second Thessalonians, which was popularized by Trilling, is known as the "form-critical investigation."[61] Similar to form criticism, this argument looks at certain units in Second Thessalonians and compares them with similar units found in First Thessalonians. For instance, the introductory and concluding greetings are virtually identical in both epistles, which is something unusual to Paul's writing style. By examining this from the perspective of form criticism, it appears, according to those against Pauline authorship, that Second Thessalonians is not addressed to any congregation in particular, but is only instructive concerning the coming judgment and return of the Lord. The conclusion, then, from the form-critical analysis of both the initial and final greetings of the letters, presumes that Second Thessalonians is not as personal as First Thessalonians and therefore is not Pauline. Trilling concludes that the final greeting in Second Thessalonians has a more authoritative tone than a personable one.[62] The result of such form-critical analysis contends that, although the units are similar in these letters, they address either different situations or congregations. This has led Trilling and

---

59. Marshall, *1 and 2 Thessalonians*, 34.
60. Wanamaker, *Epistles to the Thessalonians*, 23.
61. Ibid., 23–25.
62. Ibid., 25. See also R. Collins, *Letters*, 222–23; G. S. Holland, *Tradition That You Received*, 59–63; Schmidt, *Syntactical Style*, 383–93.

other recent scholars to conclude that Second Thessalonians was not only pseudonymous but that:

> über solche einzelnen vagen Ansatzpunkte führt nur ein Urteil über den Charakter des Briefes im ganzen hinaus. Dafür muß wohl eine so weite Zeitspanne von ca. 80 n. Chr. bis in das frühe 2 Jahrhundert offengelassen werden.[63]

In other words, adherents of the form-critical argument contend that the introductory thanksgiving of 2 Thess 1:3–12 should be regarded as proof of inauthenticity, since it does not address any specific situation or community but is more didactic and concerned with instruction about the final judgment and the Day of the Lord. Since this does not coincide with Paul's normal writing of thanksgivings, some contend that the epistle must be pseudonymous. But this reasoning is faulty and lends itself to the question: what exactly is normative? For instance, Galatians, a letter predominately held as Pauline, does not include a thanksgiving; rather Paul began with a severe reprimand, which was certainly not normal for the apostle.[64] It seems most probable, then, that it was contextual situations that dictated why Paul wrote. The church in Galatia seemingly wanted to vindicate their desire to live under the old covenant of the law. Paul sternly addressed such a notion and reminded the Galatians of the true gospel. Likewise, in Second Thessalonians, the apostle addressed actual circumstances that surrounded the Thessalonian believers. Namely, they were experiencing persecutions for the sake of the gospel and needed more instruction regarding the return of the Lord and their final vindication (2 Thess 1:4–7). Furthermore, Paul *does* incorporate other didactic thanksgivings (2 Cor 1:3–7).[65]

Another reason based on form criticism for the pseudonymity of Second Thessalonians centers upon the eschatological teaching of 2:1–12. It is assumed that this section was based on material passed down from tradition and, therefore, would not be understood by a church comprised mainly of Gentiles.[66] However, this fails to convince for three reasons. First, in 1 Thess 4:13–18, Paul referred to the traditional teach-

---

63. Trilling, *Der zweite Brief*, 28.
64. Ibid., 24.
65. Marshall, *1 and 2 Thessalonians*, 35.
66. See, for example, Menken, *2 Thessalonians*, 28–29; Goguel, *Introduction au Nouveau Testament*, 335.

ing about the eschaton that came from Jesus himself and would have arguably been familiar to Gentiles (Matt 24:31). Second, Paul seemed not to have any reservations about using material that had been handed down as tradition (1 Cor 11:23–26, 15:3–7; Phil 2:6–11).[67] Third, as was his custom, when Paul arrived in Thessalonica, he entered into the synagogue to preach the gospel (Acts 14:1, 17:1–2, 17:17, 18:4). Jews, along with proselytes and God-fearing Gentiles, were present in the synagogue and would have heard Paul preach the gospel (Acts 13:16, 14:1, 17:4, 17:12, 18:5).[68] Undoubtedly, these Gentiles would have been familiar with the Old Testament since it was read and taught every Sabbath. Since the Gentiles who made up the Thessalonian church were "God-fearing Greeks," a stronger argument can be made that the predominate Gentile congregation in Thessalonica *would* have been familiar with the traditional Jewish apocalyptic teachings. The assumption, then, that the Thessalonian church would not have been familiar with traditional Jewish material is more than likely unfounded.

Finally, the form-critical argument often tries to prove pseudonymity based on the concluding salutation. Advocates for inauthenticity maintain that the final greeting is not only less personal and more authoritative but is also used as a means to deceive his audience to view the letter as Pauline. The apostle wrote in 3:17, "I, Paul, write this greeting with my own hand, and this is a distinguishing mark in every letter; this is the way I write." Scholars such as Bailey note that the apostle did not usually write his own signature and this verse was an attempt to alleviate the suspicion of a pseudonymous writer since in all likelihood there were letters circulating in Paul's name.[69] Others such as Perrin and Duling contend that 3:17 was written by a member of a "Pauline school" in order to deceive the readers that the epistle was written by Paul.[70] However, this understanding may be countered with the following critiques. First, if Second Thessalonians is believed to be pseudonymous because of a supposed impersonal addendum, then what is to be made of the authenticity of other Pauline letters? Such reasoning could lead

---

67. These first two reasons are from G. Green, *Thessalonians*, 62.

68. For further discussions regarding the presence of Gentiles in the synagogues see de Boer, "God-Fearers in Luke-Acts," 50–71; Gager, "Jews, Gentiles, and Synagogues," 91–99; Stenschke, *Luke's Portrait*, 310–15.

69. See Bailey, "Who Wrote II Thessalonians?" 138.

70. See Perrin and Duling, *New Testament*, 208–9.

to the conclusion that Romans and Galatians must be pseudonymous since they each contain more authoritative than personal concluding salutations.⁷¹ However, both epistles are predominately held to be unquestionably Pauline. Again, the perception that an alleged impersonal tone substantiates inauthenticity is baseless.

A second weakness of this argument is that it fails to consider the context of the Thessalonians' situation. According to 2 Thess 2:2, some form of false instruction under the pretext of Paul's name had been circulating regarding the Lord's return.⁷² By examining 2:2 in relation to 3:17, J. Hill asks, "How else would the real author [Paul] have approached such a misunderstanding?"⁷³ It could be that the most reasonable solution is that the false information that the church had received regarding the Day of the Lord prompted Paul to include the addendum of 3:17 to validate that the epistle was genuinely from him. Finally, Perrin and Duling contend that a member of a "Pauline school" composed the ending. However, as Wilder argues, "this theory presupposes *without external evidence* that a Pauline school existed after the death of that apostle."⁷⁴

Regarding the context of the epistle and the reference to the inaccurate information the church received regarding the Day of the Lord, it may be best to understand 3:17 as the apostle's way of informing the Thessalonians that the letter came from him and that the instructions within it were true. This would have arguably provided much relief to the Thessalonian congregation who had somehow received inaccurate information regarding the Lord's return (2 Thess 2:2).

The third argument used to defend the pseudonymity of Second Thessalonians is concerned with the theology between the two letters. Green has observed that proponents of inauthenticity maintain that "the

---

71. See Still, *Conflict at Thessalonica*, 53; Wanamaker, *Epistles to the Thessalonians*, 25.

72. There is however, an issue that centers on the phrase ὡς δἰ ἡμῶν. Does it refer strictly to ἐπιστολήν? See, for example, Bruce, *1 and 2 Thessalonians*, 164–65. Or does it refer to ἐπιστολυν, λόγος, and πνεῦμα? See, for example, Best, *Commentary*, 278–80. For a fuller discussion of the issue see Still, *Conflict at Thessalonica*, 52 n. 26. Still writes that "either of these readings is possible (as is the reading that takes ὡς δἰ ἡμῶν to refer to ἐπιστολυν and λόγος), but one can say with certainty that ὡς δἰ ἡμῶν goes with at least ἐπιστολήν."

73. J. Hill, "Establishing the Church," 5.

74. Wilder, *Pseudonymity*, 229; emphasis mine.

theology of the letter includes Pauline elements but lacks certain themes that are commonly identified with the apostle."[75] According to Trilling:

> Die Beobachtungen zur Theologie von II weisen in eine spätere Zeit als die des Apostels Paulus. Trotz der Bewahrung grundlegender Erkenntnisse und Aussagen der paulinischen Theologie sind doch auffallende Mangelerscheinungen zu erkennen.[76]

For instance, several scholars contend that the peculiar eschatological teachings found in both letters may reveal the inauthenticity of Second Thessalonians.[77] For example, Bailey argues that the eschatological sections of First Thessalonians makes two points; first, that the Thessalonian Christians should not grieve over the death of fellow believers because they will be resurrected on the Day of the Lord; second, that the Day of the Lord comes suddenly "like a thief in the night" (1 Thess 5:2).[78] With regard to the eschatological sections of Second Thessalonians, he further contends that:

> the eschatological teaching of 2 Thessalonians is quite different. Its purpose is to controvert the false teaching, associated with a letter supposedly or actually written by Paul, that the Day of the Lord, the final fulfillment, has already come.[79]

This is clear by the listing of events found in 2 Thess 2:3–4, which must happen prior to the return of the Lord. However, on the basis of these eschatological differences, Bailey concludes that:

> these two eschatologies [i.e., the eschatologies of 1 and 2 Thess] are contradictory. Either the end will come suddenly and without warning like a thief in the night (1 Thessalonians) or it will be preceded by a series of apocalyptic events which warn of its coming (2 Thessalonians). Paul might have said both things—in differing situations to one church, or to different churches—but he can hardly have said both things to the same church at the same time, i.e., to the Thessalonian church when he founded it.[80]

75. G. Green, *Thessalonians*, 62.

76. Trilling, *Untersuchungen*, 132.

77. See Bailey, "Who Wrote II Thessalonians?" 136; Beker, "Faithfulness of God," 73; Hughes, *Early Christian Rhetoric*, 79–83; H. Koester, "From Paul's Eschatology," 441–58.

78. Bailey, "Who Wrote II Thessalonians?" 136–37.

79. Ibid., 136.

80. Ibid. See also B. Thurston, who also argues that the two points are contradictory

It is argued that such differences in the eschatological teachings of the epistles further substantiate that the author of Second Thessalonians "was instead a follower of Paul interpreting Paul's teaching for a later generation."[81]

In short, the eschatological argument focuses on an apparent "discrepancy" between the epistles and their apocalyptic teaching. Will the Day of the Lord come suddenly as a thief in the night as First Thessalonians teaches, or will certain events precede his coming as suggested in Second Thessalonians? These "discrepancies" are viewed as proof that Paul is not the author of Second Thessalonians. Undoubtedly, there is a certain eschatological flavor found in both letters; nevertheless, the eschatological sections of both epistles address different issues, which will now be discussed.

This final argument in support of the pseudonymity of Second Thessalonians contains some weaknesses. The assumption for non-Pauline authorship is that the author of Second Thessalonians described certain events that must take place prior to the Lord's return, whereas in First Thessalonians, Paul wrote that the return of the Lord would happen suddenly like a thief in the night. Such contradictions allegedly validate the inauthenticity of Second Thessalonians.[82] Two reasons however, may reveal the failure of this argument. First, in Second Thessalonians, Paul was forced to elaborate on his eschatological teachings from First Thessalonians concerning the Lord's return. Erroneous information about the Lord's advent had somehow infiltrated the Thessalonian church (2 Thess 2:2), which apparently required more detailed instruction concerning the parousia (2 Thess 2:1–12). Consequently, proponents of this view fail to recognize that a central purpose of Second Thessalonians was to *elaborate* regarding the eschatological event as well as to encourage the church to persevere until their vindication at the Lord's return (2 Thess 1:4–5). Not only was the church experiencing persecution, but it was also facing disillusionment because they believed that the Day of the Lord had already occurred. Therefore, it may be reasonable that it was not a different author who wrote the letter but that Paul was simply

---

and thus demonstrate that Second Thessalonians is inauthentic, *Reading Colossians, Ephesians*, 160–61.

81. G. S. Holland, *Tradition*, 128.
82. See Bailey, "Who Wrote II Thessalonians?" 136–37.

encouraging the Thessalonian believers by *elucidating* what he had previously taught this congregation (2 Thess 2:5).[83]

Second, proponents who adhere to this argument possibly fail to consider that in Jewish eschatology there was both the understanding that the Lord would come suddenly like a thief in the night and that certain events would precede his return.[84] There is no dilemma with Paul's teaching of a sudden return and of certain events that would precede the parousia, since both were clearly understood from the teachings of the Old Testament, the intertestamental period, the Dead Sea Scrolls, and the gospels.[85] The importance of the apostle's heritage must not be overlooked with regard to his understanding of eschatology. R. Wayne Stacy has commented that "though the language [Paul] uses to express himself is Greek, his thought-world is thoroughly Jewish. He was at home in the world of Jewish apocalypticism (1 Thess 1:10)."[86]

It is evident from the above discussion that the authorship of Second Thessalonians is a much debated issue. Though the majority of scholars adhere to the authenticity of First Thessalonians, this is certainly not the case with Second Thessalonians. Nevertheless, it has been demonstrated that the three arguments most commonly used to support the pseudonymity of Second Thessalonians fail to convince. Both First and Second Thessalonians, in their contexts, address specific situations that the church at Thessalonica needed to hear. Consequently, Pauline authorship of the Second Thessalonians may be legitimate. And yet, regarding the present state of the question surrounding the authorship of Second Thessalonians, it seems fair to adhere to the conclusion offered by Michael D. Goulder, who writes:

> We cannot assume [Second Thessalonians] to be Pauline, since so many scholars dispute that; but we cannot assume it to be irrelevant, when so many of the major commentators have thought Paul to be its author.[87]

---

83. See Longenecker, "Paul's Early Eschatology," 85–95.
84. See, for example, Ezek 38–9; Joel 3–4; *1 Enoch* 6–71; *t. Levi* 1–19; 4Q174; 4Q215; Mark 13.
85. Schürer, *History*, 2:514–47; Marshall, *1 and 2 Thessalonians*, 37.
86. Stacy, "Introduction," 177.
87. Goulder, "Silas in Thessalonica," 96.

1.3 CONCLUSION

This chapter has sought to prepare us for the study of 2 Thess 1. Through the discussion of the historical background surrounding the city of Thessalonica, it seems clear that this city was vital to Rome for the following reasons. First, Thessalonica was strategically located as the prominent port city in the Aegean Sea. This allowed Rome easy access to all the major port cities in the Macedonian region. Additionally, the city also provided access to the inland country via the Egnatian Way, which was the primary trade route that not only provided an ample amount of commerce but also made for easy and faster travel. Second, Thessalonica had tremendous loyalty to Rome, which was demonstrated by the city's willing subservience in order to maintain its elite status. Preserving a favorable relationship with Rome was imperative for the citizens of Thessalonica because it afforded them many privileges and freedoms. In fact, such devotion to Rome meant that "the city enjoyed the benefits of the imperial government without the burden of its presence."[88] Thessalonica was granted the status of a "free city," the ability to govern itself. Such privileged status would not be compromised, and this has tremendous implications for understanding the situation Paul and the Thessalonian church encountered.

The next issue discussed was authorship. Prior to World War II, Pauline authorship was agreed upon for both First and Second Thessalonians. However, resulting from the higher criticism of the twentieth century, authenticity of Second Thessalonians has come under intense scrutiny. While it is still the consensus that Paul wrote First Thessalonians, the tide has shifted concerning the second epistle. Many scholars believe that Paul did not write Second Thessalonians and that it was probably a pseudonymous letter. However, the arguments predominately offered in support of inauthenticity seem to display several weaknesses and could be used, in all likelihood, to validate the authenticity of Second Thessalonians.

The purpose of this introductory chapter has been to address preliminary issues surrounding the Thessalonian correspondence. A survey of the historical background and scholarly debates surrounding the epistle's authenticity are essential for a proper understanding of the context Second Thessalonians and, as it will be demonstrated below, lends to a

---

88. G. Green, *Thessalonians*, 20.

greater appreciation for the apostle's purpose in incorporating judicial language in the letter.

Since Pauline authorship of Second Thessalonians could reasonably be considered viable, it will be assumed throughout this work. Therefore, the following chapter will discuss the apostle's theological heritage and how such a background influenced his use of forensic language throughout 2 Thess 1.

2

Paul's Heritage and Theological Background

THE PREVIOUS CHAPTER DEMONSTRATED two important facets surrounding the Thessalonian correspondence. First, as a favored city, the Thessalonian citizens wanted to remain loyal to Rome so that they would continue to be at peace with the empire. Thessalonica's commitment to Rome arguably impacted the hostile environment Paul and his associates encountered during their stay in Thessalonica. Second, while scholarship is divided regarding Pauline authorship of Second Thessalonians, it was suggested that the primary arguments proposed for the pseudonymity of the letter may not be as substantial as once thought and that it may be reasonable to conclude that Second Thessalonians is authentic. This led to the conclusion that if Paul authored the epistle, then his familiarity with the Old Testament likely served as his theological background for the use of forensic language found in 2 Thess 1. Such an understanding would arguably provide credence not only for the theological basis of the judicial language but would also seemingly provide a more precise interpretation of the author's original intent.

Assuming that Paul authored Second Thessalonians, the purpose of the present chapter seeks to explore two aspects of the apostle, which will arguably enhance the understanding of Second Thessalonians. First, a brief examination of Paul's upbringing and Jewish heritage; and second, whether or not Hellenism influenced Paul's *theology* when he wrote Second Thessalonians. In other words, to what degree, if any, was the apostle's theology generated from the Hellenistic milieu in which he lived? Conversely, an exploration as to what extent his Jewish heritage and understanding of the Old Testament influenced his instruction to the Thessalonian church will occur.

2.1 PAUL'S UPBRINGING AND JEWISH HERITAGE

In the quest to understand Paul and Second Thessalonians, "reference must be made to his Jewish background and the influence of that background upon him."[1] Appreciating Paul as a Jewish disciple of Jesus proves crucial for understanding and properly interpreting his biblical writings, which comprise the majority of the New Testament. Coupled with Luke's information in Acts, it is primarily in these letters that a brief glimpse of Saul the staunch Pharisee—a devoted Jew, zealous for the Torah and adamant on destroying this new Jewish sect that pledged allegiance to a crucified and risen Messiah—is revealed. But his writings also reveal Paul the converted Christian whom the risen Jesus apprehended on the road to Damascus and commissioned as the apostle to the Gentiles. As a result of Paul's transformation and appointment by the risen Lord this former persecutor of the church was now missionary, ambassador for Christ, minister of reconciliation, and dedicated to advancing the gospel of Jesus.

Nevertheless, knowledge about Paul's life is limited. In fact, Polhill has commented that "a biography of the apostle is impossible. Our sources are too limited to compose one. We know virtually nothing of his birth and childhood."[2] Furthermore, his letters were not meant to be biographical; rather they were written to churches and individuals for the purpose of addressing certain situations in specific contexts.[3] Thus, Hengel has argued that the writings of the apostle are:

> fragments from Paul's thirty years' work as the preacher of a new message, as a theological thinker, founder of churches and pastor,—though even compared with ancient literature generally—these fragments are in their way unique.[4]

This, however, does not make an investigation into Paul's heritage meaningless. In fact, Hengel has observed that:

> by the standards of ancient history the little that we do know is relatively quite a lot, and the fragmentary accounts, which despite their fragmentariness, still deserve the name "history."[5]

1. Longenecker, *Paul's Christianity*, 21.
2. Polhill, *Paul and His Letters*, 1.
3. See, for example, Freed, *Apostle Paul, Christian Jew*, 2.
4. Hengel and Schwemer, *Paul*, 2.
5. Ibid., 2.

It goes beyond the scope of this work to revisit every detail about Paul's life and Jewish heritage.[6] However, brief mention of certain areas, which pertain to his background, are arguably essential for the present study of Second Thessalonians. The focus will be those epigrammatic accounts found in the New Testament writings, particularly those biographical statements recorded by the apostle as well as those recounted in the book of Acts. Exploring these statements will seemingly promote a more complete understanding of Paul the Jewish Christian and hopefully achieve the overall goal of exploring his use of judicial idioms in 2 Thess 1 for the purpose of encouraging the church.

In the few instances where Paul recounted his "former life" in his letters, he frequently made mention of Jerusalem and the importance of the holy city, but never referenced Tarsus, the city of his birth. Consequently, if the Pauline corpus were the only source for background information regarding the apostle, nothing would be known of his connection with Tarsus. As a result, Hengel notes that it is at this point where:

> people have been ready to believe Luke, because if Paul came from Tarsus it was possible to connect him broadly with Hellenistic education and culture and with the syncretistic practices of Syria and Asia Minor for his earliest youth.[7]

In Acts 22:3, Luke recorded Paul's defense before the Jews at Jerusalem. The apostle began by stating, "ἐγώ εἰμι ἀνὴρ Ἰουδαῖος, γεγεννημένος ἐν Ταρσῷ τῆς Κιλικίας." Tarsus was a Hellenistic city well known for its culture and education. The geographer Strabo, writing some time in the early first century, commented that:

> the people of Tarsus have devoted themselves so eagerly, not only to philosophy, but also to the whole round of education in general, that they have surpassed Athens, Alexandria, or any other place that can be named where there have been schools and lectures of philosophers.[8]

Aside from its educational stature, Tarsus was also an important port city situated on the fertile plain of eastern Cilicia. The city's loca-

---

6. For more exhaustive treatments of Paul's background, see Becker, *Paul*; Bornkam, *Paul/Paulus*; Bruce, *Paul*; Hengel, *Pre-Christian*; den Heyer, *Paul*; J. McKay, *Paul*; Murphy-O'Connor, *Critical Life*; Polhill, *Paul*; Wood, *Life, Letters and Religion*.

7. Hengel, *Pre-Christian*, 2.

8. Strabo *Geography* 14.5.13.

tion promoted the growth of the flax plant, which allowed the city much prosperity in the linen weaving industry.⁹ During the reign of Augustus, Tarsus enjoyed special status and privileges such as the exemption from imperial taxation, along with a variety of other liberties.¹⁰ It is not surprising, then, that Paul refers to Tarsus in Acts 21:39 as οὐκ ἀσήμου πόλεως.

Two issues are raised, however, when considering that Paul was born in Tarsus. First, how did Paul obtain Roman citizenship? Second, Acts 22:3 recounts that Paul was "brought up in this city (Jerusalem), and educated under Gamaliel," which begs the question of Paul's tenure in Tarsus. Simply put, did he reside long enough in Tarsus to receive any type of Hellenistic education? If so, is it possible that such an education influenced the theological substance of his letters in the allusions, metaphors, and idioms that he used? Moreover, did the cultural milieu of Hellenism have any impact on Paul's theology when he wrote his epistles, particularly Second Thessalonians?

Interestingly, Paul never mentioned his Roman citizenship in his epistles. This information comes strictly from the book of Acts (16:37–39; 22:25–29; 23:27; in 25:6–12 it is implied).¹¹ The majority of scholarship, however, adheres to the historical accuracy of Luke regarding this issue, maintaining that Paul was a Roman citizen.¹² Bestowal of Roman citizenship typically occurred in several ways: (1) by birth, (2) by manumission, (3) on completion of military service, (4) by reward, (5) by *en bloc* grant, or (6) for financial considerations.¹³

According to Luke's account, found in Acts 22:25–30, Paul informed the commander, who had ordered his scourging, that he was "actually born a citizen." Here Paul is able to eclipse the commander,

---

9. See Bruce, *Paul*, 35; Gasque, "Tarsus," 6:333; McRay, "Thessalonica," 23; A. N. Wilson, *Paul*, 24.

10. See Bruce, *Paul*, 35.

11. This has caused a few scholars to contend that Luke made up Paul's Roman citizenship for narrative effect. See Stegemann, "War der Apostel" 200–229. Stegemann argues that Rome would have never granted citizenship to Paul's family because of their societal status. They were tentmakers and not social elites.

12. See Bruce, *Paul*, 37–40; Hemer, *Book of Acts*, 127; Hock, "Paul's Tentmaking," 555–64; Hengel, *Pre-Christian*, 4–14; Van Minnen, "Paul the Roman Citizen," 43–52; Murphy-O'Connor, *Critical Life*, 41; Polhill, *Paul*, 15. Ramsay, *Cities of St. Paul* 169–91; Schnabel, *Paul*, 2:924.

13. Rapske, *Book of Acts*, 86.

who had purchased his citizenship.[14] Since the apostle was actually a born citizen,[15] the issue, then, is how his grandfather or father obtained Roman citizenship.

Numerous conjectures abound as to how Paul's family acquired their citizenship.[16] William Ramsay has argued that Paul's family was settled in Tarsus by a Seleucid king who wanted to strengthen his hold on the city, and in the process of this relocation, the apostle's ancestors were granted full citizenship.[17] He further argues that Paul came from a wealthy family, which would have made him a social elite.[18] This has led Ramsay to postulate that it was not until after Paul's conversion that he practiced his trade of tentmaking. He further suggests that because of Paul's conversion his family would have considered him an "apostate" to the Jewish faith and disowned him, which therefore left him poor and forced Paul to demean himself by learning a trade.[19]

While this view is certainly plausible, it does contain some weaknesses. First, according to second-century rabbinic tradition, fathers were required to teach their sons a trade. While this tradition is late, Hengel notes that it:

> probably goes back to the early Pharisaic period in the first century BCE; for the Pharisaic scribes in the period before 70 also needed a secure way of earning their bread, and all that time crafts were "golden opportunities."[20]

---

14. The purchasing of citizenship was a predominate feature during the reign of Claudius; see Dio Cassius 60.17.5–7 where he writes that Claduius "granted citizenship to others quite indiscriminately, sometimes to individuals and sometimes to whole groups."

15. See Cadbury, *Book of Acts*, 68. Cadbury reasons that the term γεγέννημαι "suggests plainly the Latin word *ingenuus*, which is the technical term for a birthright citizen."

16. See Hengel, *Pre-Christian*, 11–14; Rabello, "Legal Condition," 662–70; Rajak, "Jews and Christians," 247–62; Rajak, "Roman Charter," 107–123; Smallwood, *Jews under Roman Rule*, 285–88; Tajra, *Trial of St. Paul*, 14–21.

17. See Ramsay, *Traveler*, 32.

18. Others who follow Ramsay's view that Paul was from a family of wealth and standing include Bornkamm, *Paul/Paulus*, 6; Bruce, *Paul*, 38; Nock, *St. Paul*, 21; Schnabel, *Paul*, 2:926.

19. Ramsay, *Traveler*, 34–37. Ramsay does admit that this is only conjecture but believes that it is the most probable.

20. Hengel, *Pre-Christian*, 15–16. Cf. Hock, "Paul's Tentmaking," 555–64, who argues that this rabbinic tradition is strictly from the second century.

Furthermore, since Paul's father was a Pharisee (Acts 23:6), he more than likely was not a social elite but rather a middle-class citizen who would have practiced a trade. Predominately, the Pharisaic movement was comprised of local laymen who took the study and adherence of the Torah extremely seriously. It was their social status that enabled them to remain influential among the people.[21] The common Jew felt they could better relate to the Pharisees than, for instance, the Sadducees who were primarily rich aristocrats.[22] It is likely, then, that Paul did not begin to practice tentmaking after his conversion, but probably grew up learning to ply the trade that his father, a devout Jew,[23] would have taught him, since " a student of the Law always had a trade by which he could live."[24] Thus, Ramsay's argument does not seem to adequately explain how Paul's ancestors obtained Roman citizenship.

Another view argues that Paul's grandfather or father had performed some admirable service in the Roman military and was awarded citizenship.[25] It is assumed that as tentmakers, Paul's ancestors may have provided Caesar or Antony's armies with tents and in return were granted citizenship.[26] Although there were Jews who served in the Ptolemaic and Seleucid armies, this view is highly improbable since a devout Jew serving in the Roman army during the first and second centuries is rare.[27] The reason for this is explained by Applebaum, who writes:

> Roman army life revolved extensively around the ruler-cult, the consecrated standards and the *auguria*; this and the constant tension between the Jews and the Roman power more particularly in Judea during the first century of the current era, made

---

21. For further information regarding the Pharisees, see Josephus *Antiquities* 13.10.5–6, 17.2.4, 18.1.3; *Jewish War* 2.8.14; Nickelsburg and Stone, *Faith and Piety*, 25–30; Neusner, *Rabbinic Traditions*; Saldarini, *Pharisees, Scribes and Sadducees*; Scott, *Backgrounds*, 202–6; Silva, "Pharisees," 395–405; Stemberger, *Jewish Contemporaries of Jesus*.

22. See Josephus *Antiquities* 18.1.4, where he writes that "they [Sadducees] accomplish practically nothing, however. For whenever they assume some office, though they submit unwillingly and perforce, yet submit they do to the formulas of the Pharisees, since otherwise the masses would not tolerate them."

23. See *m. Qiddushin* 7:1.

24. Nock, *St. Paul*, 21.

25. See J. McKay, *Paul*, 24; Witherington, *Paul Quest*, 71.

26. See J. McKay, *Paul*, 24.

27. See Applebaum, "Legal Status," 1:429–32, 459.

> Jews as reluctant to enlist as it made the authorities to accept them. Exceptions of course occur, and more may be found in the future.[28]

Furthermore, as early as 50 BC Jews were exempt from serving in the Roman military under the order of the consul Lucius Lentulus.[29] Thus, it seems doubtful that Paul's ancestors obtained Roman citizenship by means of military service.[30]

A final consideration, offered by Hengel, suggests that Paul's family acquired their Roman citizenship through manumission,[31] although it has been argued that Jews who had been emancipated from slavery would not have desired Roman citizenship for fear that they would compromise their faith.[32] In fact, Stegemann maintains that it is doubtful that Paul's father and even Paul himself would have been a devout Jew and a Roman citizen at the same time.[33] But this argument fails to understand the evidence. For instance, in the ancient writings of Horace, Seneca, and Juvenal, Jews who were Roman citizens were not only devoted but were zealously involved in proselytizing.[34] In addition, Philo writes that Jews who had been enslaved by Pompey at Rome were later set free and allowed to live in the city as citizens. Furthermore, with regard to Rome allowing Jews to remain devout and practice cultic requirements, Philo writes:

> But he [Gaius] never removed them from Rome, nor did he ever deprive them of their rights as Roman citizens, because he had a regard for Judea, nor did he ever mediate any new steps of innovation or rigor with respect to their synagogue, nor did he forbid their assembling for the interpretation of the law, nor did he make any opposition to their offerings of first fruits; but

---

28. Ibid., 459.

29. See Cadbury, *Book of Acts*, 74; Schürer, *History*, 22; Josephus *Antiquities* 14.228–40.

30. See Hengel, *Pre-Christian*, 12. Hengel points out that while Jews were exempt from Roman military service, it must be remembered that "in the late Republic and the period of the early Empire the Roman army was made up of volunteers." It is possible that Paul's ancestors volunteered, but this is mere speculation.

31. See Hengel, *Pre-Christian*, 11–15; Polhill, *Paul*, 16.

32. Stegemann, "War der Apostel," 225.

33. Ibid.

34. See Stern, *Greek and Latin Authors*, 1:321–27, 1:429–34, 2:94–107; Whittaker, *Jews and Christians*, 85–91.

he behaved with such piety towards our countrymen, and with respect to all our customs.[35]

The argument that emancipated Jews would have shunned Roman citizenship seems to be unfounded.

Is the inference that Paul's ancestors obtained citizenship by means of manumission the best solution? In his commentary on Philemon, Jerome stated that Paul's parents lived outside the Judean city of Gischala and that they were carried off as prisoners of war to Tarsus.[36] Hengel has argued that if Jerome's account is correct, then " we might presuppose that Paul was only a *libertus* and not a full Roman citizen."[37] But this conflicts with Acts 22:28, which states that Paul was born in Tarsus and was, therefore, a full citizen. However, Photius, the patriarch of Constantinople, attempted to reconcile Jerome's misunderstanding by claiming that Paul was conceived in Gischala and born in Tarsus.[38] Furthermore, Harnack has argued for the probability that Paul's parents were slaves of Varus in 4 BC.[39] Fuks has shown that they may have been slaves even earlier.[40] Therefore, the evidence, though somewhat limited, suggests that "it seems most likely that Paul's forebears . . . were given the privileged status of citizenship—unasked for—when they were freed by a Roman citizen."[41]

With regard to the arguments discussed above, it seems most plausible that Paul's relatives obtained their Roman citizenship through manumission.[42] However, a definitive answer is impossible, and all arguments remain speculative. And yet, knowing that Paul was a Roman citizen arguably enables a better understanding of the situation he encountered at Thessalonica with regard to the severity of the charges

---

35. Philo *On the Embassy to Gaius* 157.
36. Jerome *Commentariorum Epistolam Ad Philemonem* 653.
37. Hengel, *Pre-Christian*, 14.
38. Photius *Ad Amphilochium Quaestio* 116. See also Deissmann, *Paul*, 85–110.
39. See von Harnack, *Mission und Ausbreitung*, 63–64 n. 1.
40. Fuks, "Freedmen," 26–32.
41. Hengel, *Pre-Christian*, 14.
42. For additional support that Paul's ancestors acquired citizenship through manumission, see Bauckham, ed., *Book of Acts*, 371–72; Black, "Paul and Roman Law," 209–218; Van Minnen, "Paul the Roman Citizen," 43–52; Schnabel, *Paul*, 2:926.

brought against him and the civil action he could have faced had the residents been able to locate him (Acts 17).[43]

The second issue for discussion regarding Paul's birthplace in Tarsus pertains to his tenure in that city. Did Paul stay in Tarsus long enough to receive a Hellenistic education? If so, is it possible that such an education influenced the theological substance of Paul's letters in the allusions, metaphors, and idioms he used? In other words, did the cultural milieu of Hellenism have any impact on Paul *theologically* when he wrote his epistles, specifically Second Thessalonians?

In the biographical section of Acts 22 Paul defended himself before the Jews declaring, "ἐγώ εἰμι ἀνὴρ Ἰουδαῖος, γεγεννημένος ἐν Ταρσῷ τῆς Κιλικίας, ἀνατεθραμμένος δὲ ἐν τῇ πόλει ταύτῃ, παρὰ τοὺς πόδας Γαμαλιὴλ πεπαιδευμένος κατὰ ἀκρίβειαν τοῦ πατρῴου νόμου, ζηλωτὴς ὑπάρχων τοῦ θεοῦ." It seems, then, that Jerusalem was the nucleus of Paul's upbringing and education. But some scholars contend that such an understanding is inaccurate. For instance, Murphy-O'Connor argues that:

> the view that Paul received all his education in Jerusalem fails to meet the objection that it was in Luke's interest to attach Paul as closely as possible to the city which Luke saw as the culmination of Jesus' ministry and the starting point of all missions.[44]

Dibelius and Kümmel also contend that Paul grew up in Tarsus and received some Hellenistic education.[45] Other scholars, such as Richard Reitzenstein, maintain that Paul not only received Hellenistic education but that he was even influenced by the mystery religions of the day.[46] Reitzenstein suggests that "Paul possibly had been initiated into two or three mystery religions or at least had become acquainted with the language and perspectives of their communities in personal intercourse."[47] Furthermore, Hyam Maccoby believes that the mystery religions influenced Paul in such a way that he even practiced moderate anti-Semitism. Maccoby writes, "[Paul's] anti-Semitism, however, is of an intermediate kind, somewhere between that of Gnosticism and that

---

43. See chapter 3 for a thorough discussion of Paul's Roman citizenship with regard to the situation he encountered at Thessalonica and its significance for this study.
44. Murphy-O'Connor, *Critical Life*, 46.
45. Dibelius, *Paul*, 30.
46. Reitzenstein, *Hellenistic Mystery-Religions*, 533.
47. Ibid.

of later Christianity."[48] But this line of thinking has been questioned and refuted by W. D. Davies, who contends that "Paul belonged to the mainstream of first-century Judaism, and that elements in his thought, which are often labeled as Hellenistic, might well be derived from Judaism."[49] Moreover, in those epistles where the apostle references his background, he always stresses his Jewish heritage and upbringing (Gal 1:13–24; Phil 3:4–7). Regarding the aforementioned evidence, is it justifiable to conclude that the education Paul received was predominately Hellenistic?

Certainly the apostle was not ignorant of his culture, since Hellenism permeated his known world. The issue, however, as K. Ehrensperger notes, is "how and to what extent Paul was influenced by Hellenism, especially how and to what extent Hellenism impacted Paul's theological thinking and form of argumentation."[50] Before settling on this, two issues must be considered. First, as mentioned above, Paul himself never indicated any influence from a Hellenistic education in his epistles, but rather accentuated his Jewish heritage and upbringing (Phil 3:4–7). This has led Hengel to suggest that caution must be taken:

> to see Paul [strictly] as a "Hellenistic Diaspora Jew," that in his own testimonies, in the letters, the Pharisee connected with Jewish Palestine stands in the foreground, to whom Jerusalem seems to be more important than anywhere else.[51]

Secondly, an examination of the language and syntax of Acts 22:3 may help to determine whether the origin of Paul's upbringing and education were influenced by Hellenistic or Jewish society or both. The exegetical issues of this verse are twofold. First, what is an appropriate understanding of the three participles γεγεννημένος, ἀνατεθραμμένος, and πεπαιδευμένος? Second, is the placement of the comma after ταύτῃ correct? It seems that understanding the three participles is crucial for a proper interpretation. Upon a brief examination of each, a conclusion will be offered that may enable a more complete perception of where Paul received his education.[52]

48. Maccoby, *Paul and Hellenism*, 182–83.

49. Davies, *Paul and Rabbinic Judaism*, 1.

50. Ehrensperger, *Mutually Encouraged*, 126. Cf. Campbell, *Paul*, 10–11; Van Unnik, *Tarsus or Jerusalem*, 259–320.

51. Hengel, *Pre-Christian*, 1.

52. For a more complete discussion of the exegetical issues see, Van Unnik, *Tarsus or Jerusalem*, 259–320.

The temporal participle γεγεννημένος is literally translated as "having been born," since perfect participles are typically antecedent to the main verb.[53] The term denotes that Paul was simply born in Tarsus. Many scholars who believe that Paul received a predominately Hellenistic education contend that this term should be understood to mean that the apostle was not only born in Tarsus but that he also grew up there.[54] But this arguably forces a meaning on γεννάω that does not seem possible and may lead to the impression that such an interpretation could have been, as Van Unnik comments simply, "smuggled in to prove the case."[55] Paul is silent about his tenure in Tarsus, and imposing on γεννάω more than it is capable of bearing is poor exegesis.

The second participle, ἀνατεθραμμένος, is more involved. This compound form found only in Luke–Acts (Luke 4:16; Acts 7:20, 7:21, 22:3) and once in the Septuagint (Wis 7:4), denotes the idea of nurturing or rearing a child with respect to feeding and physical care.[56] More predominant is the synonym τρέφω, which denotes this same basic meaning (Gen 48:15; Matt 25:37; Luke 4:16, 23:29; Jas 5:5; Rev 12:6, 12:14).[57] For example, during Stephen's defense in Acts 7:20–21, the author used ἀνετράφη and, in the subsequent verse, ἀνεθρέψατο to explain that Moses was cared for in his father's house three months before Pharaoh's daughter raised him as her own son. Similarly, in Luke 4:16 the verb τεθραμμένος was used to show that Jesus "grew up" in Nazareth. Luke seems to demonstrate that he understood ἀνατρέφω to convey the idea of a child being raised or nurtured in the parental home. It is reasonable, then, to understand Acts 22:3 to convey such a meaning. Therefore, it can be deduced that "although Paul was born in Tarsus, it was in Jerusalem that he received his upbringing in the parental home just as it was in Jerusalem that he received his later schooling for the rabbinate."[58] As a result, Luke made a distinction in verse 23 between ἀνατεθραμμένος and the final participle πεπαιδευμένος.

---

53. More comprehensive discussions regarding the nuances of perfect participles are found in Porter, *Verbal Aspect*, 394–401; Wallace, *Greek Grammar*, 626–27.

54. See Murphy-O'Connor, *Critical Life*, 46–47; Roetzel, *Paul*, 11–16.

55. Van Unnik, *Tarsus or Jerusalem*, 271.

56. See Josephus *Antiquities* 2.232; P.Cair.Zen. 59379. 1–2; P.Oxy. 1873.9; Balz, "ἀνατρέφω," 94; Spicq, "ἀνατρέφω," 115–16.

57. See Josephus *Antiquities* 9.125; P.Lips. 28.17–19; BDAG, 1015; LSJ, 1814.

58. Van Unnik, *Tarsus or Jerusalem*, 301.

It has been demonstrated that the first two participles in Acts 22:3 were likely used to convey distinct meanings regarding different stages of Paul's life; namely that he was γεννάω, "born" in Tarsus and that he was ἀνατρέφω, "raised" in his parental home as a child in Jerusalem. Luke's purpose for incorporating the third participle πεπαιδευμένος was possibly to accentuate that Paul's education came from the tutelage of Rabbi Gamaliel, strictly according to the law of the fathers.

In the Septuagint, παιδεύω is oftentimes found in contexts of God's instruction to Israel, such as his instruction as to how the nation should live. Adherence to God's commands brings blessings, while disobedience produces punishment (Deut 4:36, 8:5; Hos 7:12, 10:10). References are also found with regard to the instruction of a father to his children (Prov 3:11, 15:32–33). However, παιδεύω is often found in reference to God's discipline upon corporate Israel for their sins (Lev 26:28, 28), as well as the punishment meted out by a father on his children (Deut 21:18; Prov 13:24, 19:18). Likewise, in the New Testament παιδεύω is predominately found in contexts of discipline or punishment (Luke 23:16, 23:22; 1 Cor 11:32; Heb 12:6, 12:7, 12:10). However, in certain contexts παιδεύω can also mean "to impart instruction" (Acts 7:22, 22:3).[59] In this later understanding the term should probably not be limited to mere intellectual education, but as training or instruction of the whole self.[60] For instance, it is such a meaning that Luke may have intended to communicate in his account of Stephen's defense in Acts 7:20–22. As Stephen recounted Moses's life, he explained that he was ἐγεννήθη (born) and he was ἀνετράφη "cared for" in his father's house before being ἀνεθρέψατο (raised) by Pharaoh's daughter and then ἐπαιδεύθη (educated) in all the learning of the Egyptians. Likewise, Philo also made use of the same schema in his rendition of Moses's life.[61] It seems evident then, from the above discussion, in tandem with the context of Acts 22:3, that Luke was potentially making a three-stage distinction regarding the course of Paul's life: namely that he was born in Tarsus, that he was raised in his parental home in the city of Jerusalem, and that he received his education under Rabbi Gamaliel.

---

59. BDAG, 749.

60. Bertram, "παιδεύω," 595–625; Fürst, "παιδεύω," 775–81; Schneider, "παιδεύω," 3–4.

61. See Philo *On the Life of Moses* 6.20–24, 6.30–32.

Understanding the distinctions of each participle mentioned above arguably eliminates the problem of punctuation in Acts 22:3. Regarding the punctuation of the verse, the dilemma is whether a comma should be read after ἀνατεθραμμένος δὲ ἐν τῇ πόλει ταύτῃ, or after παρὰ τοὺς πόδας Γαμαλιὴλ. As Van Unnik simply states, "did the activity of the celebrated rabbi extend over the παιδεύειν alone or did it extend over the ἀνατρέφειν as well?"[62] With regard to the above evidence that ἀνατρέφω and παιδεύω emphasize different stages in Paul's life, it seems most plausible that a comma should be placed after ἀνατεθραμμένος δὲ ἐν τῇ πόλει ταύτῃ. It was seemingly Luke's intent for his readers to understand the distinct stages in Paul's early life that he was raised in Jerusalem and educated under Gamaliel. Furthermore, as Van Unnik notes, "Greek readers, who knew the significance of ἀνατρέφω in such a context, would of course have regarded it as quite foolish to connect 'at the feet of Gamaliel' with that word."[63]

It can be deduced, then, from this brief discussion, that in all likelihood Luke incorporated the three verbs γεννάω, ἀνατρέφω, and παιδεύω to demonstrate three distinct stages in Paul's life. Furthermore, in his epistles the apostle is silent about the impact of his birth city but frequently stressed his residency in Jerusalem, as well as his Jewish heritage. This has led Hengel to conclude that "we must therefore take very seriously Paul's report that he was a Hebrew of Hebrews, i.e. a Palestinian Jew, and moreover a Pharisee and pupil of the scribes."[64] However, even with the evidence presented above, a dogmatic answer to the question of whether Paul received any type of Hellenistic education remains debatable. If the above understanding of the verb ἀνατρέφω is correct, can it be assumed that this took place in Paul's earliest childhood? Unfortunately, the many issues regarding Paul's family background, especially his early childhood years, are unknown.[65] Nevertheless, the majority of Paul's formative years seem to have been spent in Jerusalem, but this may not have occurred until his preteen years. Thus, it may not be as certain as

---

62. Van Unnik, *Tarsus or Jerusalem*, 272.
63. Ibid., 295. See also Bruce, *Paul*, 43; Haenchen, *Acts of the Apostles*, 624–25.
64. Hengel, *Pre-Christian*, 34.
65. See Wedderburn, *First Christians*, 79–88; Barclay, *Jews*, 65–70; C. Noack, *Gottesbewußtsein*, 5–6 n. 15; Schnabel, *Paul*, 2:924. Schnabel contends that if Paul grew up in Tarsus his education would have been similar to that of Philo, "his contemporary in Alexandria."

Van Unnik presumes that Paul's parents moved to Jerusalem during the earliest years of his life.[66] Further knowledge about Paul's education, which is further difficult to ascertain, is that:

> Luke himself quite deliberately sets Paul's skills in speaking Greek and Aramaic side by side, in the same way as he does his being a citizen of Tarsus and growing up in Jerusalem. In so doing he demonstrates the bi-lingual and bi-cultural character of his hero.[67]

In other words, Hengel observes that because Paul had such a command of the Greek language, he could not have merely learned it as a secondary language; he probably grew up with it in the Hellenistic city. But this proves little since there are several inscriptions from Palestine written in Greek, which demonstrate that one did not necessarily have to grow up in Tarsus to master the Greek language. The epigraphic evidence clearly shows that he could have grown up using the Greek language *in Jerusalem*.[68]

An answer to the present question with any degree of certainty is not possible. With regard to the exegetical evidence, the manner in which Luke used γεννάω, ἀνατρέφω, and παιδεύω to apparently stress distinct phases in Paul's life, coupled with the reality that "at no point does Paul prize the Greek *paideia* which was valued so highly by Jews like Aristeas and Philo."[69] In conjunction with the fact that the apostle emphasized his Jewish upbringing and education throughout his epistles, and along with the epigraphic evidence, it seems reasonable to conclude that Paul's education was in all likelihood predominately Jewish. However, Campbell notes that "Paul's theologizing did not take place in a vacuum, nor was it an additional abstract structure of thought imposed from without."[70] Yet it was his faith in Christ and commitment to Israel's Scriptures that dictated how he utilized theology in the midst of a Hellenistic society.

To review the chapter thus far, the intent of the above discussion was not to revisit every detail of Paul's background, since it goes beyond

---

66. See Van Unnik, *Tarsus or Jerusalem*, 301.

67. Hengel, *Pre-Christian*, 34.

68. Benoit, "L'Inscription Grecque," 112–13; Dittenberger, ed., *OGIS* 598, 294–95. For additional inscriptions, see Mussies, "Greek in Palestine," 1040–64; Fitzmyer, "Language of Palestine," 501–531.

69. Barclay, *Jews*, 383.

70. Campbell, *Paul*, 11.

the primary objective of this work. However, brief mention of certain areas pertaining to the apostle's background is essential for the ensuing study of Second Thessalonians. Brief examination of the biographical accounts of Paul found in the New Testament writings, recorded by the apostle, as well as those recounted in the book of Acts, have been discussed. Two issues were considered, which surround the fact that Paul was born in Tarsus. First, how did Paul's ancestors become Roman citizens? Second, a brief discussion of the exegetical issues surrounding Acts 22:3 was provided to determine Paul may have been influenced by Hellenistic education, and, if so, whether it affected the way he wrote his second epistle to the Thessalonians.

While much remains conjecture, it seems reasonable to conclude that Paul's family, devout Jews, most likely obtained their Roman citizenship through manumission. Consequently, Paul was born a Roman citizen in the Hellenistic city of Tarsus. His tenure in this city, however, seems to have not been long, since Paul related that he was born in Tarsus, but spent his childhood being raised in Jerusalem and educated under Rabbi Gamaliel. Therefore, since Paul was apparently a "Hebrew of Hebrews," who was raised as a devout Jew and likely received strictly a Jewish education, this leads to the discussion as to whether Hellenism had any religious or theological influence on the apostle to the Gentiles.

2.2 PAUL AND HELLENISM

It does not serve the purpose of this work to engage in a lengthy dialogue regarding the extent of influence Hellenism may or may not have had upon Paul. This has been the subject of much debate among New Testament scholars for years. Nevertheless, living in the first century, Paul would not have been ignorant of the Hellenistic culture. Though it has been argued that Paul not only grew up in Jerusalem but received a Jewish education, this does not imply that he was oblivious to the world around him. The more relevant issue for the present study is, did Hellenism have any impact upon Paul's biblical writings? In other words, did Paul incorporate idioms, metaphors, allusions, etc., from the Hellenistic culture, or did he simply draw from the Old Testament when instructing his churches, particularly the church at Thessalonica?

New Testament scholars in previous generations, and some in the modern era, have argued that Paul was heavily influenced by the

Hellenistic culture of his day.[71] This has caused many to contend that the gospel Paul preached was not based on the Old Testament Scriptures or even the teachings of Jesus Christ. Consequently, this has led to the conclusion by some that Paul was not only the founder of Christianity but that he Hellenized the message of the gospel, in order to make it applicable to the Gentiles in the early churches he founded.[72] Some have even suggested that Paul's *theology* was indebted to Hellenism. Edwin Burtt writes:

> Paul also absorbed from his Hellenistic environment, at Tarsus and elsewhere in the east Mediterranean region, religious ideas which dominated the non-Hebraic world of his day, and for which he felt a deep personal need. Graeco-Roman culture at this time was swept by a host of so-called "mystery cults," promising personal immortality to their converts though mystic identification with a savior-god who had died and then triumphed over death by resurrection to a renewed divine life.[73]

In fact, after his conversion, Burtt contends that Paul's theological mindset:

> may be briefly described as a remolding of the moralized cult of Yahweh, developed by the Hebraic prophets, into a mystery religion or personal salvation, in which the crucified Jesus of Nazareth appears not merely as the promised Messiah but also as a savior-god.[74]

A further claim regarding how Hellenism may have influenced Paul's theology is made by George Holley, who suggests:

> In his view of man's constitution, the apostle [Paul] stands with the Greek philosophers rather than with the Hebrew Scriptures. With Plato he thinks of a human being as consisting of an outer man and an inner man (2 Cor 4:16), and with Greek philosophy in general he thinks of the body as a prison of the spirit (Rom 7:24; 8:23). With the Orphic faith he holds the doctrine of original sin and locates the evil principle in the "flesh," where it has been enthroned since the hour of Adam's transgression (Rom

---

71. See Becker, *Paul*; Bultmann, *Theology of the New Testament*, 187–89; Maccoby, *Mythmaker*, 14–18; Roetzel, *Paul*.

72. See Maccoby, *Mythmaker*, 16–17.

73. Burtt, *Types of Religious Philosophy*, 35.

74. Ibid., 36.

5:12). The dual aspect of his thought comes to its classic expression in Rom 7:15–18.[75]

More recently, Troels Engberg-Pedersen has argued for a certain element of Stoicism, particularly in Paul's letter to the Philippians.[76] Pedersen does not contend that Paul was a Stoic philosopher; nevertheless, with regard to Philippians he does believe that:

> Paul attempts to reach his aim by interweaving with his basic Christian ideas (the apocalyptic framework and the ideas set out in the Christ hymn) a number of equally basic ideas in Stoic ethics and politics. There is tension in the picture that results, but not between the Christian and the Stoic ideas. Rather, it is a tension within Paul's Christian understanding and practice itself.[77]

Such arguments have led many to a consensus that Paul incorporated Hellenistic idioms, metaphors, allusions, etc., in his writings to make the message of the crucified and risen Messiah more manageable for his Gentile audience. Some, such as Bultmann, have maintained that Paul's use of the Old Testament Scriptures is eccentric, since their teachings would have been completely foreign to non-Jews. In fact, Bultmann contends that:

> The Old Testament is still the word of God, though not because it contains his word spoken to Israel in the past, but because it is directly typological and allegorical. The original meaning and context of the Old Testament sayings are entirely irrelevant.[78]

Is this a correct understanding of Paul? Is it reasonable to think that a Hebrew of Hebrews, a strict Pharisee grounded in the Old Testament, would stray from the teachings of the Scriptures in order to reach his audience? Why do so many scholars seem to contend that the background for the New Testament is Hellenistic rather than Jewish? Were not all the authors of the New Testament (excluding Luke), devout Jews familiar with the Old Testament?

These are important questions in the pursuit for adequately understanding Second Thessalonians and Paul's use of judicial language and

---

75. Holley, *Greek Thought*, 85.
76. See Engberg-Pedersen, ed., "Stoicism in Philippians," 256–90.
77. Ibid., 290.
78. Bultmann, *Primitive Christianity*, 187. See also Grech, "'Testamonia,' and Modern Hermeneutics," 318–24; Lindars, "Place of the Old Testament," 59–66.

imagery. If Hellenism influenced Paul *theologically*, then how does this affect the interpretation of Second Thessalonians? Conversely, if Paul was not influenced *theologically* by Hellenism, then the most appropriate backdrop for his letters is seemingly the Old Testament. Again, Paul was aware of the cultural milieu in which he lived; however, the immediate concern is, did such a culture influence the *theology of his biblical writings*?

In order to realize why numerous scholars argue for a Hellenistic understanding of Paul, it is important to consider the accuracy of their methods as well as the sources they use for interpreting the New Testament. Tom Holland has suggested several flaws that have arguably steered many exegetes in the wrong direction.[79] For the purposes of this work, only two will be addressed. The two misconceptions that Holland contends address significant confusion with regard to language are first, how scholars understand the meaning of words, and second, the methods of language training.

Any competent exegete knows that language is always in flux. The meanings of words change over time. The mistake of earlier and modern New Testament scholars seems to be the presupposition that the meaning of words remained the same throughout time. Holland contends:

> Thus to establish the meaning that a word had two thousand years earlier is of little help in understanding its meaning when used by a completely different generation. What determines any word's meaning is not how earlier generations understood the particular word, but how the generation that has produced the text under consideration understands it. This can be known through carefully reflecting on both its immediate and it wider context.[80]

Furthermore, one of the predominant methods among modern scholarship, in terms of understanding Paul's *theological* insights, is the reliance upon the Pseudepigrapha for interpreting the New Testament. Undoubtedly, these documents are valuable for gaining insights into the Second Temple period. In fact, with the discovery of the Dead Sea Scrolls, several of the writings in the Pseudepigrapha (*Jubilees*, *First Enoch*, and fragments from the *Twelve Patriarchs*) have been proven to be

---

79. See T. Holland, *Contours*, 51–68.
80. Ibid., 51.

early as well as Jewish, making them useful for New Testament studies.[81] Nevertheless, the Pseudepigrapha must be used with caution for several reasons. First, T. Holland claims that there is ignorance regarding the "theological schools" in which the literature of the Pseudepigrapha was written. In other words, it is uncertain if these documents came from the theological mindset of the Pharisees, Sadducees, Essenes, or Zealots, making it extremely difficult to understand the meaning of the various terms and ideas. Many theologies existed in intertestamental Judaism. In fact, Julius Scott suggests that:

> The society, culture, and faith of intertestamental Judaism were not a monolithic whole by a conglomerate. They contained diverse elements which both individually and together must be taken into account in attempting to understand the period.[82]

Additionally, Scott writes:

> The four sect division of Judaism (Pharisees, Sadducees, Essenes, and the fourth philosophy) of the first-century historian Josephus is an inadequate description of the diversities of the time. There were divisions within each of theses sects; there were also other groups. Furthermore, we must recognize that the majority of Jesus' contemporaries, the average Jews, belonged to none of these sects or parties.[83]

Consequently, it seems unwarranted to assume that the theological meanings of words and ideas of the Pseudepigrapha have carried over to the New Testament text. There are certainly valuable insights from the Pseudepigrapha since they present a broad picture of Jewish ideas from the intertestamental period. But the vast diversity of Judaism during this period brings into question the wisdom of putting too much weight on the Pseudepigrapha for interpreting the New Testament. Second, it is impossible to discern how widely known these documents were. It cannot be assumed that the churches, particularly Thessalonica, to whom Paul wrote, would have been familiar with such literature.

---

81. Ibid., 59. Regarding the historical critical issues of these documents, see Charlesworth, ed., *Old Testament Pseudepigrapha*; Vermes, ed., *Complete Dead Sea Scrolls*.

82. Scott, *Backgrounds*, 21.

83. Ibid. See also Chilton and Neusner, *Judaism*, xii–xix.

In contrast, however, Beckwith has noted that the Old Testament Scriptures "existed in the New Testament period and the centuries leading up to it, which were believed to be divinely inspired and to posses divine authority."[84] As early as the second century BC, the Old Testament Scriptures were understood to be the standard of teaching about God for both Jews and Gentiles. The Old Testament was considered not only as given by God but written by God (2 Kgs 17:37; Hos 8:12). It was held as the divine authority for instruction in life and godliness. Even Jesus presupposed the supremacy of the Old Testament and understood himself to be its typological fulfillment (Matt 5:17–18; Mark 14:21; Luke 22:37, 24:27, 24:44–45).[85] Likewise, in Paul's letters, it seems apparent that he, along with the churches he founded, recognized the Old Testament as authoritative (Rom 1:2, 16:25–26; Gal 3:8).[86] It was the Old Testament that Jews and Gentiles gathered corporately to hear, read, and expounded on each Sabbath. Simply put, the Old Testament Scriptures were the divine standard for every facet of Judaism. Therefore, in all likelihood it is the Old Testament that should serve as the basic template for understanding the theological teachings found in the early church and consequently in Second Thessalonians, although significant evidence from the Pseudepigrapha will not be ignored.

A second mistake regarding New Testament exegesis as suggested by Holland is the faulty assumption scholars make regarding the Greek language. According to T. Holland, a century ago, it was believed that proper education in the Koine Greek of the New Testament should be rooted in the classics. The result of such a method advanced the perception that a firm grasp on the classics would result in proper understanding and exegesis of the New Testament. Hellenistic practices and vocabulary were advanced as the primary catalyst for New Testament theology. The apparent mistakes of such a presupposition seem obvious. The fact that the same vocabulary was used in both Hellenistic sources and the New Testament does not inevitably suggest that they have the

---

84. Beckwith, *Old Testament Canon*, 434.

85. See, for example, France, *Jesus*, 38–82; Powery, *Jesus Reads Scripture*.

86. For detailed analysis regarding the importance of the Old Testament for Paul and the early church, see, for example, Ellis, *Paul's Use*, 20–37; Nickelsburg, *Ancient Judaism*, 9–28; Hays, *Echoes of Scripture*, 1–33; Stanley, *Arguing with Scripture*, 9–71.

same meanings, particularly "when used in a religious sense in the Jewish community."[87] Furthermore T. Holland observes that:

> the Hebrew meaning had been poured into the text of the Greek translation to produce a language that had its own particular lexicon. It was Greek in its alphabet and vocabulary, but Hebrew in its mindset and essential meaning. . . . It was not from Athens that the writers of the New Testament had drawn their understanding but from Jerusalem.[88]

Consequently, it appears that earlier methods of interpreting the New Testament primarily from the Hellenistic milieu were methodologically deficient. This often displaced the primary sources with texts that were assumed to have precedence.

With the advancement of archaeology and computer technology, coupled with the discoveries of papyri, inscriptions, the Dead Sea Scrolls, etc., knowledge of the first century has been greatly enhanced. Scholars would be imprudent not to utilize such abundant resources. These writings allow for a more detailed look into the mindset of the people, everyday life, geography, religious practices, and the broad semantics of the language. Furthermore, study of these sources enables a better understanding of the culture in which Paul lived and ministered. For instance, through the exploration of primary source material, much information can be ascertained regarding the cultural situations in the city of Corinth that may have influenced the church there.[89] More importantly such material can aid in discovering the circumstances in Thessalonica, which led to the persecutions this church endured. However, it must be remembered that as a devout Jew, Paul never abandoned the religion of his heritage even after he was converted.[90] Rather, he understood his religion and the teachings of the Old Testament as not only pointing to but also being fulfilled in Jesus Christ, the crucified and risen Messiah. The apostle understood the theology of the old covenant as the type, which found its fulfillment in the anti-type, Jesus Christ and the new covenant he established.

---

87. T. Holland, *Contours*, 52.
88. Ibid.
89. See, for example, Winter, *After Paul Left Corinth*, 7–25.
90. See, for example, Davies, *Paul and Rabbinic*, 1–16; McRay, "Thessalonica," 28–30; Witherington, *Paul Quest*, 53–65.

Therefore, caution must be exercised in using Hellenistic literature as primary source materials when interpreting the *theology* of Paul's writings. The pinnacle of Paul's theological teachings, idioms, metaphors, allusions, etc., must arguably be centered upon the Old Testament. Richard Hays writes:

> To read Paul against the background of "inner-biblical exegesis" is to understand his place in the stream of tradition in a new way. He saw himself as a prophetic figure, carrying forward the proclamation of God's word as Israel's prophets and sages had always done, in a way that reactivated past revelation under new conditions.[91]

In recent years, there has been a shift to understand the prominence of the Old Testament, not only with regard to Paul but for all the authors of the New Testament.[92] Renewed interest in the unity between the Old and New Testaments is increasing. Furthermore, it seems that the Old Testament is being used with more credence as the principle for interpreting the New Testament. James Dunn has argued that the first Christians were Jews, who:

> in no sense felt themselves to be a new religion, distinct from Judaism. There was no sense of a boundary line drawn between themselves and their fellow Jews. They saw themselves simply as a fulfilled Judaism, the beginning of the eschatological Israel.[93]

It seems prudent, therefore, to understand the writings of the New Testament from a Jewish mindset. By reading the Pauline corpus from such a Jewish perspective, it can arguably be discovered that his letters were "written by and for Jews and Gentiles concerned with the Jewish context of their new faith in Jesus as the Jewish Messiah."[94]

Primary source materials that may help inform the understanding of the cultural situation, which surrounded the Thessalonian Christians, will be examined in this study. However, the Old Testament will be the foundation for the *theological* understanding of Second Thessalonians.

---

91. Hays, *Echoes*, 14.

92. See Beale and Carson, eds., *Commentary*; Beker, "Faithfulness of God," 10–16; Dodd, *Scriptures*; T. Holland, *Contours*; D. Hubbard, "Hope," 33–59; B. Noack, "Jewish Gospel," 45–55; VanGemeren, *Progress of Redemption*, 329–474.

93. Dunn, *Unity and Diversity*, 239.

94. Nanos, *Mystery of Romans*, 4.

Paul addressed a certain situation that caused great turmoil among the Thessalonians. Examining what the apostle wrote to this church will reveal that his teaching regarding the parousia of Christ was likely understood as the fulfillment of the Day of the Lord motif found throughout the Old Testament. The Thessalonian Christians would have not only been familiar with such a concept but would likely been comforted, knowing that the final assize would be their vindication.

2.3 CONCLUSION

In this chapter, the argument has been made that a proper understanding of Paul begins with his Jewish heritage. He was a devout Jew, a "Hebrew of Hebrews," who was educated in Jerusalem, steeped in the Old Testament, and zealous for his ancestry amidst a culture dominated by Hellenism. Even after his conversion, he remained a faithful Jew who had come to the realization that Jesus was the promised Messiah, the fulfillment of the "law and the prophets." Paul seemingly drew his theology from the well of the Old Testament, which culminated in Christ. It is from the same well that this study will draw, coupled with various examinations of extrabiblical literature that may be applicable, in order to understand his use of legal language and allusions in 2 Thess 1.

3

Acts 17:1–9 and the Conflict at Thessalonica

IT HAS BEEN ARGUED that maintaining a loyal relationship with Rome was important to the citizens of Thessalonica. Obedience to the empire's authority not only allowed the residents a peaceful life but also afforded certain privileges to this Roman city. Therefore, familiarity with the historical relationship between Rome and Thessalonica not only allows a better understanding for why Paul experienced conflict with the Roman authorities, which ultimately forced his departure from the city, but also seemingly explains why the newly converted disciples faced persecution from their neighbors.

The purpose of this chapter is to conduct an exegetical study of Paul's ministry at Thessalonica as recorded in Acts 17:1–9. The results of this inquiry intend to provide a better understanding of what transpired in Thessalonica during Paul's brief tenure there and how this led to his use of legal language and allusions found in his second letter to this persecuted church. Before conducting this study, a brief mention regarding the historical reliability of the book of Acts is warranted. Revisiting the arguments regarding the consistency or inconsistencies of Acts is not the goal of the chapter; however, since Acts 17:1–9 is the only source of information regarding Paul's ministry at Thessalonica, a few disclaimers must be mentioned.

3.1 THE HISTORICITY OF THE BOOK OF ACTS

While not as intently debated in the modern era, the historicity of Acts is still questioned by some New Testament scholars.[1] It is argued that Luke's theological motivations in Acts have tainted the historical reliability of

---

1. See, for example, H. Koester, *History and Literature*, 108; Richard, *First and Second Thessalonians*, 6; J. T. Sanders, "Christians and Jews," 433–45.

the book.² For instance, J. T. Sanders writes, "One cannot turn to Acts for direct information about Christianity. My own working assumption is not to accept information from Acts unless it can be corroborated."³ Such criticism has resulted in a disregard for Luke's historical acumen. Those who question the trustworthiness of Acts argue that the book should be read strictly as a "theology" and not a "history." Consequently, the book of Acts is oftentimes viewed as an illegitimate source of information regarding Paul's ministry. Some have even concluded that Acts is largely a work of entertainment.⁴ If Acts, as supposed by some, offers no historical credibility, then what, if anything, can be known about the situation Paul encountered at Thessalonica? Additionally, what can be known about Paul's ministry to the Thessalonian church?

Acts 17:1–9 has been understood by some scholars to be a fabrication. For example, H. Koester comments that "all the individual events of Paul's activity in [Thessalonica] are legendary."⁵ Likewise, E. J. Richard suggests that "the Acts account of the mission [in Thessalonica] owes more to Luke's project and remote acquaintance with the apostle's role than to first-hand data."⁶ Such negative criticisms, however, regarding the historicity of Acts have been demonstrated by several scholars to be unfounded.⁷ Although the practices of ancient historiography are quite technical and do not serve the overall purpose of this chapter, a few comments regarding ancient historiography are in order.⁸

In the ancient world, certain criteria were applied if an author's "history" was to be considered valid. According to Hemer, such criteria included but were not limited to:

> the stress of eyewitness participation; the importance of interviewing eyewitnesses; the limitation of coverage to material where the writer has privileged access to evidence of guaranteed

---

2. See Still, *Conflict*, 61.
3. J. T. Sanders, "Christians and Jews," 435.
4. Pervo, *Profit with Delight*, 1–11.
5. H. Koester, *History and Literature*, 108.
6. Richard, *First and Second Thessalonians*, 6.
7. See, for example, Barrett, "Historicity of Acts," 515–34; Hemer, *Book of Acts*; Hengel, *Acts*; Jervell, *Unknown Paul*; Jewett, *Chronology of Paul's Life*; Marguerat, *First Christian Historian*; Marshall, *Historian*.
8. For examinations of ancient historiography see: Cadbury, Jackson, and Lake, "Greek and Jewish Traditions," 7–29; Hemer, *Book of Acts*, 63–100; Hemer, "Luke the Historian," 28–52; Mosley, "Historical Reporting," 10–26.

quality; the stress on travel to the scene of events; the prospect then (and for us) of checking details with contemporary documents; the occasional insistence on the use of sources for speeches; and the vigour of the concept of "truth in history" as it actually happened.[9]

A close examination of Acts may reveal that Luke seemingly followed the customary expectations for ancient historians in his day.[10] Moreover, ancient historians such as Dionysis of Halicarnassus[11] and Lucian[12] advise those venturing to compose historical works to be brief and concise, to exclude details not pertaining to their central theme, and to write with integrity.[13] In his study on the Hellenistic practices of ancient historiography, W. C. van Unnik has argued that Luke was simply following standard protocol when he composed Acts, "doing precisely what would be expected of a historian in his own day."[14] Furthermore, it seems apparent that Luke not only adhered to the Greco-Roman standards for historians, he also followed the typical protocol for Jewish historians.[15] The main objective for both Greco-Roman and Jewish historians was to record the events truthfully, but it was their understanding of truth that differed. Concerning this distinction Daniel Marguerat comments that:

> there is a fundamental epistemological difference here. Greek and Jewish historians both understood their tasks as a search for truth, a quest for the ἀληθὴς ἱστορίας (the requirement of veracity in history is the watchword of ancient historiography); yet the former establish the plausibility of the event, while the latter ex-

---

9. Hemer, *Book of Acts*, 63–100. See also M. A. Powell, "Reading Acts as History," 49–62; Van Unnik, "Luke's Second Book," 37–60. Van Unnik demonstrates that there were at least ten standards that ancient historians were expected to follow.

10. The authorship of Acts is a separate issue and will not be discussed. It is possible to view Acts as historically reliable and not hold to Lukan authorship. See, for example, Still, *Conflict*, 61 n. 2, who views Acts as a reliable yet anonymous writing.

11. See Dionysius *Roman Antiquities* 5.56.1.

12. Lucian *How to Write History* 39. Although Lucian wrote later than Luke (AD 166–68), Marguerat has argued that "there are strong reasons to think that this [work] (Lucian attacks the incompetence of the historians of his time) fixes a much earlier scholarly tradition" (*Christian Historian*, 13).

13. See M. A. Powell, "Reading Acts as History," 49–62.

14. Van Unnik, "Luke's Second Book," 37–60, esp. 51.

15. See Barrett, *Luke the Historian*, 15–19; Marshall, *Historian*, 54–7.

pose the *truth* of the God who rules the world. Greek history is illuminating, Jewish history is confessional.[16]

Luke is oftentimes paralleled with the writings of Josephus when examining the Jewish aspect of ancient historiography. There are problems, however, with such a comparison.[17] For example, Josephus's writings contain intrusions by the author, a practice that is contrary to Jewish historiography, while in Acts there are no interventions, with the exception of the "we-passages." Moreover, Loveday Alexander has argued that the lack of intrusions by Luke seems to connect him more to the standards of Jewish historiography.[18]

Additional comments could be made with regard to the issues surrounding the historical reliability of Acts, but this goes beyond the scope of this work. It is arguable, however, that the book of Acts seems to display an affinity to both the Greco-Roman and Jewish practices of ancient historiography. This has led Marguerat to conclude that "Luke is situated precisely at the meeting point of Jewish and Greek historiographical currents."[19]

Therefore, the above evidence may lend to the notion that the book of Acts could be considered not only theologically but also historically valid, particularly the account of Paul's ministry at Thessalonica. Luke portrayed various sides of Paul's personality as well as specific details of his ministry among the Thessalonians that would otherwise be unknown. Certainly, the depiction of Paul in Acts is subjective, but this does not make it untrue.[20] In fact, Marshall comments that:

> there are differences between the picture of Paul in Acts and that in his own letters nobody will deny; the two pictures are independent of each other and cannot be harmonized in detail, since a man's self-portrait (even when unconsciously undertaken) will not necessarily agree with the impression of him received by other people. But this does not mean that the two pictures are irreconcilable, and we believe that the two can in fact be har-

---

16. Marguerat, *Christian Historian*, 22.
17. See Hemer, *Book of Acts*, 97–99. He offers several reasons demonstrating why the dissimilarities far outweigh the similarities between Josephus and Luke.
18. See Alexander, "Fact, Fiction," 395–99. See also Marguerat, *Christian Historian*, 22–23.
19. Marguerat, *Christian Historian*, 25.
20. See M. A. Powell, "Reading Acts as History," 59.

monized in general terms. The general outline of Paul's career in Acts fits well with what is disclosed in his letters.[21]

Furthermore, regarding the Acts account of Paul's ministry in Thessalonica, R. Riesner has noted that:

> der Gründungsbericht, den Lukas von der Gemeinde in Thessaloniki verfaßt hat, stimmt bei Berücksichtigung aller schriftstellerischen Tendenz und Verkürzung auf bemerkenswerte Weise mit den historischen, sozialen und religiösen Umständen überein, die sich aus dem Ersten Thessalonicher-Brief erkennen und durch zeitgenössisches Material illustrieren lassen.[22]

Moreover, Martin Hengel cautions scholars inclined to discredit the fidelity of Acts to be careful not to allow higher critical biases to supplant the evidence. He underscores this point in his following statement:

> Two things, above all concern me. First, to question the radical historical skepticism which is so widespread in a number of areas within [scholarship]; this skepticism is often coupled with flights of imagination which suggest a retreat from any historical research worth taking seriously. Secondly, however, I am no less vigorously opposed to the primitive ostracism of historical—and that always means critical—methods, without which neither historical nor theological understanding of the New Testament is possible.[23]

It is possible that Luke adhered to the expected procedure for historians of his day. He seems to have focused on a central issue, made use of eyewitnesses, faithfully incorporated sources, and wrote in a manner that was not only applicable but also honest with his audience. In short, Powell has argued that "the picture of Paul in Acts is a completion, a filling-up of what we have in the epistles. In order to get at the historical Paul, we cannot do without Acts."[24] Thus, Luke's record of Acts 17:1-9 may be reasonably considered a viable theological and historical source of information regarding Paul, and specifically his ministry in Thessalonica.

---

21. Marshall, *Historian*, 75.
22. Riesner, *Die Frühzeit*, 367–68.
23. Hengel, *Acts*, vii.
24. M. A. Powell, "Reading Acts as History," 59.

3.2 EXEGESIS OF ACTS 17:1-9

Acts 17:1-9 is significant because it illuminates the contextual situation that prompted Paul to write the Thessalonian epistles. Luke recounted that after Paul was forced to leave Thessalonica, he traveled to Berea (Acts 17:10-13). From Berea he journeyed to Athens, leaving Silas and Timothy behind, but commanded that they return to him as soon as possible (Acts 17:14-15). Upon being reunited with his companions, he sent Timothy from Athens to Thessalonica in order to assess the faith and resolve of these new believers (1 Thess 3:2). Timothy returned from Thessalonica and rejoined Paul in Corinth, informing him of the Thessalonians' great faith and perseverance (Acts 18:5). The results of this report led Paul to write First Thessalonians.[25] This makes the Thessalonian correspondence written during the second missionary journey and therefore, some of the earliest Pauline literature.[26]

---

25. As to the provenance of the Thessalonian epistles, several scholars assert that they were written from Corinth shortly after Timothy rejoined Paul with the news regarding the Thessalonian Christians. That Paul penned this letter from Corinth is evident. Acts 20 records that he returned to Macedonia, exhorting the brethren before moving into Greece. Therefore, Morris concludes that Second Thessalonians must precede this, "for it is hard to think of so similar a situation to that of 1 Thessalonians emerging again after Paul had had opportunity of dealing with it in person" (*First and Second Epistles*, 24-26). See also Bruce, *Thessalonians*, xxxiv-xxxv; Best, *Commentary*, 7-13; Frame, *Epistles of St. Paul*, 9-12; G. Green, *Thessalonians*, 52; Malherbe, *Thessalonians*, 71-74. Cf. Schmithals, *Paulus und die Gnostiker*, 89-157. Schmithals argues that First Thessalonians was written during the third missionary journey.

26. Regarding a possible date for the epistles, Acts 18:12 references the proconsul Gallio. Although Luke does not specify at what point Paul was brought before the governor, the Delphi Inscription reveals that it was probably shortly after Gallio took office (see *SIG* II, 801d). See also Morris, who has a brief explanation of this inscription, (*First and Second Epistles*, 25); Bruce, ed., *Book of Acts*, xxxv; Haacker, "Gallio," 901-3. Bruce writes, "The letter is dated in the period of Claudius' twenty-sixth acclamation as *imperator*, a period known from other inscriptions to have covered the first seven months of AD 52. It has usually been supposed that the letter mentions Gallio as current proconsul of Achaia; in that case, since proconsuls normally entered their tour of duty on 1 July, it would follow that Gallio arrived in Achaia as proconsul on 1 July, AD 51." It is generally understood that Paul wrote the Thessalonian epistles around AD 50-51 with a short interval between them. Although the exact time frame between the two epistles cannot precisely be determined, G. Green argues that "due to the similarity between the two letters, the most likely scenario is that the second letter to the church was written during the eighteen-month period that Paul spent in the city of Corinth on his second missionary journey" (*Thessalonians*, 52). See also Morris, *First and Second Epistles*, 26, who argues that the second epistle followed within weeks of the first. See also Carson, Moo, and Morris, eds., *Introduction*, 347-48; Jewett, *Thessalonian Correspondence*,

Acts 17:1-9 relates that following Paul's ministry and miraculous release from prison at Philippi, he traveled through the cities of Amphipolis and Apollonia, before arriving in Thessalonica. The participle διοδεύσαντες denotes that Paul traveled along the primary trade route, the Egnatian Way. It is argued that Luke used διοδεύω rather than the more common διέρξομαι to stress that the apostle and his companions traveled this main thoroughfare.[27] The term διοδεύω is oftentimes used in contexts referring to the travel of the Roman military on this central highway.[28] It could be said, then, that "the highways of the Empire became for Paul the highways of the kingdom of God."[29] Amphipolis was nearly thirty miles southwest of Philippi and was the capital city of the first district of Macedonia.[30] Apollonia was about thirty miles southwest of Amphipolis and roughly thirty-five miles east of Thessalonica.[31] The use of the article with both of these cities is strange, since names of cities are usually anarthrous and used only for special reasons.[32] BDF contends that the use of the article may be "the result of their original use as adjectives."[33] After passing through these two cities, Paul arrived in Thessalonica where he located a synagogue of the Jews and began to preach (Acts 17:1-2).

In keeping with his usual practice, verse 2 records that, while in the synagogue, Paul reasoned with the Jews from the Scriptures for three Sabbaths. Much controversy surrounds the issue of Paul's tenure in Thessalonica. Several scholars argue that he and his companions stayed anywhere from one year to one month.[34] Those who contend for a longer stay do so because Paul recorded in 1 Thess 2:9 that he was there "long enough for him to form an intimate relationship with his converts [1 Thess 2:7-8], to receive aid from Philippi "once again" [Phil 4:16], and

---

59-60; Malherbe, *Thessalonians*, 73-74.

27. Bruce, *Acts of the Apostles*, 368.

28. See *NewDocs* 1.9.

29. Bruce, *Acts of the Apostles*, 368.

30. See chapter 1, note 4 of this volume.

31. See Newman and Nida, *Handbook*, 327; Bruce, *Book of Acts*, 343; Stott, ed., *Message of Acts*, 270.

32. See Turner, *Syntax*, 171-72; BDF, §§ 261-62, pp. 136-37.

33. BDF, §§ 261-62, pp. 136-37; Turner, *Syntax*, 171-72.

34. See Donfried, "Cults of Thessalonica," 356; Malherbe, *Paul and the Thessalonians*, 13-14; Marshall, *Thessalonians*, 5; Morris, *Thessalonians*, 4; Neil, *Epistle of Paul*, xii; Wanamaker, *Epistles to the Thessalonians*, 7.

to ply his trade [1 Thess 2:9; see also 2 Thess 3:7–9]."[35] Furthermore, the prepositional phrase ἐπὶ σάββατα τρία simply denotes the temporal aspect of Paul's reasoning with the Jews in the synagogue. This phrase does not reveal how long Paul and his companions ministered in the city of Thessalonica. Understanding Paul's tenure in Thessalonica as only three Sabbaths may stretch the meaning of the preposition too far.[36] Three weeks seemingly does not allow sufficient time for Paul to accomplish all that he did in Thessalonica, and thus, Rudolf Pesch has argued, "darf man annehmen, daß er einige Wochen mehr bleiben konnte."[37] Although the length of the apostle's stay in Thessalonica is impossible to determine, periods ranging from four to six months seem most probable.[38]

It was ἀπὸ τῶν γραφῶν that Paul reasoned with those in the synagogue. In other words, it was the Old Testament that served as the platform for Paul's rational. The two participles in verse 3, διανοίγων and παρατιθέμενος, indicate the means by which Paul used the Scriptures; namely explaining and demonstrating what the Old Testament spoke concerning the Christ. The word διανοίγων literally means "open or to open."[39] It appears only eight times in the New Testament,[40] seven in the Luke–Acts corpus and in Mark 7:34. In half of the occurrences it simply has the meaning of "open" such as the opening of a womb (Luke 2:23) and Jesus' opening of blind eyes to regain sight (Mark 7:34); it also is used in the account of the stoning of Stephen when he saw the heavens opened up and the Son of Man standing at the right hand of God (Acts 7:56) and when Jesus opened the disciples' eyes so they could recognize him (Luke 24:31). The remaining instances are found in contexts of explaining with the intent of making someone understand (Luke 24:32, 24:45; Acts 16:14, 17:3). It is this later interpretation that in all probability fits best within the immediate context, since διανοίγω is connected with παρατίθημι. The term παρατίθημι carries the idea of demonstrating

---

35. Still, *Conflict*, 67.

36. See BDAG, 367; Harris, "Prepositions and Theology," 1193–96.

37. Pesch, *Die Apostelgeschichte*, 126.

38. See Barrett, *Acts*, 2:809; Donfried, "Cults," 356 n. 92; Lührman, "Beginnings of the Church," 237–49; Malherbe, *Paul*, 13–14; Ramsay, *Paul the Traveler*, 228. See also Murphy-O'Connor, *Paul*, 102, who argues that Paul stayed in Thessalonica a minimum of one year.

39. See BDAG, 234, for the various interpretations.

40. It is also used several times in the Septuagint and once in the Apocrypha (2 Macc 1:4).

through teaching. This is evident in Acts 28:23; while under house arrest in Rome, Paul explained the kingdom of God to a large crowd.[41] Following the participles in verse 3, the ὅτι clause unpacks specifically the central theme of Paul's argument: that the Christ had to suffer and rise again from the dead. The pronoun οὗτός, used here in direct discourse, is best understood as the subject of the clause, with ὁ χριστὸς functioning as the predicate and Ἰησοῦς in apposition to ὁ χριστὸς. In other words, Paul explained that the one who fits the description as the Christ revealed in the Scriptures is Jesus.[42] Preaching a crucified and risen Messiah in the synagogue led to a number of converts and also provoked much hostility among the Jews towards Paul, Silas, and later the Thessalonian church. This is significant because in 2 Thess 1:10, Paul reminded these persecuted Christians of their genuine belief regarding his testimony when he explained to them from the Scriptures that Jesus was the Christ.

The outcome of Paul's preaching in the synagogue resulted in several ἐπείσθησαν.[43] Paul's message convinced some Jews, a large number of God-fearing Greeks, and leading women of the truth that Jesus was the Messiah, and they joined themselves to Paul and Silas.[44] This "joining" to the missionaries denotes the idea of following as disciples. This

---

41. Further evidence for this meaning is found in Matt 13:24, 13:31.

42. The textual variant in this verse is worth noting. The majority of manuscripts read ὁ χριστὸς Ἰησοῦς. Vaticanus, however, inserts the article before Ἰησοῦς. If this reading of codex B is accepted, then ὁ Ἰησοῦς could be in apposition to οὗτός. But this view should not be accepted for at least three reasons. First, the more difficult reading is always preferred. It appears that the article was inserted before Ἰησοῦς to alleviate an apparent problem of how the reader should understand Ἰησοῦς. Second, the external evidence overwhelmingly supports the ὁ χριστὸς Ἰησοῦς reading. Third, it makes better sense in the immediate context to read Ἰησοῦς as anarthrous. Paul is in the synagogue explaining what the Old Testament teaches about the Messiah. The climax of his testimony is the revelation that the Messiah is Jesus. Understanding Ἰησοῦς being in apposition to ὁ χριστὸς not only fits the context but ensures that there is no confusion in the identity of the Messiah. The literal translation of the verse would read: "that the Christ had to suffer and rise from the dead and that this is the Christ *namely* Jesus, whom I am proclaiming to you." For further discussion of this variant and its syntax see Bruce, *Acts*, 369; Barrett, *Acts of the Apostles*, 2:810–11; Culy and Parsons, *Acts*, 326; Read-Heimerdinger, *Bezan Text of Acts*, 256–58; McGaughy, *Toward a Descriptive Analysis*; B. Metzger, *Textual Commentary*, 401; Wallace, *Greek Grammar*, 43–46.

43. BDAG, 792.

44. For a discussion as to why Luke mentions Silas, see Kaye, "Acts' Portrait of Silas," 13–26.

concept of discipleship is further strengthened by the ensuing datives, which likely demonstrate a close association.⁴⁵ Luke's aim was simply to indicate that a number of people were convinced that the Old Testament taught that the Messiah had to suffer and rise from the dead. It was the success of such preaching that led to the opposition Paul and Silas encountered. Before discussing the antagonism these missionaries faced, a brief mention of the σεβομένων Ἑλλήνων and τῶν πρώτων γυναικῶν is pertinent.

The largest group of converts resulting from Paul's message about the Messiah stemmed from the σεβομένων Ἑλλήνων. Luke's mention of "God-fearers" and the prominence afforded to this group in Acts has caused scholars to question Luke as a historian because, as Levinskaya comments, "until recently the very existence of such a category of Gentiles was questioned."⁴⁶ However, certain evidence has revealed that "God-fearers" were not only a legitimate group but also had a close relationship with Jews, as they frequently worshiped in the synagogue and adhered to the laws of God.⁴⁷ However, they were not considered proselytes (full converts of Judaism) because they abstained from circumcision.⁴⁸

The phrase γυναικῶν τε τῶν πρώτων presents an interesting dilemma. Typically this phrase translates as "and the leading women." But it is possible to translate it as "wives of the leading men." The Western text emphasizes this later translation with the variant καὶ γυναῖκες.⁴⁹ But this reading of the Western text should not be followed for two reasons.

---

45. Barrett, *Acts*, 2:811 notes that the verb προσεκληρώθησαν is a *hapax legomenon* the New Testament. Outside the biblical writings, the term denotes the meaning of *to be assigned* (possibly by lot); see Josephus *Jewish War* 2.567. However, Barrett comments that "one is tempted to translate freely *they threw in their lot with Paul and Silas*; but Luke held a predestinarian view of conversion (Acts 13:14, 16:14) and may have thought that those who attached themselves to Paul and Silas did so because God had allocated them to this end."

46. Levinskaya, *Book of Acts*, 51.

47. Ibid., 51–82. See also Balz, "σέβομαι," 236; Forester, "σέβομαι," 169–72; Günther, "σέβομαι," 91–94; J. S. Wright, "God," 85–86; Feldman, "Proselytes and 'Sympathizers,'" 265–305; Lake, "Proselytes and God-Fearers," 74–96; Romaniuk, "Die 'Gottesfürchtigen,'" 66–91.

48. Referring to the inscriptions from Aphrodisias, Feldman lists twenty-eight factors that attracted "God-fearers" to Judaism ("Proselytes and 'Sympathizers,'" 282–97). He also observes that the inscriptional evidence reveals some Gentiles did become full proselytes to Judaism (ibid., 298–305).

49. See Bruce, *Acts of the Apostles*, 369; B. Metzger, *Textual Commentary*, 401–2; Witherington, *Acts of the Apostles*, 506.

First, the external evidence for γυναικῶν τε τῶν πρώτων is far superior and, secondly, throughout the context of Luke-Acts women are often depicted as important figures within Jesus' ministry and the early church (Luke 23:55–24:35; Acts 5:1–11, 9:32–42, 16:13–34).[50] Furthermore, regarding such women, Winter has commented that:

> there were certainly some in the church who were wealthy and therefore potential private and public benefactors. . . . There were not a few of the leading women who became converts, according to Acts 17:4. As such, they were not precluded from giving public and private benefactions as illustrated by the inscription to Junia Theodora of Corinth AD 43. Even if the Acts account contained no references to people of status in the church in Thessalonica, the existence of a few wealthy members would need to be presupposed.[51]

Some, however, have simply understood this phrase to be a title of honor.[52] Regardless of the translation followed, the meaning of verse 4 is not altered. Luke related that a large number of the social elite women (whether or not they were married is uncertain) were converted to Christianity.

A transition from the preceding paragraph into verse 5 is evident by the particle δέ.[53] The unconverted Jews in Thessalonica became ζηλόω, indicating that they had intense negative feelings over another's success (Acts 7:9, 13:45; 1 Thess 2:14–16).[54] Furthermore, in the book of Acts ζηλόω is oftentimes used to depict the hostility Jews felt toward the gospel message (Acts 5:17, 13:45).[55] The term can also denote a positive sense, such as having great zeal for something or someone (Acts 21:20, 22:3).

---

50. For detailed analysis regarding women in the early church, see Cassidy, *Society and Politics*, 57–59; Witherington, *Women*.

51. Winter, *Seek the Welfare*, 46–47. See also J. Hill, "Establishing the Church," 212–13; Portefaix, *Sisters Rejoice*, 155–58.

52. See *NewDocs* 1, no. 25 (1981) 72; Barrett, *Acts*, 2:812; Witherington, *Acts*, 506 n. 160.

53. See, for example, Levinsohn, *Textual Connections*, 86–120; Thrall, *Greek Particles*. Levinsohn comments that "whenever de/ is used in the narrative of Acts, it introduces something distinctive. This distinctive information is usually presented in a sentence, which is introduced by de/" (*Textual Conenctions*, 95).

54. BDAG, 427; Hahn, "ζῆλος," 1166–68; Popkes, "ζῆλος," 100–1; Stumpff, "ζῆλος, ζηλόω, ζηλωτής, παραζηλόω," 877–92.

55. See Stumpff, "ζῆλος, ζηλόω, ζηλωτής, παραζηλόω," 887.

In the context of the passage, however, Luke likely used ζηλόω in the former sense. The unbelieving Jews at Thessalonica became infuriated and even envious at the success of Paul's ministry. With a large number of God-fearing Gentiles and leading women following Paul and Silas, the Jews viewed Paul's message as a threat to Judaism and synagogue life. This has led Rapske to conclude that:

> the jealousy of the Jews in the Diaspora was not solely on account of the numbers of converts but what those numbers represented. They raised serious questions regarding the acceptable terms for inclusion and constituted a diminution of power for the ruling elites in the Jewish community. Significant numbers of conversions from among the God-fearers would have diminished Jewish standing and protection with the Gentile community, particularly when converts were or had connections, with the Gentile ruling elites.[56]

But even more serious than the potential loss of Gentile converts, the Jews arguably believed that Paul's message opposed the teachings of the Torah. Both of these convictions provoked an aggressive jealousy among the unbelieving Jews, and they vehemently resisted Paul's message and wanted him either out of the city or dead (1 Thess 2:14–16). These zealous opponents could not allow Paul to continue his ministry, and they conspired to do whatever was necessary to have him and his companion removed from Thessalonica.[57] The result of such hostility produced false accusations against the missionaries, namely that "ils troublent l'ordre public, ils s'opposent à Céasar."[58]

In order to carry out these false accusations, the unbelieving Jews coerced a group of τῶν ἀγοραίων ἄνδρας τινὰς πονηροὺς to instigate an insurrection. While the term ἀγοραῖος often connotes a public speaker or a court day, in the immediate context of verses 1–9, it seems most prob-

---

56. Rapske, "Opposition," 247 n. 32. See also Barrett, *Acts*, 2:812; Bruce, *Acts of the Apostles*, 370; Haenchen, *Acts of the Apostles*, 507; Murphy-O'Connor, "Lots of God-Fearers?" 418–24; Polhill, *Acts*, 361. Bruce argues that "the Jewish authorities probably looked on the God-fearing Gentiles as potential proselytes, so that in preaching to them Paul was poaching on their preserves."

57. See, for example, Seland, *Establishment Violence*, 223–303. He provides a thorough discussion of the aggressive zeal Jews had against the Christian message in order to maintain Judaism. This is further evidenced in Dio Cassius 49.22.4, where he writes, "the race [referring to Jews] is very bitter when aroused to anger." See also 2 Cor 11:24; Rom 15:31; Josephus *Jewish War* 1.7.5 § 150, 2.18.3 § 466.

58. Taylor, *Les Actes*, 272.

able that Luke used ἀγοραῖος to refer to idlers who spent the day loafing in the market place looking for an opportunity to cause trouble.[59] This word is used only twice in the New Testament, here and again in Acts 19:38 where it refers to a court day. Several Greek writers, however, use this term to refer to hooligans, troublemakers, or agitators.[60]

Falsely accusing Paul and Silas of causing a riot enabled their Jewish opponents to take legal action against the missionaries. As a "free" Roman city, Thessalonica had the privilege of handling legal issues and meting out punishment locally.[61] If the missionaries were found culpable for the riot, they would suffer punishment under Roman law, which could have included exile, imprisonment, or corporal punishment.[62] For instance, Josephus recorded that Varus of Syria searched the country looking for the individuals who were responsible for insurrection (they supported the potential king Judas). Upon their capture, he writes, "those who appeared to be less turbulent individuals Varus imprisoned; those most culpable, in number about two thousand, he crucified."[63] This may have been exactly what the Jews intended for Paul and Silas. Since any sort of public disturbance would not be tolerated, the opponents attempted to locate Paul and Silas in order to bring them to court. The angry mob "rushed" Jason's house in search of the missionaries to bring them before the city authorities. The term ἐφίστημι with the dative often signifies the idea of rushing upon someone with the intent to harm or attack.[64] Unable to locate Paul and Silas, the Jewish mob dragged Jason and other believers to court.

The identity of Jason has been the subject of much discussion. Because Jason seems to have played a pivotal role within the newly

---

59. See Bruce, *Acts of the Apostles*, 370; Field, "ἀγοράζω," 267–68; Still, *Conflict*, 71; L&N, 88.251; Schneider, "ἀγοράζω," 23.

60. See Aristophanes *Frogs* 390 (1015); Herodotus *Histories* 2.141.4; Plato *Protagoras* 210 (347c); Xenophon *Hellenica* 6.2.23; Theophrastus *Characters* 6.2.

61. For a discussion of the privileges of "free cities" within the Roman Empire, see Jones, *Greek City*, 131–32; Sherwin-White, *Roman Society*, 96.

62. See, for example, Showerman, *Rome and the Romans*, 410–17.

63. Josephus *Jewish War* 2.71–75. This is also made evident with the insurrection of Andriscus. As previously mentioned, Andriscus, the self-proclaimed son of King Perseus, was imprisoned for igniting a rebellion against Rome. He was later released because the empire no longer considered him a threat. See Diodorus Siculus 32.15.

64. BDAG, 418; L&N, 39.47. This meaning is also evident when the Jews at Corinth attacked Paul and brought him to court (Acts 18:12).

formed Thessalonian church, a brief examination regarding his importance is warranted. It appears that Jason functioned as the guarantor that Paul would not return to Thessalonica, and this resulted in the apostle's truncated stay in the city, which may have served as one of the catalysts for writing the Thessalonian correspondence.

Many commentators have understood Jason to be a Hellenistic Jew. For instance, Rudolf Pesch comments that "Jason steht als griechischer Name im hellenistischen Judentum häufig für Jehoschua [oder] Jesus."[65] While the ethnicity of Jason is unknown, it is possible that he was the same Jason that Paul mentioned in Rom 16:21.[66] But even if the Jason of Acts is identical to the one in Romans, there is still much that is unknown about him.[67] Several scholars contend that the newly formed Thessalonian church met in Jason's house, which has led to the conclusion that Jason may have been a man of wealth and status.[68] Gillman has even suggested that Jason's arrest and ability to post bond for the missionaries depicts that he was not only host to the young Thessalonian church but that he was a leader within the congregation.[69] While much remains unknown about Jason, it seems that his house became the central location for Paul's ministry since it was here that the angry mob attacked, determined to bring Paul and Silas before the δῆμος.[70] In

---

65. Pesch, *Die Apostelgeschichte*, 2:123 n. 10. See also Bruce, *Book of Acts*, 326; Schneider, *Die Apostelgeschichte*, 224 n. 30. This is contra Meeks, *First Urban Christians*, 63, who believes that Jason is a Gentile with a Greek name.

66. See, for example, Cranfield, *Epistle to the Romans*, 805–6; Moo, *Epistle to the Romans*, 934; Schreiner, *Romans*, 807. This is contra Käsemann (*An die Römer*, 404) and Meeks (*First Urban Christians*, 62–3), who disagree and argue that the Jason of Acts is not the same person found in Rom 16:21.

67. See Morgan-Gillman, "Jason of Thessalonica," 40. Gillman believes that the reference of Jason in Romans is probably best understood as the Jason in Acts. However, in trying to decipher all those in the New Testament called Jason he concludes that the information given is too insignificant and, therefore, a definitive answer is unattainable.

68. See Jewett, *Thessalonian Correspondence*, 120; Malherbe, "Inhospitality of Diotrephes," 223–26; Winter, *Seek the Welfare*, 46–47. This is contra Theissen (*Social Setting*, 95). Theissen argues that Jason's social status is uncertain. See further Murphy-O'Connor, *St. Paul's Corinth*, 153–161. Murphy-O'Connor discusses the archaeological evidence for houses in Greek cities that were of substantial size and would have been more than adequate for Christian assemblies.

69. Gillman, *Thessalonian Correspondence*, 41 n. 7.

70. Cf. Malherbe, *Paul*, 13–14. Malherbe comments that "Paul's mission suggests that we should understand Jason's house as having been the base for Paul's work among the Gentiles after his separation from the synagogue, as Titius Justus' house would be

the Septuagint, δῆμος normally translates מִשְׁפָּחָה meaning family or tribe (Num 1:20, 1:22; Judg 13:2). However, in later instances the term translates עַם signifying "people" (Dan 8:24, 9:16).[71] Free cities, like Thessalonica, were considered self-governing, and it was the function of the δῆμος to implement governmental and legal action as necessary.[72] However, when the missionaries were accused of violating the decrees of Caesar, the politarchs were responsible for administering punishment.[73] Failing to locate Paul and Silas, the angry mob determined that Jason along with some of the brethren were credible substitutes and forcefully brought them before the city officials in order to take legal action. While legal responsibility was placed upon Jason (17:9), it is important to remember, as Alexandru Neagoe notes, that "there is no question that what is being judged here 'before the politarchs' is *Paul's* case and that 'Jason and some of the brethren' are only substitutes (17:6)."[74]

Jason and some of the brethren were brought to court before τοὺς πολιτάρχας. Much has been discovered about the office of the politarchs, which has enhanced the understanding of the situation at Thessalonica. With regard to the most recent data concerning the office of the politarchs, G. H. R. Horsley writes:

---

in Corinth (Acts 18:6-7)."

71. BDG, 223; LSJ, 386-87; Balz, "δῆμος," 296; Josephus *Antiquities* 14.259; Gundmann, "δῆμος," 63. The Septuagint, however, usually incorporates the typical Greek word λαός to denote the idea of "people." In Hellenistic cities δῆμος connoted the idea of a group of people gathering together to conduct business. Furthermore, Gundmann notes that δῆμος "can have the derogatory nuance of the mob as distinct from the aristocracy. But it can also have a proud ring, as in Athens, where it is used for the free and self-governing citizens."

72. See, for example, Bruce, *Acts of the Apostles*, 370; Stambaugh and Balch, *Social World*, 32–34; Tajra, *Trial of St. Paul*, 33; Witherington, *Acts*, 507. Regarding the function of the δῆμος, Tajra writes, "The popular assembly had an important role in the civic life of Thessalonica since it enjoyed a certain number of legislative and juridical prerogatives. Under the Republic the people seemed to have exercised their power to legislate on many matters, but with the introduction of the Principate the main function of the popular assembly was the election of magistrates or priests with real and effective power passing more and more to the magistrates and notables in the local Senate."

73. See, for example, Donfried, "Cults," 343; Judge, "Decrees," 5. Judge contends that the decrees of Caesar refer to the "oath of loyalty to the Emperor," which the politarchs were responsible for upholding and thus mandated their involvement.

74. Neagoe, *Trial of the Gospel*, 190. See also Still, *Conflict*, 73, who notes the use of αυτούς in 17:5 and 6.

There are known today possibly as many as 70 non-literary references to politarchs. Almost all of these occur in inscriptions. Over 80% of them are from Macedonia, and more than 40% of all the attestations are from Thessalonike alone, some 28 to date.[75]

The politarchs were generally comprised of the social elite who carried out administrative and police duties.[76] Moreover, they were liable for maintaining civic order and possessed legal authority (Acts 17:6–9). F. Gschnitzer has noted that "die Politarches waren also als Kollegium . . . für die Ordnung in der Stadt und für die Überwachung und Verfolgung aller Friedensbrecher verantwortlich."[77] Furthermore, Horsley has commented that they also had an administrative function, "for they appear to be responsible for convening the *boule* and introducing motions to it, and confirmed its decisions."[78] While politarchs were not present in every city, those that did have politarchs usually had more than one serving in office, with the number depending upon the populace of the city.[79] It seems, however, that the number of politarchs serving at one time was typically five.[80] Jason and some of the brethren probably appeared before at least five politarchs and were indicted with serious allegations that required legal action.[81]

The Jewish opponents presented two charges against Paul and Silas.[82] The first accusation against the missionaries was τὴν οἰκουμένην

---

75. Horsley, "Politarchs," 422–23. See further Schuler, "Macedonian Politarchs," 96–98, for a listing of thirty-one inscriptions mentioning the politarchs.

76. See Haenchen, *Acts of the Apostles*, 507–8; Tajra, *Trial of St. Paul*, 34.

77. Gschnitzer, "Politarches," col. 491.

78. Horsley, "Politarchs," 425.

79. See Horsley, "Politarchs," 425, who points out that there is one instance where a Macedonian community had a single politarch for one year.

80. However, the inscriptional evidence attests that the number of politarchs ranged anywhere from three to seven; see *IG* 126, 127, 133, 137. See also Tajra, *Trial of St. Paul*, 34, who notes that "Thessalonica was governed by a college of five (later six) Politarchs, which was headed by a presiding Politarch."

81. For further study regarding the politarchs in Macedonia, see Burton, "Politarchs," 598–632; W. D. Ferguson, *Legal Terms*, 65; Schuler, "Macedoninan Politarchs," 90–100; Hatzopoulos, "Greek and International Scholarship," 109–115.

82. Some scholars contend that the opponents actually brought three charges against Paul and Silas: causing a riot, defying the decrees of Caesar, and proclaiming another king called Jesus; see, for example, Cassidy, *Society and Politics*, 89–90; Pohill, *Acts*, 362; Sherwin-White, *Roman Society*, 103. But this likely misunderstands the function of λέγοντες. The participle is simply functioning as a complement to the main verb by

ἀναστατώσαντες. In the surrounding context this phrase arguably incorporated a political nuance. While the term οἰκουμένην typically means "world" or "inhabited world," in certain contexts it is translated as "the empire" or "Roman Empire" (Luke 2:1; Acts 24:5).[83] Furthermore, the following term, ἀναστατόω, denotes the idea of someone attempting to cause sedition (see Acts 21:38).[84] Pohill even contends that ἀναστατόω carries the notion of a political agitator.[85] In the immediate context, then, it seems imperative not to overlook the political overtones of this first accusation. Simply put, the Jewish opponents accused the missionaries of instigating a revolution against the empire. L. T. Johnson emphatically states that "the political connotation here is unmistakable, and any other translation would miss the point of the charge."[86] The antagonists understood that convincing the politarchs and their fellow citizens that Paul and Silas were insurrectionists would force them to carry out legal action against the missionaries. Therefore, the city authorities desperately wanted to find Paul and Silas because, as Lyall notes, "failure to suppress such sedition might have brought severe punishment and loss of their city's status upon them."[87]

The second charge against Paul and Silas was their defiance of the decrees of Caesar, namely proclaiming another king known as Jesus (v. 7). This is the only instance where such a charge is made against Paul, and the obscurity of this allegation has produced much discussion. Two

---

"unpacking" how Paul and Silas were acting contrary to the decrees of Caesar—namely proclaiming another king. See also Barrett, *Acts*, 2:816; Dunn, *Acts*, 228; Neagoe, *Trial of the Gospel*, 191 n. 71; Still, *Conflict*, 75 n. 60; Talbert, *Reading Acts*, 157; Witherington, *Acts*, 507.

83. BDAG, 699; *CIG* 3:4416; L&N, 1.83; *OGIS* 666.4, 668.5; P.Oxy. 7.1021.5ff; L. T. Johnson, *Acts of the Apostles*, 307; Michel, "οἰκουμένη," 157; Weitbrecht, "World Upside Down," 526–27; Louw and Nida note that in the appropriate context, "the meaning of οἰκουμένη is simply the Roman Empire as a region, a governmental entity, and a population" (1:83 n. 14).

84. BDAG, 72; Bruce, *Acts of the Apostles*, 371; Cassidy, *Society and Politics*, 90; Judge, "Decrees," 7; L&N, 39.41; Pohill, *Acts*, 362 n. 59. Judge proposes, "There may have been an imperial edict covering Jewish messianic agitation which the Thessalonian informer invoked . . . however, accusations of disturbing the peace in general were always a good lever to open a case." See Neyrey, "Symbolic Universe," 271.

85. See Pohill, *Acts*, 362 n. 59.

86. L. T. Johnson, *Acts of the Apostles*, 307.

87. Lyall, *Slaves, Citizens, Sons*, 234. See also Davies, *Gospel and the Land*, 234. Davies argues that the Roman authorities in Thessalonica knew the accusation of sedition was false.

questions with regard to the decrees of Caesar are relevant for the present work: first, what are the decrees of Caesar, and second, what bearing does this have on the Thessalonian correspondence?

There is proliferating disagreement regarding the exact identity of the decrees of Caesar. Several scholars contend that the decrees refer to the violation of civic law by causing sedition.[88] As discussed above, inciting a riot was a serious offense and demanded swift legal action. However, Bruce has noted that causing an insurgence was "an offense against public law that required no special decree of Caesar to make it illegal."[89] If this was the case, then the decrees of Caesar possibly referred to some sort of imperial edict mandated by the emperor. It was not uncommon for the emperor to issue certain decrees that would preserve his rule. For example, in AD 16, Tiberius instituted an edict that made it illegal for anyone to predict the death or the usurping of rulers:

> But for all the other astrologers and magicians and such as practiced divination in anyway whatsoever, he put to death those who were foreigners and banished all the citizens that were accused to still employing the art at this time after the previous decree by which it had been forbidden to engage in any such business in the city.[90]

There is further evidence of a decree referred to as "the oath of loyalty to Caesar."[91] This oath applied to all Roman and non-Roman citizens who were expected to pledge their allegiance to and even worship the emperor. Adherence to this oath is illustrated by the citizens of Paphlagonia, who swore a personal oath of loyalty to Caesar so the Romans could do business among them:

> I swear . . . that I will support Caesar Augustus, his children and descendants throughout my life, in word, deed, and thought . . . that in whatsoever concerns them I will spare neither body nor soul nor life nor children . . . that whenever I see or hear of anything being said, planned or done against them I will report it . . .

---

88. See, for example, Lightfoot, "Church of Thessalonica," 253–69; Stegemann, *Zwischen Synagoge*, 237; Tajra, *Trial of St. Paul*, 36.

89. Bruce, *Acts of the Apostles*, 371. See also Donfried, "Cults," 343; Judge, "Decrees," 2; Manus, "Luke's Account of Paul," 27–38; Sherwin-White, *Roman Society*, 103; Witherington, *Acts*, 508.

90. Cassius Dio 57.15.8.

91. See Cassidy, *Society and Politics*, 195 n. 22; Judge, "Decrees," 5.

and whomsoever they regard as enemies I will attack and pursue with arms and the sword by land and by sea.[92]

Jews were exempt from emperor worship, and Rome permitted them to continue cultic practices. There were, however, as Smallwood notes, stipulations regarding such immunity:

> The Roman government recognized the Jews' moral right to practice their religion without hindrance; but its duties included the maintenance of law and order and public morality, and if the Jews in any individual locality traded on their privileges to contravene Roman law or act in any way thought to endanger public order or morality, they came under the penalties of the law on equal terms with Gentile offenders.[93]

The most probable identity of the "decrees of Caesar" is that the Jewish opponents accused Paul of direct violation to the "oath of loyalty."[94] This is further substantiated by the following clause, βασιλέα ἕτερον λέγοντες εἶναι Ἰησοῦν, which specifically identifies the *particular* decree the missionaries were accused of opposing.[95] As the empire's representatives, the politarchs were responsible for upholding this oath and would have been liable to administer punishment for such disloyalty.[96]

The jealousy the Jews had towards the Christian missionaries, which they expressed by accusing them of violating "the decrees of Caesar," was in all likelihood religiously motivated. But it is also important not to overlook the political nature of the allegation. Thessalonica was a free city, and the citizens wanted to maintain that privileged status. The Jewish opponents understood the political ramifications that the city would face if Paul and Silas were not dealt with. Persuading the

---

92. Ehrenberg and Jones, *Documents*, 315, cited in Judge, "Decrees," 6.
93. Smallwood, *Jews under Roman Rule*, 210. See also Tajra, *Trial of St. Paul*, 23.
94. See Donfried, "Cults," 343; Judge, *Social Pattern*, 34–35.
95. In the preceding clause Luke recorded that οὗτοι πάντες ἀπέναντι (they all act contrary). Arguably the word "they" not only included Paul and Silas but also Jason, who would have been considered guilty and able to face legal charges. The improper preposition ἀπέναντι with the genitive is used as an indicator of hostility or strong opposition towards something. See, for example, BDAG, 101; L&N, 90.35; LSJ, 185; MM, 57; Sir 37:4.
96. See Donfried, "Cults," 344; and Judge, "Decrees," 7, who also refers to an inscription from Samos, which reveals that it was the responsibility of the local magistrates to administer the oath of loyalty and to hear the complaints and accusations of those who dishonored this oath.

residents that the missionaries were plotting treason against the emperor would have certainly brought swift action against them since it was an extremely serious offense. In fact, Tajra has commented that:

> for a Roman citizen to proclaim *regem alium* over against the sovereign head of the Empire would exact the most rigorous punishment. Indeed the text of Acts clearly shows that the crowd present in the Forum and the magistrates were shocked and angered when they heard the accusations.[97]

This was not only a serious accusation against Paul and Silas but also caused a severe predicament for Jason. The Jews knew that Jason not only aligned himself with the Christian preachers but that he also housed them. By harboring the accused, Jason would have also been charged with treason and faced legal consequences until the missionaries could be located (v. 9).[98]

The city officials made Jason legally responsible for the missionaries by forcing him to pay a ἱκανός. Simply put, the magistrates forced Jason to "be a guarantor that Paul would not return."[99] The term ἱκανός is often found in legal contexts referring to security or bail.[100] The surety was paid to the city officials and would have been forfeited by Jason if the offense was repeated.[101] Since Paul and Silas could not be found, the politarchs made Jason pledge that he would not instigate such actions and that he would ensure the missionaries' departure.[102] This would seemingly not only satisfy the citizens but also the magistrates who wanted to maintain order and prove their loyalty to Rome. Moreover, Tajra suggests that:

> the politarchs' main concern was to maintain public order and to calm the powerful passions aroused among the population. This

---

97. Tajra, *Trial of St. Paul*, 36. See also L. T. Johnson, *Acts of the Apostles*, 307, who further comments that "as in the trial of Jesus the confession of Jesus as 'Messiah' is put in the most politically inflammatory form. Such activity is generally subversive" (Luke 23:2).

98. See Bauman, *Crimen Maiestatis*, 266–92; Donfried *Paul*, 32–34; Judge, "Decrees," 2.

99. Hemer, *Book of Acts*, 186. See also Millar, "Emperor," 156–66.

100. See, for example, Mark 15:15; BGU, 530.38; *OGIS*, 629.100; P.Oxy. 2.259.29; Cassidy, *Society and Politics*, 91; Moulton, *Greek Prolegomena*, 20–21; Spicq, "ἱκανός," 221–22; Tajra, *Trial of St. Paul*, 43.

101. Newman and Nida, 331–32.

102. Barrett, *Acts*, 2:816–17; Bruce, *Book of Acts*, 345; Dunn, *Acts*, 228; Hemer, *Book of Acts*, 186.

was accomplished by Paul's *banishment*, which had the effect of putting an impassable chasm between the apostle and the newly-founded church at Thessalonica.[103]

Consequently, Paul and Silas left the city and were immediately sent away at night to Berea (17:10).

In summary, by accusing Paul and Silas of defying the decrees of Caesar, the Jews essentially indicted them for violating the oath of loyalty to the emperor. Their motives were arguably both religiously and politically charged. The Jews wanted Paul and Silas gone, since they had disrupted synagogue life by preaching a crucified and risen Messiah. In order to accomplish this they falsely accused the missionaries of plotting the overthrow of the emperor. This forced a legal response from the Roman officials to expel Paul and Silas from Thessalonica.

The second question regarding the "decrees of Caesar" is: what effect does this have on the Thessalonian correspondence? Upon the missionaries' departure from Thessalonica, the situation also proved difficult for the new Christians, who began to suffer persecution at the hand of their neighbors (1 Thess 2:14–16, 3:2–3; 2 Thess 1:4–7). The unbelieving citizens (Jews and Gentiles) living in Thessalonica likely viewed these new converts as allies of the "trouble makers" who were forced to leave. The Jewish opponents were likely a source of persecution since the Thessalonian believers continued to advance the gospel concerning the Messiah, not only in Thessalonica but also to those beyond the regions of Macedonia and Achaia (1 Thess 1:8). The Jewish unbelievers in Thessalonica had slandered Paul by portraying him and his ministry to be illegitimate, motivated by greed, and concerned with only pleasing men (1 Thess 2:1–6, 2:10). It seems probable that the Thessalonian Christians likewise suffered similar ridicule as they too were maligned as those who do not know God. This is made evident throughout the Thessalonian epistles where Paul often reiterated to these believers of their true knowledge of God (1 Thess 1:4, 1:9–10; 2 Thess 1:10, 2:13).

Moreover, the Thessalonian Christians likely suffered further persecutions from the Gentile residents of the city who likely considered the members of this church as a potential threat to their city's status and privilege with Rome. During his tenure in Thessalonica, Paul not only taught that Jesus was Lord but also that he would soon return (1 Thess

---

103. Tajra, *Trial of St. Paul*, 43.

5:2; 2 Thess 2:5). Gentiles hearing such a proclamation would have been greatly concerned by such a statement because they understood this to be a prediction of the emperor's demise and thus a direct violation of the oath of loyalty.[104] Once the instigators of such claims were banished, the Gentiles seemingly directed their rage towards the Thessalonian church. As a result, Dunn has suggested that these new believers were likewise considered to have been "turning the world (or Empire) upside down, [which] was to threaten the foundations of established order and custom."[105] The mob believed that the Thessalonian Christians had committed an offense against the emperor by proclaiming a king other than Caesar. This was viewed as a breach of the personal oath of loyalty, an oath that Paul and these new converts could not obey, and ultimately led to their persecution.

The riot and false allegations initiated by the nonbelieving Jews during Paul's ministry in Thessalonica had ongoing effects on the Christians living in the city. Similar to Paul and Silas, the Thessalonian Christians were likely seen as apostates of Judaism and enemies of Rome. Upon Paul's departure from Thessalonica, the Christians residing in the city encountered tremendous slander and persecution for their faith in Christ (1 Thess 2:14–16). It is not surprising, then, that throughout the Thessalonian epistles, Paul's great affection and kindred spirit for these new believers is manifest. Not only were they all members of the family of God, but they also stood firm together with great perseverance as they shared in the same sufferings for Christ (1 Thess 1:2–10, 2:13–16; 2 Thess 1:3–4, 2:13–15).

3.3 CONCLUSION

The foregoing study of Acts 17:1–9 is crucial for gaining an accurate interpretation of Second Thessalonians. By understanding the cultural reaction of the Thessalonian residents to the gospel message, it becomes seemingly apparent why Paul and these new converts were slandered and persecuted. For the unbelieving Jews, Paul and the Thessalonian church

---

104. The term ταράσσω denotes throwing into mental or spiritual agitation and confusion. See Spicq, "ταράσσω," 372–76, who notes that ταράσσω is also the technical term for insurrections, political agitation, or riots. For further evidence of this particular nuance, see Acts 16:8–13, 19:23; 3 Macc 3:24; BDAG, 990; BGU, 889.23; L&N, 39.44; LSJ, 1757–58; Müller, "ταράσσω," 709–711; SIG 684:13; SEG 9.168.8.

105. Dunn, Acts, 228.

posed a threat to synagogue life, and they may have been viewed as "evildoers." Prompted by jealousy, these Jews instigated a riot and accused the missionaries, along with some of the brethren, of being conspirators against the empire. Fearing that their privileged status with Rome was in jeopardy, the citizens of Thessalonica erupted and demanded legal action from the city's magistrates. As a result, Paul and Silas were banished from Thessalonica, and the newly formed church became the object of persecution from both nonbelieving Jews and Gentiles.

Despite the apostle's shortened stay, his banishment from the city, and the intense persecution from their neighbors, the Thessalonian Christians stood firm in their faith and remained steadfast in advancing the gospel (1 Thess 1:2–3). Paul rejoiced and thanked God for the kindred relationship he had with this church whose members had suffered similar persecutions as he experienced and whose faith was proven genuine as they persevered and remained devoted to Christ. Inevitably, however, these young believers grew discouraged by the regular disparagement they faced. Consequently, the Thessalonian church longed for the Day of the Lord since that would mean an end to suffering and their ultimate vindication. Understanding their need for encouragement, Paul wrote Second Thessalonians with the intent to exhort this suffering church to be resolute as they continued to advance the gospel and await their justification at the Lord's return. Although they were persecuted and slandered as enemies of God and Rome, Paul assured them that their vindication would come at the final assize. It will be argued, then, that because of the situation that Paul and these new Christians faced at Thessalonica, the apostle intentionally incorporated judicial language, allusions, and idioms drawing from the Day of the Lord motif found throughout the Old Testament in order to remind the Thessalonian church that at God's court, his faithful believers would be found not as enemies of God but rather his children. It will further be argued that by using such forensic language Paul also assured the Thessalonian Christians that those who persecuted them would be declared the Lord's enemies and found guilty at his court.

The previous chapters have seemingly demonstrated several key factors essential for interpreting Second Thessalonians. First, understanding the importance of Thessalonica's relationship with Rome may also be crucial for appreciating why Paul and the Thessalonian Christians experienced persecution and slander and thus longed for the return of the Lord. Second, demonstrating that Second Thessalonians could reasonably be considered authentic and not pseudonymous affords a more precise understanding of Paul's theological background and motivations for integrating Old Testament forensic motifs into Second Thessalonians. Third, it seems imperative to appreciate Paul as a Jew who relied primarily on the Old Testament for *theologically* instructing the recipients of his biblical writings. As a Jewish Christian, he understood Jesus to be the Messiah and the fulfillment of the Old Testament. At the same time, Paul was certainly aware of the cultural milieu in which he lived and ministered. But as a Jew, his *theological* instruction would have most likely found its basis in the Old Testament. Fourth, although not as rigorously debated as it was in years past, the book of Acts may be understood as both theologically and a historically reliable source, which provides a clearer picture regarding the conflict at Thessalonica and why the new Christians living in this Roman city longed for the Day of the Lord and their vindication.

The following chapters will examine the possible legal language that Paul arguably utilized in 2 Thess 1 and how such language affects the context, purpose, and meaning of the apostle's letter to his beloved and persecuted church at Thessalonica.

4

The Judicial Language of 2 Thess 1

THE PREVIOUS CHAPTERS HAVE laid a foundation for the study of Second Thessalonians. The historical background of Thessalonica, the probable authenticity of the epistle, the importance of Paul's Jewish background and his reliance upon the Old Testament, the historical accuracy of Acts, and the account of Paul's ministry in Thessalonica as recorded in Acts 17, have provided the necessary background for further examination of the author's original intended meaning of Second Thessalonians. In order to accomplish this objective, the following discussion seeks only to prove that 2 Thess 1 contains judicial language, imagery, and allusions for the specific purpose of encouraging the persecuted church at Thessalonica. It will be argued that Paul purposefully used such a forensic word grouping to remind the Thessalonians that, though they were defamed and ridiculed by their pagan neighbors, God would vindicate them because of their faith in Christ and resolve amid great persecution. It will be suggested that the existence of legal language not only enables a better understanding of the context of Second Thessalonians but also provides timeless applications for contemporary Christians facing similar struggles.

Since Paul's Jewish heritage has been demonstrated to be crucial for understanding his *theological* instruction, the majority of the examination will focus primarily on biblical and ancient Jewish texts. These contextual discussions of the various legal idioms throughout such literature aim to not only confirm that Paul did utilize judicial language but, by doing so, it more than likely allowed his intended meaning to be clearly understood, namely that the Thessalonian Christians must persevere until the final assize, when their vindication would come. However, because Paul was not ignorant of his cultural surroundings, secular literature will be consulted to determine what influence, if any, such writings had on how the apostle *theologically* understood the proposed forensic concepts incorporated throughout 2 Thess 1. The Thessalonian believers had suffered greatly since Paul's departure and were undoubtedly anxious for the Lord's return (1 Thess 2:14–16; 2 Thess 1:4, 6–7). Still contends that the apostle reminded the Thessalonian church that:

> although the parousia of Jesus had yet to occur, the faithful Lord would come in due course. At his coming, the harassed elect would receive rest, and the Lord would pour out vengeance on those who neither know God nor obey the gospel.[1]

Simply put, the apostle likely wrote to encourage the Thessalonian church that at the Day of the Lord he would convene his court, vindicate the believers, and punish their persecutors.

4.1 THE PROPOSED LEGAL LANGUAGE IN 2 THESS 1

The brevity of 2 Thess 1 does not negate its importance. Exegetes cannot simply give this chapter a superficial reading before moving into what is often considered the more "substantial" chapters of the epistle.[2] New Testament scholars realize that Paul typically explained the purpose and theme for his letters in the introductory greeting or shortly thereafter.[3] It should be of no surprise, therefore, that such a pattern seems obvious in this pericope, especially with the presence of the suggested judicial word clustering.

Paul began Second Thessalonians in typical fashion with an introductory greeting and thanksgiving (verses 1–4). These verses are identical to those found in First Thessalonians, except for the additional ὀφείλομεν in verse 3. O'Brien notes that this term "points neither to formality in language [or] grudging praise . . . but indicates the apostle was personally indebted to God to give thanks for the Thessalonians."[4] Paul expressed thanks to God because the faith of the Thessalonian

---

1. Still, *Conflict*, 197. See also Giblin, *Threat to Faith*, 7, who further explains that for the unbelievers the coming of the Lord to judge is "seen as a day of requital for unbelievers and the day of reward for those whose faith is being tested."

2. Much of the literature written on Second Thessalonians pertains to the identity of the "man of lawlessness" in chapter 2.

3. See Giblin, *Threat to Faith*, 6 n. 1. See also Reed, "Identifying Theme," 75–101; J. L. White, "Saint Paul," 433–44.

4. O'Brien, *Introductory Thanksgivings*, 171.

Christians had been greatly enlarged and the love they had for one another continued to grow. Consequently, the apostle spoke proudly of them to other churches because they stood firm in their faith while enduring intense persecution. The following chapter will address the introductory thanksgiving in detail; it is simply mentioned here because it prepares the examination of the suggested forensic language throughout the remainder of 2 Thess 1.

It is relatively clear that Paul was not welcome by the majority of residents in Thessalonica. His message of Jesus as both Messiah and King was offensive to unbelieving Jews and Gentiles, which led to his early departure from the city (Acts 17:1–9). However, his brief ministry at Thessalonica was by no means fruitless. The gospel message had penetrated the hearts of some, which resulted in the formation of a local Christian congregation (1 Thess 1:1; 2 Thess 1:1). According to verses 4–10, subsequent to the apostle's forced exit from Thessalonica, the unbelieving residents concentrated their enmity for the gospel message toward the Christian remnant that remained. The result of such suffering resulted in Paul further encouraging this church to remain steadfast as they awaited their vindication at the Lord's return (2 Thess 1:4–10). Such encouragement is palpable through the use of judicial language to reassure the Thessalonian Christians that, though their neighbors slandered them, God would declare them innocent at his eschatological court.

Second Thessalonians 1:5–10 begins Paul's intentional word clustering of judicial idioms. The following examination of each verse seeks to prove that the apostle understood the Day of the Lord motif throughout the Old Testament as an appointed court day, which from Paul's perspective would ultimately be fulfilled at Christ's return. As a result, it will be suggested that the apostle intentionally borrowed from this concept and incorporated legal terms, idioms, and allusions in 2 Thess 1 for the purpose of further supporting and encouraging these afflicted believers to continue persevering in their faith as they awaited the final assize.

4.1.1 ἔνδειγμα

The initial term in verse 5, ἔνδειγμα, warrants a closer examination for a possible legal connotation. Although this term is a *hapax legomena* in the New Testament, its synonyms ἔνδείχνυμι and ἔνδειξις are found throughout the Pauline corpus, oftentimes used in contexts as verification against the enemies of God and the punishment they will face at his eschatological court (Rom 2:15; Phil 1:28; 2 Tim 4:14). For instance, in Phil 1:28, Paul reminded the church that their oppressors had shown ample ἔνδειξις as enemies of the gospel, which would serve as an indictment against them and would result in their eventual destruction. Conversely, the Philippian believers' faithful partnership for the advancement of the gospel was ἔνδειξις of their soteriological exoneration. Philippians 1:28 demands that the reader understand ἔνδειγμα to denote an eschatological reference for at least three reasons. First, in the immediate context Paul had been referring to his own eschatological outlook (verse 21–24).[5] He was uncertain of the outcome of his current imprisonment; he would either live or die. However, regardless of the outcome his desire was to depart and be with Christ. For Paul, death was gain, and he wanted this future certainty embedded in the minds of the Philippians as they continued advancing the gospel in the midst of opposition (Phil 1:22–23).[6] Second, the nouns ἀπωλείας and σωτηρίας are predominately used throughout the New Testament in contexts referring to eternal destruction or eternal salvation (Matt 7:13; Rom 9:22; 1 Cor 1:18; 1 Thess 5:8–9; 2 Thess 2:13; 2 Pet 2:1).[7] Third, the pronoun αὐτοῖς could be generally understood as a dative of reference but more specifically as possibly one of disadvantage.[8] In other words, the opponents' hostility towards the gospel served as irrefutable condemning ἔνδειξις against them and would result in their future judgment at God's court. This is further emphasized with the following genitive phrase ὑμῶν δὲ σωτηρίας, which accentuates the fact that the Philippians' perseverance and advancement of the gospel was indisputable ἔνδειξις of their ultimate salvation.[9] It seems reasonable, then, that in this passage Paul

---

5. See also Fee, *Philippians*, 169.

6. Ibid., 168.

7. See Hawthorne, "Interpretation and Translation," 80–81; Loh and Nida, *Translators Handbook*, 42. They understand the terms ἀπωλείας and σωτηρίας as a reference to physical destruction and deliverance. But this fails to understand both Paul's immediate viewpoint in the passage and the predominate use of the terms in eschatological contexts.

8. See Dana and Mantey, *Manual Grammar*, 84–85; Robertson, *Grammar*, 538–39; Wallace, *Greek Grammar*, 142–44; Zerwick, *Biblical Greek*, 20.

9. See Banker, *Semantic and Structural Analysis*, 73; Beare, *Commentary*, 67–68; Fee, *Philippians*, 169–70; O'Brien, *Epistle to the Philippians*, 155–56; Silva, *Philippians*, 89–90; Wallace, *Greek Grammar*, 143–44. See also Collange, *Epistle of Saint Paul*, 74–75; Hawthorne, "Interpretation and Translation," 80–81. They argue for the variant reading ὑμῖν. This, however, fails on at least two accounts: (1) this seems to be an apparent

utilized ἔνδειξις to denote the evidence that would indict the oppressors and exculpate the Philippians at the final assize.

A further instance that seems to demonstrate the judicial quality of ἔνδειξις is found in 2 Tim 4:14.[10] In this passage, Timothy was instructed to be cautious of Alexander the coppersmith, who did much harm to Paul and vehemently opposed the gospel message. Since the text does not reveal the nature of injury, which Alexander imposed against the apostle, all suggestions remain conjecture. However, Fee has argued that:

> the harm Alexander imposed against Paul was to have him arrested. This is further supported by the fact that the verb ἐνδείχνυμι was often used with the legal sense of "inform against," and by the note in verse 15 that he strongly opposed (same verb as in 3:8) our message.[11]

Regardless of the type of impairment Alexander imposed, it seems clear from the context that his actions would serve as arraigning evidence against him at God's eschatological court. This conllusion is further strengthened by the use of the future verb ἀποδώσει, which is often found in contexts indicating the Lord's final recompense against those who disobey him (Ps 62:12; Matt 12:36; Rom 2:6–8; Rev 22:12). Moreover, Mounce observes that the judicial aspect of ἐνδείχνυμι is even more implicit if "Alexander's opposition to ἡμετέροις λόγοις in v. 15 refers to Paul's words of defense at his trial."[12] The harsh treatment that Alexander directed against Paul would serve as an imprecation against him, and as a result he would suffer God's penal vengeance.[13]

---

correction by the Majority Text to alleviate a difficult reading; (2) the antithesis is not between αὐτοῖς and ὑμῶν but rather ἀπωλείας and σωτηρίας. Paul is simply contrasting the future destruction of the oppressors and the future salvation of the Philippians.

10. While the Pauline authorship of the Pastoral Epistles is contested, there seems to be increasing evidence for their authenticity. For evidence supporting this claim, see Fee, *Timothy and Titus*, 23–31; L. T. Johnson, *Letters to Timothy*, 55–91; Mounce, *Pastoral Epistles*, cxviii–cxxix; Wilder, *Pseudonymity*, 221–27.

11. Fee, *Timothy and Titus*, 295–96. See also G. W. Knight, *Pastoral Epistles*, 467–68; Mounce, *Pastoral Epistles*, 592–93; Spicq, *Les Épîtres Pastorales*, 394.

12. Mounce, *Pastoral Epistles*, 593.

13. See also Marshall, *Pastoral Epistles*, 822; Moule, "Punishment and Retribution," 21–36. Cf. Spicq, *Les Épîtres Pastorales*, 34, who comments that "C'est une prediction, non une imprecation." But this argument is based on the weakly attested variant reading, which suggests the subjunctive ἀποδῴη. The majority of manuscript evidence supports ἀποδώσει.

Moreover, there is also apparent evidence that other New Testament authors understood the various constructions of ἔνδειγμα as forensic evidence against those at the Day of Lord (2 Pet 2:6–9; Jude 7). In Second Peter, the author denounced false teachers who had infiltrated the various churches to which the letter was addressed. In fact, Bauckhaum suggests that "2 Peter is a polemical document . . . that employs not only a denunciation but also apologetic arguments in defense of the eschatological teaching of the apostles against their objections."[14] Specifically, in 2 Pet 2:4–10, the apostle described the certainty of final judgment by using various Old Testament illustrations: angels who sinned, the ungodly in Noah's day, and Sodom and Gomorrah. Neyrey has even noted that "it is characteristic of the author to perceive in Old Testament events; not just ad hoc examples of divine judgment, but prophecies of the parousia judgment (cf. 3:5–7, 10, 13)."[15] The opponents questioned the reality of such judgment, and Peter reminded his audience that God used these two cities as ὑπόδειγμα in order to demonstrate that the actions of those who live ungodly lives would serve as evidence against them when they appear before God's final tribunal.

Arguably, however, Paul's knowledge of the judicial nuance of ἔνδειγμα stemmed from the term's usage throughout the Old Testament. The Septuagint typically translates ἐνδείχνυμι from the Hebrew גמל, לכד or ראה, which are terms often found in contexts referring to evidence in judgment or forensic matters (Deut 32:6; Josh 7:14–18; Ps 137:8; Isa 3:11, 8:15, 28:13; Jer 6:11).[16] For instance, in Josh 7:14–18 God commanded Israel to present themselves by tribes in order to punish the family who had sinned by taking the spoils of war. The nation was essentially on trial for disobedience, and God would not allow Israel's military campaign to be successful until the sin was eradicated. The legal nature of this passage is further strengthened by the word קרב. Consequently, Kühlewein has noted that when the term קרב does appear in such contexts, "it indicates appearance in legal proceedings and for a legal decision."[17] Achan

---

14. Bauckham, *Jude, 2 Peter*, 154. See also J. D. Charles, *Virtue amidst Vice*, 47 n. 14; Harrington, *Jude, 2 Peter*, 233–35; J. Knight, *2 Peter and Jude*, 57–74; Neyrey, "Form," 12.

15. Neyrey, "Form," 88.

16. For thorough discussions regarding the judicial nuances of these terms, see, for example, Carpenter, "גמל," 871–73; Lewis, "גמל," 166–67; Sauer, "גמל," 320–21; Seybold, "גמל," 29; W. Kaiser, "לכד," 479–80; Konkel, "לכד," 800–1; Fuhs, "ראה," 224–28.

17. Kühlewein, "קרב," 1165. See also Coppes, "קרב," 812; Gane and Milgrom,

was found guilty of the crime, resulting not only in his execution but also the death of his family and seizing of his possessions. R. Clements observes that:

> Achan stands accused of a uniquely heinous action, and his guilt is readily shown up by God and later openly confirmed by his confession. The necessary punishment is then inflicted by the community without compunction or mercy. . . . In a unique way it is against God that [Achan] has sinned, and all Israel is forced to suffer until his guilt is purged.[18]

In essence, the nation was subpoenaed to appear before God, who presided over the legal proceeding. The evidence incriminated Achan, and when the Lord declared his verdict, the sin was purged from the nation.

Several instances throughout both the Old and New Testaments, particularly throughout the Pauline corpus, seem to demonstrate that ἔνδείχνυμι was often used in judicial contexts. However, it should be mentioned that ἔνδείχνυμι is also found throughout secular Greek literature as a reference to legal evidence.[19] For instance, proof that ἔνδείχνυμι was often used as a forensic term is found in the writings of Philo. In his exposition of Num 5:12–31, he recounted that a woman charged with adultery must appear before the judges.[20] If she was found innocent, her husband was required to present sufficient ἔνδείχνυμι to prove that his accusations were not malevolently motivated.[21]

The preceding discussion has revealed that ἔνδειγμα was commonly used in legal contexts in both the Scripture and secular literature. It seems valid, then, to conclude that Paul may have understood ἔνδειγμα

"קרב," 138–39. Furthermore, Kühlewein notes that depending on the context, קרב can refer to people presenting themselves for punishment either by God or human authorities or it can refer to the Lord himself drawing near to deliver his verdict.

18. Clements, "Achan's Sin," 113–26. See also Auld, *Joshua*, 143–44; Stec, "Mantle Hidden by Achan," 356–59.

19. See, for example, *IG* 22.1128.18; *IG* 52 266.44; *LSJ*, 558; *OGIS* 669.45; Demosthenes 19.113; Plato 9.856C; H. A. A. Kennedy, "Epistle of Paul," 431.

20. The term "judges" should in all likelihood be understood in the context of Num 5:12–31, as the priests.

21. Philo *On the Special Laws* 3.55. Further examples abound, which demonstrate that that ἔνδείχνυμι was understood as a term denoting legal evidence throughout Hellenistic literature. See, for example, Demosthenes 20.156; *IG* 22 1128.35; *IG* 52.266.44; Isocrates 18.20; Lysias 6.15; Plato *Apologia* 32b; Philo *On the Special Laws* 3.139.

as a judicial term to denote evidence used at court, particularly God's eschatological court. Moreover, Bruce has argued that:

> the fact that [the Thessalonians] were enduring persecution and affliction for Christ's sake is sure [evidence] of God's righteous judgment, which will be vindicated in them and in their persecutors at the Advent of Christ.[22]

Therefore, in accordance with the context of 2 Thess 1 and the semantic domain of ἔνδειγμα, it may be reasonable to assume that Paul utilized ἔνδειγμα in a legal sense to signify evidence that would not only indict God's enemies but vindicate the Thessalonians when they appear before him at the final assize.

4.1.2 δικαίας κρίσεως τοῦ θεοῦ

A further possibility of forensic language in 2 Thess 1:5 is found in the genitive phrase δικαίας κρίσεως τοῦ θεοῦ. The subjective genitive τοῦ θεοῦ indicates that it is God's judgment that is right and that, "for the Thessalonians, the evidence of the righteous judgment of God consisted in their endurance of persecutions and afflictions, which Paul mentioned in v. 4."[23] Syntactically, δικαίας is simply used adjectivally to emphasize the equitable nature of God's judgment, but it should also be noted that the idea of δικαίας κρίσεως is found throughout the Pauline corpus in contexts referring to God's judgment at the final assize (Rom 2:5, 3:26; 2 Tim 4:8).[24] For instance, in Rom 1–3, scholars such as Cambier have argued that the apostle's intent was to demonstrate that "Dieu seul juge tous les hommes selon la vérité, finalement selon l'esprit de l'Evangile de Jésus-Christ."[25] Specifically in 2:5, Paul reminded the Jews that they, like the Gentiles, would also be held accountable to God. Paul condemned the arrogance of the Jews, who believed that their favored position with God would allow them to escape his judgment. As Moo points out:

---

22. Bruce, *Thessalonians*, 149.

23. Wanamaker, *Epistles to the Thessalonians*, 221. See also Best, *Commentary*, 255; G. Green, *Thessalonians*, 284; Malherbe, *Thessalonians*, 394; Morris, *Thessalonians*, 196–98. For a discussion surrounding the theological issues of the phrase whether the judgment is eschatological or present, see chapter 5.

24. See Robertson, *Grammar*, 776. He notes that in the first attributive position the adjective receives more emphasis than the substantive. Cf. Porter, *Idioms*, 116–17; Wallace, *Greek Grammar*, 306.

25. Cambier, "Le Jugement," 213.

The Jews are no better off than the Gentiles in the judgment. This is a radical departure from all Jewish tradition and implies not only a critique of the prevailing understanding of God's covenant with Israel but also that a new era in salvation history had dawned.[26]

This reality is further emphasized in 2:6–11, where Paul explained that God judges both Jew and Gentile equally. It seems that the apostle's point in verse 5, then, was to demonstrate that the impartial judicial administration of God applies to both Jew and Gentile.[27] In the end, all will stand before God, who alone possesses true δικαίας κρίσεως.

Similarly, other New Testament authors suggest a judicial nuance regarding the idiom δικαίας κρίσεως (Acts 17:31; 1 Pet 2:23; Rev 16:7). For instance, Rev 16 details the seven angels who unleash the bowls of God's wrath upon the earth. The construction δίκαιος εἶ in 16:5 is probably an intertextual translation of hwhy ht) qydc and indicates a "vindication formula."[28] With regard to such a construction Staples has mentioned that:

> this particular formula is sometimes preceded/followed by יכּ/ὅτι clause which indicates the grounds for stating (better *re*-stating) the fact that God is indeed still righteous; despite all indications to the contrary.[29]

Here the "angel of the waters" praises God because his judgments are not only fair but also justified against those who have murdered his saints and prophets. Consequently, verse 7 seemingly operates as the antiphon affirming God's judgments as both ἀληθινός and δίκαιος.[30] These final judgments, therefore, are rooted in the very nature of God's character, which is the epitome of truth and righteousness.[31]

---

26. Moo, *Romans*, 133. See also Dunn, *Romans 1–8*, 83–86; Lamp, "Paul," 37–51; Schreiner, *Romans*, 108–110.

27. See Bassler, "Divine Impartiality," 43–58; Cambier, "Le Jugement," 187–213.

28. See J. M. Ford, "Structure and Meaning," 327–331; Staples, "Revelation 16:4–6," 280–93. Cf. Betz, "Zum Problem," 391–409. According to Betz, 16:5-6 "Es handelt sich um Gerichtsdoxologie, beginnend mit δίκαιος εἶ, wie wir sie aus dem Alten Testament kennen."

29. Staples, "Revelation 16:4–6," 280 n. 3.

30. See Osborne, *Revelation*, 585. Osborne comments that "in Revelation ἀληθινός is always used of God or Christ, and it refers both to their covenant faithfulness and to the absolute reality of their deeds and judgments."

31. Ibid.

While δικαίας certainly functions as an adjective in the genitival construction δικαίας κρίσεως, it is κρίσεως that prescribes further examination, for in the context it arguably denotes a forensic understanding. The term commonly conveys the meaning of the judgment of a court, the results of a trial, acting as judge, and penal judgment.[32] In many biblical contexts, the judgment refers to the sentence of condemnation against an individual, such as in the Day of the Lord (Isa 34:8; Matt 10:15; Jude 6). Furthermore, κρίσις is oftentimes used in contexts depicting God or Christ as the Judge carrying out a legal procedure (Joel 3:12; Acts 17:31; Heb 12:23). Throughout the Pauline corpus, it appears evident that the apostle understood κρίσις as a legal term and likely utilized it in several forensic contexts (Rom 2:1–11; 1 Cor 3:15; 2 Thess 1:5; 1 Tim 5:24). An example is found in Rom 1–3 where Paul declared that all, both Jew and Gentile, are culpable and must appear before God's court. The legal context of these chapters is made evident from the various forensic idioms that Paul utilized to emphasize that *all* have a divine appointment to appear before God's tribunal.[33] The apostle's intention was arguably to demonstrate that God is impartial in his judgments and that he will judge both Jew and Gentile equally. Later in 2:5, Paul compounded δίκαιος with κρίσις, forming the *hapax legomenon* δικαιοκρισίας. The term continues the legal tone of the context. In fact, Fitzmyer has suggested that the word "has the connotation of God's condemnatory judgment, stressing the equity of the divine sentence to be issued on the Day of the Lord."[34] The judicial flavor of the text is further strengthened with the earlier use of ὀργῆς, which in the Pauline corpus typically denotes an eschatological nuance (Rom 2:8, 3:5, 5:9; Eph 5:6; Col 3:6; 1 Thess 1:10, 5:9).[35] Moreover, the forensic nature of the context is made more explicit by the modifying relative clause in verse 6, which unpacks God's actions

---

32. BDAG, 569; LSJ, 997; Büchsel, "κρίνω," 921–943; Rissi, "κρίσις," 318–21; Malherbe, *Thessalonians*, 394–96; Wanamaker, *Epistles to the Thessalonians*, 220–23.

33. See Bassler, "Divine Impartiality," 43–58; Lamp, "Paul," 37–51; Travis, "Problem of Judgment," 52–57. For discussions of the various legal terms in Rom 1–3, see, for example, S. L. Johnson, "God Gave Them Up," 124–33; Schlatter, *Gottes Gerechtigkeit*, 66. For instance, Schlatter notes that in Rom 1:24, "παρέδωκεν ist das übliche Wort für den Spruch des Richters, durch den er die Vollstreckung der Strafe anordnet."

34. Fitzmyer, *Romans*, 301–2. He notes that δικαιοκρισίας is found in the Septuagint (Hos 6:5), and in the Qumran documents (1QH 1:23, 30; 1QS 4:4).

35. Cf. Wallace, *Greek Grammar*, 101 n. 78.

at the final assize.³⁶ With regard to the immediate context of 2 Thess 1, it seems best to conclude that Paul understood κρίσις as a forensic term.³⁷

Further examples of the judicial overtones of κρίσις are prevalent throughout the New Testament (Matt 10:15, 11:20–24; John 3:18–21, 5:27–28; Jude 6; Rev 14:7). In John 5:29, Jesus explained to the crowd that God the Father had given him the power to execute judgment and that the hour would come when those in the tombs would hear his voice and come forth. When this takes place, those who had committed evil deeds would face ἀνάστασιν κρίσεως, which seems certain to be a reference to the sentence of condemnation.³⁸ John likely understood Jesus to be the eschatological Judge, to whom the Father had given all authority. Regarding John's portrait of Jesus as the final Judge, J. T. Carroll concludes that "as revealer, judge, life-giver, and vanquisher of the world ruler . . . Jesus accomplishes full in the present the primary tasks of the end-time. He embodies the eschaton."³⁹

Both the Pauline corpus and the New Testament authors seem to indicate that in certain contexts κρίσις was understood as a legal term, oftentimes in reference to God's final judgment. Nevertheless, their awareness of the forensic nature of κρίσις was arguably derived from its use throughout the Old Testament. The Septuagint translates κρίσις from the Hebrew term שׁפט, which refers to either the office or role of a judge, as seen in Moses's position as judge or in relation to the king's responsibility to carry out justice (Exod 24:14; 1 Kgs 8:32). The term also denotes judgment between persons (Gen 16:5; Exod 24:14; Num

---

36. Cf. Porter, *Idioms*, 248.

37. Cf. 2 Tim 4:1–8 where Paul concluded the letter reminding his beloved disciple that when he appears before the Lord, the δίκαιος κριτής; on that eschatological day, he would be rewarded the crown of righteousness. The judicial aspect of the immediate context seems also to be enhanced from the previous idiom τῇ ἡμέρᾳ, "which is the technical term for God's final court (2 Tim 1:12, 1:18)." See Arichea and Hanton, *Handbook*, 246–47. The authors note that this is definitely an eschatological reference when considering his use of the same idiom in 2 Tim 1:12, 1:18, although in 1:12 it is in the accusative.

38. The genitives in ἀνάστασιν ζωῆς and ἀνάστασιν κρίσεως probably express both purpose and result. Wallace, *Greek Grammar*, 101, notes that John intends to communicate "the resurrection for the purpose of *and* which results in life/judgment." See also BDF, §166.

39. Carroll, "Present and Future," 63–69. See also Carson, *Divine Sovereignty*, 136–46; Morris, *Gospel according to John*, 283–85.

25:5) and between God and humans (Isa 66:16; Ezek 17:20).[40] Even so, the Old Testament unambiguously indicates that God alone is both the universal and final Judge whose verdicts are both righteous and impartial (Job 9:15; Ps 9:19; Isa 43:26, 66:16; Jer 25:31).[41] For example, in Isa 66 the prophet declared the reality of God's final judgments against the evil nations and the restoration of his people. Particularly in verse 16, God is portrayed as a divine warrior wielding his sword, preparing to slay his enemies. Specifically noteworthy from this "trial scene" depicted in Isa 66 are the various echoes of the divine warrior motif found not only in 2 Thess 1:5–8, but also in several instances throughout Pauline literature (1 Cor 1:8, 5:5; 2 Cor 1:14; Phil 1:6, 2:10).[42] The apostle demonstrated that he understood Jesus to be the eschatological agent of the Father who would not only pour out his divine retribution upon his enemies but would also bring ultimate victory for his followers. Such a theme of victory for Paul was connected with a forensic motif, since it would not be fully evident to all until the final assize.[43] While Paul certainly understood the present reality of the victory that Christ had accomplished through his death on the cross and his resurrection (Eph 1:20–23; Col 1:9–10), he further realized that "the verdict obtained at Calvary was [also] capable of literal application eschatologically, at the judgment seat of God."[44]

It is plausible then, that in 2 Thess 1:5–8 Paul was heavily dependant upon Isa 66 and the concept of the divine warrior who renders a judicial verdict upon his enemies to remind the Thessalonians that their vindication would come at Christ's return.[45] In fact, Roger Aus contends that to understand Isa 66 as the background of 2 Thess 1:5–8 is very reasonable:

> First, Isaiah 66:9 provided [Paul] with the delaying factor he needed to convince his addresses in chapter two that the Day of

---

40. Cf. Richard Schultz, "שׁפט," 213–21.

41. Ibid.

42. See Longman, "Divine Warrior," 290–307, who notes that in these references the "Day of Christ" refers to Christ as the Divine Warrior.

43. See, for example, Sherlock, *God Who Fights*, 335–41.

44. Ibid., 354.

45. See Aus, "Relevance," 252–68; Fudge, "Final End," 325–34; Leclerc, *Yahweh Is Exalted*, 156–57; Longman and Reid, *God Is a Warrior*, 173–74; G. V. Smith, *Prophets as Preachers*, 149–53.

the Lord had not yet arrived. In the meantime, however, as a good pastor he needed to comfort them in their present tribulation. This he does by portraying in a judgment theophany in 1:7–10 how at the Lord's coming they will receive rest from their persecutions, and their persecutors will be repaid with affliction. The second impetus he had for employing Isaiah 66 in chapter one was the fact that as an OT passage describing the final coming of the Lord, it fitted his subject matter very well, especially since the birth pangs occur in 66:7, which . . . was probably already in the author's time part of a known messianic [birth pangs] tradition.[46]

In both contexts the judicial element seems evident: Isaiah prophesied of God's impending judgment upon the wicked nations and the restoration of his people. Borrowing from this concept, Paul described Christ as the eschatological Judge who will sentence his enemies to destruction and acquit the Thessalonians. Regarding such an intertextual parallel, Longmann and Reid have noted that:

> all of this points to the fact that Paul thought of the future return of Christ in terms of the Old Testament expectation of an eschatological event in which Yahweh would settle the accounts of history. God would act in Christ; but the two were not to be confused, and Paul clearly viewed Jesus as an agent of this divine enterprise.[47]

This allusion seems to demonstrate that Paul not only understood the forensic nature of κρίσις as stemming from the Old Testament but also that it could act as a link between the teachings of the Old Testament and his theological instruction concerning the parousia of Christ. In fact, Roger Aus has further argued that "the author of Second Thessalonians used Isaiah 66 as the main background for his portrayal of Jesus' final coming in 2 Thess 1."[48] Clearly, both the Old and New Testaments establish the judicial meaning of κρίσις, and while the concept of God's eschatological judgment is evident throughout the Old Testament, it is developed further in the New Testament, particularly with regards to Christ fulfilling the role as the final Judge depicted in 2 Thess 1.[49]

---

46. Aus, "Relevance," 264–65.
47. Longman and Reid, *God Is a Warrior*, 173.
48. See, for example, Aus, "God's Plan," 546.
49. See Schultz, "שׁפט," 220.

The use of κρίσις as a forensic term also functions outside the biblical writings in various legal contexts.[50] In Jdt 16:17, the author declared woe upon any nation rising up against God's people. The author warned that if they did, the Lord Almighty would take vengeance upon them in the ἡμέρα κρίσεως. Similar to the biblical text, Yahweh is portrayed as exercising righteous judgment on his enemies at the final assize.[51]

The genitive phrase δικαίας κρίσεως τοῦ θεοῦ in 2 Thess 1:5 should in all probability be understood as a judicial idiom. While the syntax of the sentence does refer to God's character in his judgment, ample evidence seems to have demonstrated that throughout Scripture and ancient literature the phrase δικαίας κρίσεως and the term κρίσεως have distinctive legal connotations. It seems, as Green has suggested, that the apostle likely wanted to reassure the Thessalonian Christians that they:

> had suffered rejection and dishonor at the hands of their contemporaries (1 Thess 2:14), but in God's plan the source of social shame is transformed into a sign of honor. God counts them worthy of the kingdom of God and their sufferings are a mark of dignity.[52]

Therefore, when God returns to set up his court, he will vindicate the Thessalonian Christians in the presence of their enemies because of their growing faith, love for one another, and perseverance, which have proven them worthy of the kingdom of God.

4.1.3 δίκαιον

The next term that demands a forensic understanding is δίκαιον, which appears in verse 6 and is often found in judicial contexts throughout the

---

50. Demosthenes 19.232; Didorus 17.80.2; *OGIS* 669.39; P.Oxy. 9.1203.29; Plato *Phaedrus* 249a; Polycarp 2.1; Ep Jer 54, 64; Jdt 16:17; 2 Macc 4:43, 7:35; Wis 6:5, 9:3. Also as late as Lysias 13.35.

51. Cf. Moore, *Judith*, 255–57. See also Polycarp *Philippians* 2.1, who understood the eschatological aspect of God's final judgment to be clearly in view. Regarding the judicial nature of Polycarp's interpretation, Bovon-Thurneysen has argued that "in Philippians 2.1 endet ein altes zweiteiliges Glaubensbekenntnis mit dem Kommen Christi als Weltenrichter . . . ihm nun wurde alles Himmlische und Irdische unterworfen, ihm dient jeder Odem, er kommt als Richter über Lebende und Tote, sein Blut wird Gott von denen fordern, die ihm nicht gehorchen" ("Ethik und Eschatologie," 242).

52. G. Green, *Thessalonians*, 284. See also Bruce, *Thessalonians*, 149; Giblin, *Threat to Faith*, 7; Wanamaker, *Epistles to the Thessalonians*, 223.

Scriptures (Gen 18:25; Deut 32:35; Rom 6:13; Heb 10:38).[53] In certain contexts, the term and its derivatives are used to describe someone who is morally right or who has righteous conduct (Rom 6:13, 6:16; 2 Cor 9:9–10; Eph 5:9). However, Williams has argued it should be understood that "for the Hebrews generally and for Paul in particular, righteousness is primarily a *legal* standing, not an ethical virtue."[54] The context of 2 Thess 1:6 seems to reveal that this is in relation to God's impartiality in his eschatological judgment.

Typically δίκαιος and its synonyms are often found in contexts referring to God's declaration of individuals to be "right" with him (Rom 1:17, 3:21–22, 5:19; 2 Cor 5:21; Phil 3:9). In other words, δίκαιος is often understood to convey "a quality or state of juridical correctness with focus on redemptive action."[55] Paul particularly used δίκαιος in judicial settings with reference to either a person's legal standing or the character of God's judgment (Rom 2:13, 3:4, 3:20, 3:24; 1 Cor 4:4, 6:11; Gal 2:16). In Gal 2:16 Paul used the verb δικαιόω to emphasize the fact that none are righteous from the works of law but rather are acquitted by God on the basis of faith in Christ. The forensic nuance of δικαιόω seems evident from the context since it is likely that Paul was not stressing that individuals are *made* righteous but rather that they are *declared* righteous by God.[56] The message that Paul seems to have intended the Galatians to understand was that those who self-vindicate by trying to keep law would not be exonerated. The entire context of the letter seems to indicate that only those who have faith in Christ would be confirmed innocent by God.

Not only does the Pauline corpus reveal that δίκαιος and its variations are best understood as judicial language, there is also evidence of this throughout the New Testament (Matt 25:31–46; Heb 10:38; Rev 16:5). For instance, Matt 25:31–46 concludes the Olivet discourse with Jesus' description of his eventual return as the eschatological Judge who

---

53. Schneider, "δικαίως," 324; Van der Minde, "δίκη," 336; Schrenk, "δίκαιος," 182; Spicq, "δίκαιος," 318–327. See also Best, *Commentary*, 254–56; Frame, *Epistles of St. Paul*, 226–27; G. Green, *Thessalonians*, 283–86; Wanamaker, *Epistles to the Thessalonians*, 220–23.

54. Williams, *Paul's Metaphors*, 155.

55. BDAG, 247.

56. See Morris, *Apostolic Preaching*, 283–87. See also Barrett, *Commentary*, 50, who notes that "δικαιόω does not mean to make virtuous, but to grant a verdict of acquittal."

would pronounce his sentence on the righteous and the unrighteous.[57] His act of judgment is depicted as separating the sheep from the goats, which was arguably a direct parallel to Ezek 34, where God judges between the sheep, rams, and goats.[58] Matthew seems to have applied this principle of separating the sheep from the goats (a common practice among shepherds since goats cannot tolerate cold temperatures as well as sheep)[59] to the concept of the universal final assize when all must appear before Christ's judgment seat. In the context, the sheep are those who receive Jesus' messengers and are viewed as righteous because they in essence receive Jesus and are rewarded eternal life. In contrast, the goats do not receive the gospel emissaries, an act that is considered a blatant rejection of Jesus himself, and as a result they are sentenced to eternal punishment. Matthew's intention in the passage is to demonstrate that:

> Jesus is both judge and the focus of the final judgment, spelling disaster to those who ignored him on this side of that day. The nations will be judged according to how they respond to the gospel and its messengers.[60]

At the final assize the sheep will be declared δίκαιος by the Judge and consequently given the place of honor at his right hand.[61]

Paul's understanding of the judicial semantics of δίκαιος in all likelihood stemmed from his knowledge of the term's usage throughout various Old Testament legal contexts. The Septuagint typically translates δίκαιος from the Hebrew צדק, which is often found in contexts pertain-

---

57. See Pond, "Sheep and the Goats," 201–220. He lists two reasons as to why Jesus' return is the climax of the Olivet discourse. "First, it completes Jesus' answer to the disciples' questions, 'Tell us, when will these things happen, and what will be the sing of your coming, and the end of the age?' (24:3). Second, the previous references to this coming in 24:29–31 links two major subsections of the discourse: a presentation of signs preparatory to Christ's return (vv. 4–28) and lesson and parables for disciples in light of his delayed return (24:32–25:30)" ("Sheep and the Goats," 202).

58. See Heil, "Ezekiel 34," 698–708.

59. See Davies and Allison, *Matthew*, 3:423; Morris, *Gospel According to Matthew*, 636.

60. Keener, *Matthew*, 360. See also Chae, *Jesus*, 219–27; Court, "Right and Left," 223–33; Heil, "Double Meaning," 3–14; Sim, *Apocalyptic Eschatology*, 116–28; Weber, "Image of Sheep," 657–78; A. I. Wilson, *When*, 238–47.

61. See Manson, *Sayings of Jesus*, 250. Regarding this passage in Matthew he comments that "it is judgment, not trial, for which court is assembled. The right hand is the place of honor; and, in this connection, the left had the place of rejection."

ing to the equity of God's judgment (Gen 18:25; Exod 23:7; Deut 32:35; 1 Kgs 8:32; Pss 54, 59, 103:6, 109; Isa 41:21–29). In fact, Morris observes that:

> The noun and the adjective from this root reveal the same essentially forensic significance. The righteous are those acquitted at the bar of God's justice, and righteousness is the standing of those acquitted.[62]

Furthermore, Colin Brown has noted that "when δίκαιος translates the root צדק (and even other roots as well), the forensic sense is almost always present."[63] For instance, Isa 41:21–29 seems to describe a courtroom setting where Yahweh summons the gods of the foreign nations to present their case before him. In this context, Yahweh challenges these gods to present evidence of their workings in the past or to predict the future, both of which they are unable to do. Consequently, God provides sufficient verification that he alone controls the events in history. Regarding this passage, D. Hill has noted that "Israel's history is proof of Yahweh's power and he wins the case and is declared 'in the right.'"[64] God's judgments, therefore, are seen to be righteous as he vindicates his people and punishes the foreign nations who have oppressed them.

While δίκαιος is found throughout the Old Testament in contexts of judgment (both human and divine), it is most often utilized in the Psalms in a legal sense denoting God's character in judgment.[65] In one example, the Psalmist writes that he has been falsely accused by his enemies and cries out to God for legal vindication (Ps 7:1–17). The forensic overtones of this passage are further evidenced by the term הושיעני in verse 2, which often serves as an Old Testament technical term referring to a legal cry for help.[66] In essence, the Psalmist maintains his innocence regarding the judicial charges brought against him and implores the true Judge to give him reprieve. Yahweh is then depicted as a divine warrior wielding deadly weapons in order to judge the accusers and vindicate

---

62. Morris, *Apostolic Preaching*, 260.
63. C. Brown, "δικαιοσύνη," 358.
64. D. Hill, *Greek Words*, 89 n. 2.
65. See Reimer, "צדק," 759–63. He notes that "the צדק word group is employed more often in the Psalms than in any other book of the OT, appearing 139 times and thus comprising about 26.6 percent of the total occurrences."
66. Cf. Boecker, *Redeformen des Rechtslebens*, 61–66; R. L. Hubbard, "Dynamistic and Legal Language," 67–104; Schroeder, *History*, 109–119.

the Psalmist. The chapter concludes with the author giving thanks to Yahweh for adjudicating the case.

Both the Old and New Testaments generally use δίκαιος in judicial contexts. However, the forensic nuance of the term is also found throughout extrabiblical writings.[67] In 2 Macc 12:1–6, the Jewish residents of Joppa (believing they were at peace with their neighbors), were deceived by some of the governors in the surrounding regions. The governors invited the women and children of Joppa to accompany them on boat rides, which resulted in the drowning of two hundred innocent Jews. When Judas Maccabeus heard of this deceitful act, he called upon God to righteously judge the tyrants and vindicate the death of his fellow Jews who were murdered.[68]

Ample evidence seems to have demonstrated that δίκαιος was commonly found in forensic contexts, oftentimes with reference to God's equity in judging his enemies and vindicating his children. With regard to Paul's use of the term in 2 Thess 1:5 and throughout his biblical writings, it seems best that δίκαιος be understood to mean a quality or state of juridical correctness.[69] Particularly in the context of 2 Thess 1, Paul used δίκαιος as a reference to God's juridical precision in dealing with the Thessalonian Christians and their oppressors. The Thessalonians' faith in Christ and perseverance amid intense persecution was evidence that they were worthy of God's kingdom when Christ returned at the eschatological assize. Paul stressed that because of Christ's righteous judicial integrity, he would exonerate the Thessalonians before their enemies. Therefore, as Schrenk has observed, "we may note both a juridical and theological use of the term."[70]

---

67. 2 Macc 12:1–6; Wis 5:18, 12:16; Sir 10:29, 42:2; 1 Clement 14:1, 21:4; P.Oxy. 3.653; P.Ryl. 119.14.

68. Further evidence regarding the forensic nature of δίκαιος is also found in the documents from Qumran. In various writings from the community it is clear that the term δίκαιος denotes God's character in judging between his enemies and those committed to him. Cf. 1QH 7:12; 1QM 11:14; D. Hill, *Greek Words*, 111 n. 2 and 3; Vermes, *Dead Sea Scrolls*, 174–75, 249–52. Additional proof that δίκαιος was understood as a legal term is also found in both Josephus and Philo. See Josephus *Antiquities* 11.268, 17.206, 18.176; Philo *On Drunkenness* 95. For instance, Josephus related how Emperor Tiberius was slow to hear the cases of prisoners who had been declared guilty and condemned to death because he wanted them to suffer anguish as they awaited their execution; see *Antiquities* 18.178.

69. BDAG, 247.

70. Schrenk, "Concept of Law," 175. See also G. Green, *Thessalonians*, 284; Malherbe,

4.1.4 παρὰ θεῷ

Continuing in verse 6, another legal idiom is the prepositional phrase παρὰ θεῷ. While παρὰ with the dative is used to express a variety of nuances throughout Scripture, it is strictly context that determines meaning. Syntactically, the term θεῷ functions as a dative following a preposition where the emphasis suggests the idea of "sphere," which would literally be translated as the phrase, "in the sight of or before God."[71] However, oftentimes the preposition παρὰ with the dative portrays a forensic meaning referring to the judge before whom the parties appear, as well as denoting the relevance of one's viewpoint in the judgment of someone.[72] With regard to the context of 2 Thess 1, it is arguable that Paul intended the idiom παρὰ θεῷ to convey a forensic idea of having to appear before God's judgment bench. In fact, Malherbe argues that "the image of the divine tribunal is present in the phrase παρὰ θεῷ."[73] In addition, Paul used the particle εἴπερ to underscore the fact that it is unquestionably just in the sight of God to punish the oppressors and grant rest to the Thessalonians.[74] The apostle reminded the Thessalonians that their vindication would come at the final assize when their enemies would appear before God's judgment seat and justice would be served.

Further evidence can be found throughout Paul's writings that he at times understood παρὰ θεῷ as a legal idiom (Rom 2:11, 2:13; 1 Cor 3:19; Gal 3:11). In Rom 2:13, Paul instructed his audience that those who are merely hearers of the law are not righteous παρὰ θεῷ; instead, those who obey the law will be justified. While some scholars see a contradiction here in Paul's writing regarding his teaching of justification by faith,[75] others have concluded that the apostle's argument in this context is not to demonstrate how people can be justified but rather that the divine

---

Thessalonians, 394–96; Wanamaker, *Epistles to the Thessalonians*, 220–23.

71. See BDF, §238; Porter, *Idioms*, 167–68; Turner, *Syntax*, 273; Wallace, *Greek Grammar*, 378.

72. BDAG, 757; LSJ, 1303; Harris, "παρά," 1202; Köhler, "παρά," 13; Riesenfeld, "παρά," 732; G. Green, *Thessalonians*, 286; Malherbe, *Thessalonians*, 397; Wanamaker, *Epistles to the Thessalonians*, 224.

73. Malherbe, *Thessalonians*, 397.

74. See chapter 5 for a discussion regarding the exegetical issues surrounding this particle.

75. See, for example, Räisänen, *Paul and the Law*, 103; E. P. Sanders, *Paul, the Law*, 125.

standard is required if one is to be justified.⁷⁶ For Paul, only perfect obedience to the law could result in justification, and he quickly affirmed that this was an impossibility (3:20, 3:28) and denounced any notion that "the Jews [could] depend on their covenant relationship to shield them from the consequences of this failure."⁷⁷ It seems, then, that Paul may have used παρὰ θεῷ in 2:13 forensically to stress that those who desire to obey the law must obey it perfectly in order to stand before God's eschatological court justified. Simply put, the apostle was likely setting the stage for all Jews' need of the gospel and their justification by faith in Christ alone (3:24–26).

A similar judicial idea of παρὰ θεῷ is found in Gal 3:11. In this passage Paul reminded the church that no one is justified by the law παρὰ τῷ θεῷ and that the righteous man lives by faith in the Lord Jesus. In this context, those in the Galatian church encountered certain opponents who insisted on strict adherence to the law as a requirement for salvation (Gal 6:11–13).⁷⁸ Regarding these outsiders Gunther has argued that:

> Paul's opponents held that to receive and to be led by the Spirit are inseparable from the requirement of subjection to the law (3:2, 3:5, 5:18, 5:23, 6:1–2). They considered law and grace to be compatible (2:21, 5:4).⁷⁹

Thus, Paul reminds the Galatians that a return under the old covenant of the law was essentially a denial of the gospel (1:6–7). The apostle reiterated that when they appear before the Judge at his final court, the works of the law would not make them righteous. He enforced this point with allusions from Gen 15:6 and Hab 2:4, accentuating that the true heirs of God are those who, like Abraham, are of faith.⁸⁰ As a result, the

---

76. Moo, *Romans*, 148. See also Jewett, "Law," 341–56; Schreiner, "Did Paul Believe," 131–58; Stuhlmacher, *Paul's Letter*, 41–47; Thielman, *Paul and the Law*, 167–73; Tobin, *Paul's Rhetoric*, 113–15.

77. Moo, *Romans*, 148. Cf. Jewett, "Coexistence," 341–56; Schreiner, "Did Paul Believe," 131–58; Stuhlmacher, *Paul's Letter*, 41–47.

78. See, for example, Dunn, *Theology of Paul's Letter*, 8–12; Gunther, *St. Paul's Opponents*, 59; Jewett, "Agitators," 198–212; Nanos, *Irony of Galatians*, 159–83.

79. Gunther, *St. Paul's Opponents*, 59.

80. See, for example, Fung, *Epistle to the Galatians*, 143–54; Garlington, "Role Reversal," 85–121; Hays, *Faith of Jesus Christ*, 163–207; Thatcher, "Plot of Gal 3:1–18," 401–10; Young, "Who's Cursed and Why?" 79–92. See also Silva, *Interpreting Galatians*, 165–67, who argues that Gen 15:6 and Hab 2:4 are expounding the same idea.

Galatians' desire to be under the law would only prove to be condemning when they appear before God at the final assize.

The judicial idiom παρὰ θεῷ was used primarily within the Pauline corpus. Still, there are few instances where other New Testament authors seem to demonstrate a forensic understanding of παρὰ θεῷ (Jas 1:27; 1 Pet 2:20; 2 Pet 2:11, 3:8). For example, 2 Pet 2:11 recounts the punishment that the false teachers who had infiltrated the church would face when they appear before the Lord. The reference here seems to be an allusion to standing before the final judgment seat of God.[81] However, with regard to the use of παρὰ θεῷ outside of Paul's literature, Harris has noted that the idiom:

> indicates the ultimate standard—the purity of the divine life and clarity of the divine vision—by which all aspects of thought and conduct, whether human or angelic, should now be assessed and will in the end be judged.[82]

Although παρὰ θεῷ was used mainly by Paul as a likely correlation from the Day of the Lord motif in reference to God's judgment seat, the legal nuance of the idiom is in some contexts seemingly apparent throughout other New Testament writings (Jas 1:27; 1 Pet 2:20; 2 Pet 2:11, 3:8).

Paul's familiarity with the judicial meaning of παρὰ θεῷ was grounded in his knowledge of the Old Testament, where the idiom was often used in legal contexts to denote God's court or standing before God at trial (Job 9:2; Isa 49:4). For instance, in Job 8, Bildad insisted that Job's sin had caused his suffering and that if he was truly innocent he should seek a legal decision from God, who would certainly deliver him from distress.[83] Job's response in chapters 9–10 begins a courtroom scene between Job and God.[84] Particularly in 9:2, the author questioned

---

81. However, παρὰ κυρίῳ is the alternate reading supported by, ℵ B C K P 88 1739 arm *al.* The Nestle-Aland 27th reads παρὰ κυρίου supported by p⁷² 056 0142 330 *al.* See Bauckham, *Jude, 2 Peter*, 258; B. Metzger, *Textual Commentary*, 763. Metzger explains that the reading παρὰ κυρίου is preferred because it is the more difficult reading, although παρὰ κυρίῳ has much better external evidence. He writes, "In order to avoid attributing βλάσφημον κρίσιν to God, scribes altered κυρίου to κυρίῳ or omitted the prepositional phrase entirely." Whatever reading is preferred, the context of judgment is still clear.

82. Harris, "παρὰ," 1202.

83. See, for example, Perdue, *Wisdom in Revolt*, 131.

84. See Paul, "Unrecognized Biblical Legal Idioms," 231–39; Roberts, "Job's

how a man can be in the right παρὰ κυρίῳ. Job is not concerned with his righteousness before God, for he knows he is blameless, but rather, Job desires to be vindicated as a righteous man, as several scholars have argued with regard to the forensic nature of the context.[85] In fact, Clines has suggested that "Job is not lamenting the impossibility of *defeating* God in a lawsuit, but of *defending himself* in such a way to *compel* God to vindicate him. However, Job fully understood that a lawsuit against God would certainly prove unsuccessful."[86] Nevertheless, in response to Bildad, Job continued firmly adhering to the claim that he was blameless and that his suffering was not a direct result of any transgression. Despite the inevitable outcome of standing trial before God, Job adheres to his innocence and knows that he will be vindicated (9:20–22).[87]

Extrabiblical literature likewise makes use of the idiom παρὰ θεῷ in various legal contexts, primarily as a reference to being in favor in the sight of God or human beings.[88] For instance, Appian related how Perseus was being publicly accused of disloyalty to Rome before the Senate. In return, he sent ambassadors to plead his case to the Senate, vowing complete loyalty to the empire. His ambassadors challenged the opponents to present their case παρ' ὑμῖν (before the Senate) regarding the charges brought against him.[89]

The above discussion has demonstrated that throughout both the Scriptures and nonbiblical literature the prepositional phrase παρὰ θεῷ in certain contexts could be understood forensically. In all probability, Paul used this idiom in 2 Thess 1:6 to carry on the legal nature of his exhortation, namely to remind the Thessalonian church that their vindication would come when they and their oppressors appear before God's judgment bench at the Day of the Lord.

Summons to Yahweh," 159–65; Van der Lugt, *Rhetorical Criticism*, 110–23; Waddle, "Dubious," 81–90.

85. See, for example, Clines, *Job 1–20*, 226–27; Magdalene, "Scales of Righteousness," 151–52; Scholnick, "Meaning of *Mišpāṭ*," 521–29.

86. See, for example, Habel, *Book of Job*, 189, who comments that "in spite of [Job's] conviction that litigation is futile, he progressively moves to state his case."

87. See, for example, Van der Lugt, *Rhetorical Criticism*, 123; Roberts, "Job's Summons to Yahweh," 160; Waddle, "Dubious," 85.

88. *IG* 12.91.6; Appian *Macedonian Affairs* 11.8; Josephus *Antiquities* 6.205, 7.84. There is also evidence as early as Herodotus 3.160; Thucydides 1.73.

89. Appian *Macedonian Affairs* 11.8.

4.1.5 ἀνταποδίδωμι

The final term in verse 6 that denotes a legal meaning is ἀνταποδίδωμι. Although the word itself simply carries the idea of "payback" or "vengeance" it is reasonable that Paul intended the term to have a legal connotation, which seems plausible because of the surrounding judicial word grouping in the immediate context.[90] Throughout biblical writings, the forensic nuance of this term is seemingly defensible, particularly in contexts referring to God enacting vengeance upon his enemies at the final Day of Judgment and punishing them accordingly (Deut 32:6, 32:35; Rom 12:19; Heb 10:30; Rev 20:11–15).[91]

In the Pauline corpus the term is often connected with God's recompense, both positive and negative, at the final assize (Rom 11:1–10, 11:35; Col 3:24). This seems evident from the context of Col 3:22–25, where Paul instructed Christian slaves as to how they were to conduct themselves towards their masters within the corporate body. The apostle contrasted the recompense that slaves may receive at the final judgment: either they would receive a reward for faithful service rendered or they would suffer consequences for disloyal service (3:24–25). Particularly, in 3:24 slaves are urged to serve with diligence because their ultimate master was the Lord Christ from whom they would receive τὴν ἀνταπόδοσιν τῆς κληρονομίας. With regard to the construction τῆς κληρονομίας, James Dunn has noted that "the imagery lent itself to eschatological reference (Ps 37:9; Isa 54:17)."[92] Thus, the context seems to indicate that the re-

---

90. See Frame, *Epistles of St. Paul*, 228; Giblin, *Threat to Faith*, 7–8; G. Green, *Thessalonians*, 286; Malherbe, *Thessalonians*, 397; Morris, *Thessalonians*, 199; Sand, "ἀνταπόδοσις," 107–8; Still, *Conflict*, 197.

91. See Bruce, *Thessalonians*, 149–50; G. Green, *Thessalonians*, 286; Frame, *Epistles of St. Paul*, 228; Malherbe, *Thessalonians*, 397; Witherington, *Thessalonians*, 193.

92. Dunn, *Epistles*, 257. See also Harris, *Colossians and Philemon*, 184–87; O'Brien, *Colossians, Philemon*, 228–29. See also Standhartinger, "Origin," 117–30, who contends that the background for the Colossian household code was derived from a law-code utilized by Hellenistic street philosophers. But this seems unconvincing, since there are other instances of "household regulations" in the New Testament (Eph 6:2–3; 1 Pet 3:6), which often refer to "household rules" found in the Old Testament. For instance, Eph 6:2–3 exhorts children to honor their parents, which is clearly a citation of the fifth commandment (Exod 20:12; Deut 5:16). Since Paul was a devout Jew, it seems best to understand the household codes in Col 3:18–4:1 to have derived from his knowledge of the Old Testament. See, for example, Lillie, "Pauline House-tables," 179–83, who argues for the Jewish background of the Colossian household code.

wards and punishments referred to will be given without partiality at God's final court (3:24–25).[93]

Other New Testament authors also seem to have employed ἀνταποδίδωμι and its derivatives in similar judicial contexts (Matt 16:27; Luke 14:12–14; Heb 10:30; Rev 22:12). For example, in Matt 16:27 Jesus informed the disciples that at his return he would recompense every person according to their deeds. In verses 24–26 Jesus described the cost of discipleship, namely a denial of self, taking up one's cross, and total obedience to him. The eschatological nature is emphasized in verse 25, with Jesus' statement that losing one's life now for the sake of Christ results in eternal life. To make certain that his followers understood the cost of discipleship, he explained that genuine disciples are not to be concerned with the temporal treasures of the earthly life but rather are to be focused on the everlasting life that comes from following him. Moreover, Carson contends that in verse 27, "not only Jesus' example, but the judgment he will exercise is an incentive to take up one's cross and follow him."[94] The allusion here is seemingly an intertextual echo of Ps 62:12, where the Psalmist declares that God delivers his recompense accordingly. Such an idea seems evident in verse 27, where at the eschaton Jesus will judge every individual impartially. With regard to Jesus serving as the soteriological Judge, Daniel Marguerat offers the following summary of Matt 16:27:

> Paré de la gloire divine, accompagné du cortège théophanique, le Christ-Fils de l'homme viendra procéder au jugement; par le truchement d'un motif stéréotypé, le v. 27 place son avènement sous le signe de la rétribution. La comparution eschatologique, conformément à l'idéologie régnante au sein du bas-judaïsme, est conçue comme l'exercice d'une justice rétributive, appliquée à l'individu et axée sur ses actes concrets.[95]

---

93. The legal nature of the term is further evident in Rom 2:6 where Paul emphasized that both Jew and Gentile would each have their day at court, where God would deliver his unbiased ἀνταποδίδωμι. See also Bassler, "Divine Impartiality," 48; Davis, *Lex Talionis*, 156–57; S. L. Johnson, "God Gave Them Up," 124–33; Plevnik, *Paul and the Parousia*, 225–26. In fact, Plevnik convincingly argues that "Romans 2 indicates, above all, God's impartiality: God will reward the good done by everyone, Jew or pagan, and he will punish sin committed by everyone. The judgment is here presented as a day in court" (225).

94. Carson, "Matthew," 379.

95. Marguerat, *Le Jugement*, 96. See also Schlatter, *Der Evangelist Matthäus*, 523.

Paul's understanding of the legal nuance of ἀνταποδίδωμι, however, was in all probability derived from his knowledge of the Old Testament. The idea that God would not only dispense judicial recompense upon his enemies but also upon his covenant people for their disobedience was a familiar teaching throughout the Old Testament Scriptures. In the Septuagint, ἀνταποδίδωμι and its various constructions are translated from נָקַם or גְּמוּל, which are frequently found in contexts relating to God's eschatological vengeance (Ps 27:4–5, Prov 24:12; Isa 61:2, 63:4, 66:6; Jer 51:6).[96] In Isa 63:1–6 the prophet changed from the theme of future salvation, which Yahweh would bring (chapters 60–62), to the announcement of his enacting vengeance on Edom and Bozrah. In the context, God is depicted as having "tread the wine press," which was a metaphor often used to emphasize the setting of judgment (Jer 25:30; Lam 1:15; Joel 3:13; Rev 14:19, 19:15).[97] In the immediate context of Isa 63:1–6, Yahweh is portrayed as a punitive Judge who unleashes his ἀνταποδόσεως upon the pagan nations, thereby bringing vindication for his covenant people.[98]

Finally, the forensic use of ἀνταποδίδωμι in extrabiblical literature is also evident.[99] Secular writers, however, used the term to denote the idea of rewarding an individual for something they had done—good or bad.[100] For example, Josephus writes regarding a decree issued by Julius Caesar during a court session commanding both the Senate and the citizens of Rome to express their gratitude to Hyracanus and the Jewish people for the benefits and loyalty they had given Rome.[101]

It seems evident from both Scripture and secular literature that ἀνταποδίδωμι was often used in legal contexts referring to the recompense one would receive at court for what they had done, whether positive or negative. In 2 Thess 1, it is likely that, in keeping with his judicial premise, Paul utilized ἀνταποδίδωμι to remind the Thessalonian Christians to continue in their perseverance, for when God returned, he

---

96. See the discussion in Plevnik, *Paul and the Parousia*, 225–27.

97. See also Peels, *Vengeance of God*, 172 n. 371.

98. See Neufeld, *Armour of God*, 15–47, who sees a distinct parallel between Isa 59 and 63:1–6.

99. Josephus *Antiquities* 14.212; P.Hib. 30.17, 31.6–7, 198.69, 202.6; P.Tebt. 29.6, 8.

100. See, for example, Josephus *Antiquities* 19.358; Tob 10:14; Ep Jer 34; Sir 3:31; 1 Macc 2:68, 10:27. Also as early as Herodotus 1.43; Thucydides 1.43.

101. See Josephus *Antiquities* 14.212.

would justly repay their persecutors for the afflictions they had caused these believers. Paul understood that only God, the righteous Judge, was able to adequately repay their oppressors when they would face him at the eschatological court.

4.1.6 ἀποκάλυψις

The term ἀποκαλύψει in verse 7 deserves brief consideration. While used infrequently by Paul in an eschatological sense, the term in the setting of 2 Thess 1 denotes a judicial significance.[102] In contexts related to Christ's second coming, Paul often used the term as a synonym of παρουσία. He typically incorporated ἀποκάλυψις to denote the revealing of knowledge, visions, or something unknown, such as the mystery of the gospel (Rom 16:25). However, he does integrate the term as metaphorical imagery to reference Christ's return, specifically drawing from the Day of the Lord concept of the Old Testament (Rom 2:5, 8:18; 1 Cor 1:7, 3:13).[103] In the context of 2 Thess 1, Paul seems to be alluding to Isa 66:15, where the prophet described that at the revelation of the Lord's coming he would pour out his retribution and judge with fire.[104] In fact, Plevnik has noted that for Paul, "the word ἀποκάλυψις . . . is usually employed for an event associated with the Lord's coming, such as judgment."[105] With regard to the immediate context of Second Thessalonians, Paul arguably had this in mind as he instructed the Thessalonians that at the Lord Jesus' ἀποκαλύψει he would perform judgment and mete out punishment to those who have rejected God.[106]

Other New Testament uses reveal that in certain contexts authors used ἀποκάλυψις idiomatically as a legal term to depict the revealing of Christ for judgment (Luke 17:30; 1 Pet 1:7, 1:13, 4:13). For instance,

---

102. See, for example, Ahn, "Parousia," 224 n. 113.

103. See, for example, Aus, "Relevance," 263–68; Glasson, "Theophany and Parousia," 259–70.

104. Glasson, "Theophany," 259–70.

105. Plevnik, *Paul and the Parousia*, 3. See also Oepke, "ἀποκαλύπτω," 582–83, who observes that throughout the epistles ἀποκάλυψις was often understood, "not as an impartation of supernatural knowledge, but as the coming of God, as the disclosure of the world to come, which took place in a historical development up to the person and death and resurrection of Jesus in the last time (1 Cor 10:11, Heb 1:1f.) and which will culminate in the cosmic catastrophe at the end of history."

106. See, for example, G. Holland, "Let No One," 327–41; Shires, *Eschatology of Paul*, 65–67; Vos, *Pauline Eschatology*, 78–79.

in Jesus' eschatological discourse in Luke 17:22–37, he instructed the disciples about the nature of the coming judgment; that it was both unexpected and severe. He illustrated his point with two Old Testament examples of Noah and Lot where the ungodly living in those days were suddenly destroyed by God's judgment. In similar fashion, the final judgment would commence unexpectedly when Christ was ἀποκαλύπτεται. Moreover, as Fletcher-Louis has noted:

> At the very least the Son of Man here acts as God's divine agent or judicial representative. . . . It is implicit in the context of the whole, which is framed by concern for the kingdom of God, that is the manifestation of God's justice, his vindication of the elect and punishment of the wicked.[107]

In the context of the passage it seems clear that Luke understood ἀποκάλυψις to denote the suddenness of the final tribunal where both judgment and exoneration reside.

The concept of the Lord's judgment is abundant throughout the Old Testament. However, ἀποκάλυψις was seldom used to convey the Jewish idea of final judgment and vindication (Ps 98:2). The Old Testament prefers to describe the theophany of Yahweh's judgments through either the exhibition of fire, smoke, lightning, etc., or in reference to the future judgment by the standard prophetic phrase the Day of the Lord.[108] With regard to the Day of the Lord, the prophets understood this as Yahweh's divine tribunal where he would pour out judicial retribution upon Israel for his people's covenant unfaithfulness, as well as upon pagan nations who blatantly defied God (Isa 13:2–16; Amos 5:18–20). This day is described as both tragic and victorious, as God himself will preside as Judge, rendering impartial verdicts.[109] Thus, it is probable that Paul borrowed the Day of the Lord concept from his knowledge of the Old Testament and applied it to the second coming of Christ and his revealing. Regarding the apostle's understanding of the second advent of Christ corresponding to the Day of the Lord, Glasson observes that:

> the doctrine of the Parousia was not new; all the essential details are found in the O.T. description of the coming theophany.

---

107. Fletcher-Louis, *Luke-Acts*, 229. See also Lindars, "Re-Enter," 52–72; Marshall, *Commentary on Luke*, 656–64; Mearns, "Son of Man," 8–12.

108. See Ahn, "Parousia," 71.

109. See, for example, Bloesch, *Last Things*, 62–86.

> Broadly speaking, the Christians took over the O.T. doctrine of the Advent of the Lord, making the single adjustment that the Lord was the Lord Jesus.[110]

Moreover, Joseph Young-Sik has also suggested that:

> Paul used the Day of the Lord concept to designate the Second Coming of Christ. Paul modifies, however, the traditional concept including at the following points: 1) whereas the traditional picture of the Day of Yahweh portrayed God himself as its chief figure and the One coming; Paul puts Christ in this role; 2) whereas traditionally the Day of Yahweh was viewed as the time when God would overcome the forces of evil, Paul proclaimed that they have already been decisively, though not finally, defeated.[111]

While ἀποκάλυψις is not often found in judicial contexts in the Old Testament, this does not prevent the acceptance of Paul's use of the term in a forensic sense in 2 Thess 1 for two possible reasons. First, the above evidence seems to demonstrate that the apostle understood the parousia of Christ as a direct fulfillment to the Old Testament concept of the Day of the Lord.[112] Second, with regard to the judicial word clustering of the immediate context, coupled with the two succeeding prepositional phrases, ἀπ' οὐρανοῦ μετ' ἀγγέλων δυνάμεως αὐτοῦ, which seemingly describe a judgment scene and explain the manner of Christ's revealing as judge, it may be reasonable to understand Paul's use of ἀποκάλυψις as an idiomatic expression referring to the Day of the Lord. The impending judgment against those who had persecuted the Thessalonians would be revealed when Christ returns as Judge, declaring his righteous verdict upon them.[113]

---

110. Glasson, *Second Advent*, 176. See also Witherington, *Thessalonians*, 194, who contends that from Paul's perspective the Day of Yahweh corresponds to the Day of the Lord Jesus.

111. דנה, "Parousia," 151.

112. See, for example, Witherington, *Thessalonians*, 194–95.

113. It should be noted that in Hellenistic literature ἀποκάλυψις was not typically used in judicial contexts. The usual term was παρουσία, which is occasionally found in legal documents; BGU 4.1127.37, 1129.127; and as late as P.Gen. 68.11; P.Oxy. 6.903.15.

4.1.7 ἐν πυρὶ φλογός

Paul continued his use of legal language in verse 8 with the idiom ἐν πυρὶ φλογός in order to explicate what the Day of the Lord would entail for those who had persecuted the Thessalonian church. He explained that the Lord would return from heaven with his mighty angels ἐν πυρὶ φλογός.[114] The word πυρὶ is oftentimes used as a judicial term in connection with the last judgment as well as a reference to God's punishment of sinners (Deut 32:33; Isa 29:6, 66:24; Acts 2:19; Rev 9:17–18).[115] Throughout the Pauline corpus, the idiom is used in only three passages with reference to the eschatological judgment (Rom 12:20; 1 Cor 3:13–15; 2 Thess 1:8).[116]

In 1 Cor 3, Paul addressed the quarrels within the church that stemmed from an improper allegiance to certain teachers of the faith (verses 1–7). Such misguided allegiances not only caused factions within the congregation but also hindered the growth of the church. The apostle reminded the Corinthians that the church was built upon the foundation of Christ alone, who in turn allows his followers to be involved as fellow workers in the building process (verses 8–9). In verses 10–15 Paul continued to address not only the labor he and Apollos had carried out among the Corinthians but also the service of Christians in general.[117] Paul warned that all work conducted by the apostles as well as believers would be tested by fire at the final judgment. In fact, William has argued, "the fire serves to reveal the quality of the work so that the person can be judged for reward or loss."[118] The imagery continues with those who build the church upon the foundation, which Christ had laid, being rewarded because their work would prove imperishable. However, those whose work was consumed would suffer loss, even though they would be saved. Regarding the concept of suffering loss, Witherington comments that:

---

114. For a discussion regarding the phrase ἐν πυρὶ φλογός and whether it is anaphoric or cataphoric see chapter 5. See G. Green, *Thessalonians*, 288–89; Malherbe, *Thessalonians*, 401–2; Wanamaker, *Epistles to the Thessalonians*, 226–27. However, scholars such as Best, *Commentary*, 259, and Morris, *Thessalonians*, 202, understand this to be anaphoric. Best writes, "The flaming fire emphasizes the glory of the appearance of the Lord, an appearance like that of a theophany."

115. See Malherbe, *Thessalonians*, 400; Witherington, *Thessalonians*, 195.

116. Lang, "Divine Judgment," 944.

117. See, for example, William, "Judgment and Community," 217.

118. Ibid., 212.

the purpose of the eschatological fire will be to test or prove the strength and endurance of the superstructure. Those who have built well will be rewarded; those who have not will not be rewarded. The reward is not heaven or salvation. The reward is, rather, the sort of heavenly rewards that Jesus talks about (Matt 5:12). Paul might call them rewards on earth at the eschaton.[119]

In the context of 1 Cor 3, it seems that Paul used fire not as a reference to eternal damnation but rather as the means to reveal both the motives and quality of ministry of the apostles, and furthermore all Christians who are responsible for building Christ's church.[120] Particularly in 2 Thess 1, Paul likely understood πυρὶ φλογός to not only emphasize the awesome and powerful sight of the return of the Lord, but also his coming as the divine Judge to allocate retribution upon his enemies and provide vindication for the Thessalonians.[121]

Other New Testament authors demonstrate that πῦρ was often used in relation to divine judgment (Matt 3:11, 25:42; Luke 3:16; Heb 10:27; 2 Pet 3:7; Jude 7). For instance, the fire of God's judgment is evident in Jude 1–7. In this context the author seemingly wrote to persuade his audience to beware of certain ungodly persons who had crept in unnoticed with the intention of defaming the Lord Jesus Christ. Drawing from several Old Testament examples, the author instructed his readers that just as the ungodly in the Old Testament suffered God's divine judgment so also their intruders who denied Christ and made a mockery of the faith would suffer the same fate.[122] Jude's reference to Sodom and Gomorrah in verse 7 was probably used to remind his audience that just as those immoral cities experienced judgment by fire, so likewise, their ungodly opponents would face the eternal fire of God's condemnation. With regard to the use of πῦρ in this pericope, J. D. Charles notes that:

> in line with the Hebrew prophets of old, Jude reinforces for his readers the fate of the ungodly. Judgment by fire was manifest

---

119. Witherington, *Conflict*, 134. See also Fee, *Epistle to the Corinthians*, 135–45; Thiselton, *Epistle to the Corinthians*, 301–315. See also Proctor, "Fire in God's House," 9–14, who convincingly argues that in 1 Cor 3:13–15 Paul is alluding to the fire of God's judgment in Mal 3.

120. See, for example, Fiore, *Function of Personal Example*, 168–75; William, "Judgment and Community," 217.

121. Lang, "Divine Judgment," 944.

122. See Bauckham, *Jude, 2 Peter*, 46–7; J. D. Charles, *Literary*, 92–101; Joubert, "Persuasion," 75–87; Watson, *Invention, Arrangement, and Style*, 48–57.

in past history and serves as a reminder to his audience in the present.[123]

It appears, then, that Jude was reminding his audience that God's enemies would appear before him at the final tribunal where he would sentence them to eternal punishment by fire.

It seems further substantiated that Paul understood πυρὶ φλογός to denote a judicial nuance based on the idiom's usage throughout the Old Testament. Lang has noted that throughout the Old Testament, fire is "primarily a common image for the judicial wrath of God (Isa 29:6, 66:15–16; Jer 4:4, 5:14; Ezek 21:36, Zeph 1:18)."[124] The Septuagint predominately translates πῦρ from the Hebrew אֵשׁ, which is used to signify divine justice.[125] For instance, Gen 19:23–24 records God's destruction of Sodom and Gomorrah by means of fire and brimstone. Earlier in the chapter Yahweh had sent his delegates to investigate the sinfulness of Sodom and to rescue Lot's family. At sunrise, upon their safe arrival at Zoar, God unleashed his divine wrath upon the city.[126] In the context of Sodom and Gomorrah's destruction, Bovati has noted that the forensic nature seems clear, as "God reveals himself at daybreak with a judicial verdict which re-establishes justice."[127] Furthermore, the severity of Yahweh's judgment is accentuated from the Hebrew idiom וְאֵשׁ גָּפְרִית, which seems to illustrate strongly the judicial outpouring of Yahweh's vengeance upon these wicked cities.[128]

Finally, there is also sufficient evidence throughout ancient literature demonstrating that πῦρ was understood in certain contexts referring to God's forensic judgment.[129] In 4 Macc 8–13, the author recounted

---

123. J. D. Charles, *Literary*, 99.

124. Lang, "Divine Judgment," 935.

125. See Fields, *Sodom and Gomorrah*, 134–42; Hamilton, "אֵשׁ," 76–77; Hamp, "Fire," 424–28; Naudé, "אֵשׁ," 532–37.

126. Interestingly, the Old Testament authors oftentimes describe the morning as the favored time for Yahweh's juridical intervention (Exod 14:24; Josh 6:15–21; Jer 21:12; Zeph 3:5). See also Bovati, *Re-Establishing Justice*, 367–68; Seeligmann, "Zur Terminologie," 278.

127. Bovati, *Re-Establishing Justice*, 368.

128. See Avishur, *Stylistic Studies*, 182–91; Fields, *Sodom and Gomorrah*,138–39; Le Tellier, *Day in Mamre*, 170–72.

129. See 4 Macc 8–13; 1QpHab 10:5–13; 1QS 2:15; Josephus *Antiquities* 1.70; Josephus *Adam and Eve* 49.3; Philo *Allegorical Interpretation* 2.57; Philo *On Flight and Finding* 59. Also as late as 2 Clement 17; Ignatius *Ephesians* 16:2.

the vicious torture and killing of seven brothers and their mother. In chapter 12 the seventh brother remained steadfast in his faith even unto death, as did his brothers before him. In verse 12 he informed the tyrant that because he had acted so wickedly by killing his siblings, when he stood before God at the final judgment he would face Yahweh's forensic justice by eternal πῦρ.

It is arguable that from the context of 2 Thess 1 Paul used the idiom πυρὶ φλογός to illustrate the judicial aspect of the Lord's return. Drawing from various judgment theophanies throughout the Old Testament, (particularly Isa 66:15–16) the apostle incorporated this idiom to depict Jesus' judicial power as being carried out with flames of fire at the Day of the Lord. This would have more than likely been great encouragement for the Thessalonians, as the apostle reminded them of their vindication from their persecutors in the presence of the righteous Judge at the final assize.

4.1.8 ἐκδίκησις

The next possible judicial term in verse 8 is ἐκδίκησις. The word connotes the idea of parceling out justice or legal remedies. In fact, Williams has observed that:

> when Paul enlists a word from the group "to avenge, vengeance, and avenger" he uses these terms [judicially]—as in his description of God as "an avenger" (1 Thess 4:6) and as wrecking "vengeance" on wrong doers (Rom 12:19; 2 Thess 1:8).[130]

Paul's use of the term demonstrated his intention to continue the forensic nuance of 2 Thess 1. Regarding the apostle's incorporation of ἐκδίκησις, Findlay writes that "it connotes *justice* in the penalty, punishment determined by a lawful process."[131] The term here is also used with the dative, which brings out the idea of declaring a sentence of punishment incorporated to wrongdoers in the final judgment.[132] This has led Wanamaker to conclude that "not only would the persecutors of the Thessalonians be subject to divine vengeance at the Day of Judgment

---

130. Williams, *Metaphors*, 147.

131. Findlay, ed., *Epistles of Paul*, 149.

132. BDAG, 301; LSJ, 504; Goldstein, "ἔκδικος," 408; G. Green, *Thessalonians*, 289–90; Schrenk, "ἐκδικέω, ἐκδίκησις, ἐκδίκησις," 443–46; Best, *Commentary*, 259; Wanamaker, *Epistles to the Thessalonians*, 227.

but they belong to a much larger group that would also be punished."[133] Furthermore, Green writes, "This 'vengeance' is the result of a judicial decision and disposition against those who have rejected God and his gospel."[134]

In other instances throughout his writings, Paul demonstrated that ἐκδίκησις, along with its various constructions, was a courtroom term referring to either God or humans exacting punishment (Rom 12:19; 2 Cor 7:11, 10:6; 1 Thess 4:6).[135] Quoting Deut 32:35, the apostle exhorted the church at Rome that they were to not only treat one another with respect but they were, as far as was possible, to be at peace with all people.[136] However, when treated unjustly, they were not to retaliate but rather display love for their enemies because vengeance ultimately belonged to God, who would repay their antagonists. The command for Christians not to seek revenge is further strengthened with the two ἀλλά phrases in verses 20–21, where believers are instructed to perform acts of kindness to their enemies.[137] Only God can repay justly, and those who continually spurn the gospel would ultimately receive their just recompense at his final court.[138]

Other New Testament authors also seem to validate the judicial understanding of ἐκδίκησις (Luke 18:7, 21:22; Acts 7:24; Heb 10:30; 1 Pet 2:14). In Luke 18:1–8 the author used ἐκδίκησις to depict the idea of apportioning legal punishment. In this parable, Jesus related how a widow persistently asked the unjust judge for legal protection from her opponent. Although the judge was unwilling to grant her request immediately, he gave her the legal protection she desired because she was relentless and he no longer wanted to be troubled by her. Jesus instructed the disciples that if the unjust judge granted the woman her request because she was persistent how much more, then, would God, the just

---

133. Wanamaker, *Epistles to the Thessalonians*, 227. Cf. Frame, *Epistles of St. Paul*, 233; G. Green, *Thessalonians*, 289–90; Malherbe, *Thessalonians*, 400; Still, *Conflict*, 202; Witherington, *Thessalonians*, 195.

134. G. Green, *Thessalonians*, 290.

135. See Williams, *Metaphors*, 157 n. 50.

136. See Yinger, "Romans 12:14–21," 74–96. Yinger argues that since Paul is addressing the church in chapter 12 the persecution is not coming from outside the community but from within.

137. See J. N. Day, "Coals of Fire," 414–20.

138. See, for example, Barram, "Romans 12:9–21," 423–26; Klassen, "Coals of Fire," 337–50.

Judge, bring about ἐκδίκησις for his elect? Furthermore, Bock has suggested that the point of Jesus' parable is that God the Father "will bring about justice in the face of trouble. He will judge those who persecute the righteous."[139]

Paul's understanding of ἐκδίκησις as a forensic term arguably came from his knowledge of the Old Testament, where ἐκδίκησις is commonly used to denote judicial punishment (Jer 11:20; Ezek 16:41, 25:17; Hos 9:7; Mic 7:4). The Septuagint employs ἐκδίκησις in the place of several Hebrew terms used to express the meaning of penal retribution or sentence.[140] An example is found in Ezek 16:38–41, where God informed Jerusalem that because of the abominations she had committed, he would "execute a court judgment" upon them and burn their houses with fire and bring punishment upon them.[141] Furthermore, Malul contends that the forensic nature of the context seems evident from verse 2, "where the usage of the verb ידע, has already introduced the readers to the legal atmosphere of the chapter."[142] In fact, several scholars have observed that all of chapter 16 could be construed as a subpoena of Jerusalem where God pronounces his judgments upon the nation for her covenant unfaithfulness.[143] It seems probable, then, that throughout Scripture ἐκδίκησις likely denoted the idea of legal punishment typically handed down by God.

Numerous examples of κδίκησις are also found throughout extrabiblical literature in contexts referring to judicial retribution.[144] In 1 Macc 2:67 the author praised Judas for his military talent and leadership during the Hasmonean revolt. Judas's success resulted with the people essentially "setting up court" for the purpose of avenging the wrong that

---

139. Bock, *Luke*, 1446–55. See also Cassidy, *Jesus, Politics, and Society*, 34–35; Curkpatrick, "Dissonance," 107–121; Weaver, "Luke 18:1–8," 317–19.

140. Such terms include תובה, נקם, נקמה, פקדה, שפטים. See also Schrenk, "ἐκδικέω, ἔκδικος, ἐκδίκησις," 445.

141. See Bovati, *Re-Establishing Justice*, 207; P. L. Day, "Adulterous Jerusalem's Imagined Demise," 285–309.

142. Malul, "Adoption of Foundlings," 114 n. 9.

143. See Greenberg, *Ezekiel 1–20*, 292–306; Malul, "Adoption of Foundlings," 98; Zimmerli, *Ezekiel 1*, 333–53.

144. See 1 Macc 2:67; Sir 7:17; Jdt 8:35, 9:2; Josephus *Antiquities* 17.291, 20.126; *Jewish War* 2.237. There is also evidence that the term meant a public advocate, prosecutor, or legal representative; see P.Oxy. 2.261.14.

the Jews had suffered from Gentiles and rededicating themselves to the observance of the law.¹⁴⁵

Regarding 2 Thess 1, the context strongly suggests that Paul understood ἐκδίκησις as a legal term denoting vengeance or retribution at court. The apostle referred to the just punishment that God would confer on those who persecuted the Thessalonian church at his eschatological tribunal. With the use of ἐκδίκησις in the immediate context, it is possible that Paul intended to emphasize that the Lord would act as the Divine Judge and punish the unjust with terrible retribution at the final assize.¹⁴⁶ The Thessalonians could take heart in the midst of their sufferings, knowing that their vindication awaited them at God's final court.¹⁴⁷

4.1.9 οἵτινες δίκην τίσουσιν

The forensic nature of Paul's message continues in verse 9, where he explained the verdict against the persecutors who had caused the Thessalonian church to suffer with the idiom οἵτινες δίκην τίσουσιν. This seemingly legal construction typically refers to judicial punishment, action, and in various contexts a judicial hearing.¹⁴⁸ Green has further noted that this phrase "comes from the world of jurisprudence meaning to pay the consequence for some action."¹⁴⁹

---

145. See Barton and Muddiman, eds. *Oxford Bible Commentary*, 714–16; Bovati, *Re-Establishing Justice*, 173–74; Metzger and Murphy, eds. *New Oxford Annotated Bible*, 189–92; Rahlfs, ed., *Septuaginta*, 1046.

146. Williams, *Metaphors*, 157 n. 50.

147. Before moving into verse 9, brief mention should be made regarding the term ὑπακούω. Paul informed the Thessalonians that the recipients of God's judicial punishment are those "who do not know God or obey the gospel of our Lord Jesus Christ." The dominate meaning of ὑπακούω throughout Scripture is simply obedience. However, there are instances where ὑπακούω is used in judicial contexts to refer to a judge who listens to a complaint as well as legal parties that appear before the court. Unfortunately, there appear to be no biblical examples of this term used judicially or in forensic contexts. The examples of this term in legal contexts outside of Scripture are primarily found in the classical period. See, for example, Demosthenes 19.257, 19.290; Xenophon 8.1.18.

148. Schneider, "δίκη," 336. See also BDAG, 250; LSJ, 430; Ellingworth and Nida, *Translator's Handbook*, 148; Schrenk, "δίκη," 181–82; Spicq, "δίκη," 318–27; Williams, *Metaphors*, 154.

149. G. Green, *Thessalonians*, 291. See also Frame, *Epistles of St. Paul*, 234–35; Malherbe, *Thessalonians*, 402; Morris, *Thessalonians*, 204.

The judicial aspect of the idiom is in all probability generated by the term δίκη.¹⁵⁰ Apart from the compound καταδίκη, found in Acts 25:15, δίκη is used only three times throughout the New Testament (Acts 28:4; Jude 4–8; 2 Thess 1:9).¹⁵¹ In every instance, however, where δίκη is used, Schrenk has noted that "it always [has] the sense of 'penal justice,' or 'punishment,' with no distinctive features."¹⁵² Since δίκη was used by Paul only in the current passage, the discussion here will focus on the term's usage in other New Testament authors before examining the Old Testament's treatment of δίκη.

In Acts 25, after a two-year interval (24:27),¹⁵³ Paul finally went to trial before Festus regarding charges brought against him by some leading Jewish men (25:1–3). In his defense, the apostle pleaded innocent to the accusations that he had committed crimes against the Jewish or Roman law (verse 8). Festus encouraged Paul to go with him to Jerusalem and stand trial, but the apostle refused and appealed to Caesar. According to Tajra, his appeal to Caesar was crucial because:

> for the apostle, Festus' request that there be a change of jurisdiction was disastrous. Paul's overall strategy consisted of doing all within his power to remain under Roman jurisdiction. To accept the governor's proposal meant embarking on the road to a legal lynching.¹⁵⁴

With Paul's appeal granted, Festus was forced to send a letter with the accused to Caesar's tribunal explaining the particulars of the indictment. He enlisted the help of King Agrippa who was already knowledgeable regarding the details of Paul's case. Luke recorded that Festus presented Paul's case before Agrippa, informing him that the apostle was left as a prisoner of Felix and that the chief priests and elders who had brought the allegations against him sought a judicial sentence of καταδίκην for

---

150. It should be mentioned that τίνω is used as a legal term referring to one experiencing forensic retribution. However, this is strictly found in classical Greek literature. The term is a *hapax* in the New Testament and appears only twice in the Old Testament (Prov 20:22, 27:12), neither of which are judicial contexts.

151. Frame, *Epistles of St. Paul*, 234; G. Green, *Thessalonians*, 291–92; Morris, *Thessalonians*, 205–7; Malherbe, *Thessalonians*, 402; Schrenk, "δίκη," 181.

152. Schrenk, "δίκη," 181.

153. See, for example, Rosenblatt, "Under Interrogation," 221.

154. Tajra, *Trial of St. Paul*, 142. See, for example, Skinner, *Locating Paul*, 142. This idea is further emphasized from Barrett's translation of με . . . χαρίσασθαι, "make a present of me" (*Acts* 2:1120, 1130).

him. In the context, καταδίκην reveals that Festus understood that the Jewish leaders sought a legal punishment for Paul. Moreover, Tajra advocates that the statement αἰτούμενοι κατ' αὐτοῦ καταδίκην reflects the real essence of the Sanhedrin's demand: they wanted Paul transferred to the Jewish high court, where his condemnation would be a foregone conclusion."[155] The apostle was then brought before Agrippa, where he made his defense by giving a bold proclamation of the gospel (26:14–23). Paul's affidavit was extraneous in the Roman court, and thus the text indicates that he would have been released had he not appealed to Caesar (26:32).[156]

From the limited usage of δίκη it seems apparent that the authors of the New Testament understood the term judicially. Their understanding, however, in all probability derived from the term's usage throughout various contexts in the Old Testament indicating legal retribution (Exod 21:20; Lev 26:25; Deut 32:41–43). While δίκη better expresses the Hebrew idea of צדק and משפט for judicial punishment, it is used very infrequently throughout the Septuagint.[157] Nevertheless, there is evidence that the term connotes the idea of forensic punishment. For instance, in Exod 21, after God had given Moses the Ten Commandments, he gave further ordinances, which his people were commanded to follow. If they disobeyed any of the ordinances, they would suffer consequences. In 21:20, God commanded that if a man struck his male or female slave with a rod and the slave died, the man would suffer δίκη (criminal punishment).[158] Although the text is silent regarding who should carry out the punishment on behalf of the deceased slave, the forensic nature of the passage seems evident. Regarding this context, Noth contends that the slave owner would appear before the court and "vengeance . . . [was] to be executed for the slave by the legal assembly."[159]

---

155. Tajra, *Trial of St. Paul*, 154.

156. Cf. Hickling, "Portrait of Paul," 499–503; Porter, *Paul of Acts*, 158–61; Rosenblatt, "Under," 221–22; Schwartz, "Trials," 501–513; Soards, *Speeches in Acts*, 119–26.

157. The Septuagint prefers δικαιοσύνη to express the Hebrew idea of judicial vengeance. See, for example, Quell, "Concept of Law," 2:174.

158. See Brin, *Studies in Biblical Law*, 91; Boecker, *Redeformen des Rechtslebens*, 139–41; Bovati, *Re-Establishing Justice*, 362; Lipinvski, "Obligation to Take Vengeance," 3–9; Sauer, "נקם," 767–69.

159. Noth, *Exodus*, 181. See also Childs, *Book of Exodus*, 470–71.

Sufficient evidence of the legal term δίκη is also apparent throughout secular writings.[160] Josephus recounted the incident of the chief Jews who reported to Hyrcanus concerning Herod's blatant disregard for the law, murder, and misuse of funds. These leading Jews demanded that Herod be brought to δίκη (judgment) before the Sanhedrin. Infuriated upon hearing their report, Hyrcanus summoned Herod to appear in court to stand trial for his violation of the law.[161]

Although the term δίκη was seldom used throughout biblical literature, it appears evident that most of its occurrences are in judicial contexts referring to penal retribution. With regard to 2 Thess 1:9 it is reasonable to conclude that Paul, continuing the forensic aspect of the passage, used δίκη in the immediate context to encourage the suffering Thessalonian church that God would vindicate them by sentencing their persecutors to suffer eternal punishment at his soteriological court. Such an understanding coincides both with the term's clear Old Testament roots and the other legal terminology evident in the immediate context of the passage.

4.1.10 ἀπὸ προσώπου

One final phrase in verse 9 warrants a brief discussion. While ἀπὸ προσώπου is technically not a legal idiom, the phrase arguably displays a judicial overtone. The forensic nuance is evident depending on how one understands the syntax of the prepositional phrase. The majority of English versions translate ἀπό in this context as conveying the idea of "separation from." While this is the predominate usage of the preposition, it may be that the author understood ἀπό in verse 9 to express source or origin. Green has suggested that "Paul's thought is rather that the presence of the Lord is the source from which the judgment proceeds."[162] It is widely recognized in a number of texts throughout Scripture that the presence of the Lord is frequently linked with judgment (Num 16:46; Judg 5:5; Pss 34:16, 96:13; Isa 2:10; Rev 6:16, 20:11).[163] Moreover, it is

---

160. See *IG* 7.21.8; Josephus *Antiquities* 6.288, 18; Josephus *Jewish War* 7.450; 2 Macc 8:11–13; Philo *On the Change of Names* 194; Philo *On the Life of Joseph* 48; Wis 14:31.

161. Josephus *Antiquities* 14.168.

162. G. Green, *Thessalonians*, 292. See also Harris, "ἀπο," 1180–81.

163. There is also evidence in classical Greek that πρόσωπον can mean in the presence of a legal personality. See Diogenes 4.46; LSJ, 1533.

arguable from verse 9 that Paul was alluding to Isa 2:10, where judgment is executed from the presence of the Lord (see also Isa 2:19, 2:21). This same idea is also found in Rev 20:11, where John was allowed to see the coming final judgment, which would be executed from the Lord's presence.[164]

Certainly the prepositional phrase ἀπὸ προσώπου typically denotes the idea of presence. However, with regard to the immediate legal context and the possibility that the syntax of ἀπό denotes source, Paul may have offered encouragement to the Thessalonians by reminding them that when their adversaries stand before God's tribunal, he will declare the sentence of eternal destruction. Green has further suggested that "the idea [which] v. 9 conveys is not merely that the disobedient will be excluded from the Lord's presence but that from [his] presence the everlasting destruction comes forth."[165]

4.1.11 ἐν τῇ ἡμέρᾳ

The next possible legal idiom is the dative phrase ἐν τῇ ἡμέρᾳ. Paul continues the forensic nature of the chapter explaining "that the day of the Lord's coming would be the day of judgment when sentence would be passed and executed against the opponents of God and God's people."[166] This phrase, along with its various constructions,[167] is arguably an idiomatic expression from the Old Testament for the Day of the Lord, which often carried the meaning of a legal or fixed court day in accord with God's final judgment.[168]

---

164. See, for example, Beale, *Book of Revelation*, 1031–32; Chilton, *Days of Vengenace*, 529–32; Fekkes, *Isaiah and Prophetic Traditions*, 226–27; Mealy, *After the Thousand Years*, 143–89.

165. G. Green, *Thessalonians*, 293. See also chapter 5 for a more thorough discussion of this issue.

166. Wanamaker, *Epistles to the Thessalonians*, 230. See also Still, *Conflict*, 261, who contends that this phrase may also carry political overtones. However, Paul's thought throughout the chapter is arguably judicial. The Thessalonians are awaiting their vindication at God's court where their adversaries will be judged.

167. Such derivatives include ἡμέρα κυρίου, ἡμέρα τοῦ κυρίου ἡμῶν Ἰησοῦ, ἡμέρα Χριστοῦ, ἡμέρα κρίσεως; and ἡμέρα μεγάλη.

168. BDAG, 437–38; Černy, *Day of Yahweh*, 82–84; Delling, "ἡμέρα," 948–53; LSJ, 770; Dunn, "Jesus the Judge," 398–405; R. W. Klein, "Day of the Lord," 517–25; Morris, *Biblical Doctrine of Judgment*, 60–61; J. M. P. Smith, *Day of Yahweh*, 3–31; Trilling, "ἡμέρα," 119–121.

The legal nature of ἡμέρα is seemingly found elsewhere throughout the Pauline writings (1 Cor 1:8; Phil 1:6; 1 Thess 5:2; 2 Tim 1:12, 1:18). In 1 Thess 5:2, the apostle reminded the church that the day of God's final judgment would come as a thief in the night. The Thessalonians were already familiar with the concept of the Lord's return (5:1), and Paul simply exhorted the church that they should be prepared, for at any moment the final assize could convene. For the Thessalonians, their day at court would be a day of exoneration while conversely it would be a day of condemnation for their enemies.[169]

Other New Testament authors seem to demonstrate that they likewise understood ἐν τῇ ἡμέρᾳ ἐκείνῃ and its different constructions as a judicial idiom referring to God's final court day (Matt 7:22; Luke 10:12; Heb 10:25; Rev 6:17). This idea is evident in Heb 10:25. Similar to Second Thessalonians, the author of Hebrews wrote to encourage believers who suffered because of their faith in Christ. Unlike the Thessalonians, the recipients of the Letter to the Hebrews considered relapsing back under the old covenant until persecution had ceased. The author, therefore, reminded these persecuted Christians of the supremacy of Christ over the old covenant and that receding to the law would prove detrimental. According to 10:25, some of those believers had begun to forsake the practice of assembling together for corporate worship on account of the persecutions they experienced.[170] The writer of Hebrews encouraged these believers not to forsake their assembly but rather to continue meeting despite the reproach from antagonists, in order to encourage one another as βλέπετε ἐγγίζουσαν τὴν ἡμέραν. Regarding the author's intended meaning of the clause βλέπετε ἐγγίζουσαν τὴν ἡμέραν, Spicq writes:

> Le suprême motif d'être fervent dans l'approche de Dieu, la confession de l'espérance, etc., c'est que la parousie est proche; c'est dire à la fois que l'effort ne durera pas indéfiniment, et que ce jour du Seigneur étant celui des assises judiciaires et de la rétribution il importe de pouvoir comparaître avec de bonnes oeuvres et une charité vraie.[171]

---

169. Stanley, "Who's Afraid?" 468–86.

170. See, for example, Bruce, *Epistle to the Hebrews*, 252–57; C. Koester, *Hebrews*, 450–51.

171. Spicq, *L'Épître aux Hébreux*, 2:320.

The idea here is that they were to persevere amid their various trials and edify one another as they looked forward to the court day of God where their vindication awaited.[172]

The forensic understanding of ἡμέρα was linked to its usage throughout numerous judicial contexts in the Old Testament. While the Hebrew term יום certainly has a broad semantic field, it often refers to Yahweh's intervention for judgment when used idiomatically (Isa 13:1-10; Ezek 13:5; Joel 1:15; Amos 5:18-20).[173] This seems apparent in the context of Zeph 1 where the prophet declared God's indictment against his enemies. Zephaniah proclaimed throughout chapters 1 and 2 that the Day of the Lord was fast approaching. This would prove to be a terrible day for Yahweh's adversaries, who would appear before him for judicial retribution. Moreover, King has suggested that Zephaniah's prophecy demonstrates that:

> no one will be able to avoid the judgment bar of Yahweh on this day. If some might think they can hide from the judgment Yahweh announced, "I will search" (1:12). And if any think the darkness will enshroud them, thereby enabling them to avoid the search, Yahweh expressed his intention to use lamps. Indeed the day of Yahweh is a day of inescapable, universal judgment.[174]

Furthermore, the prophet related that the Day of the Lord would be such an awesome and fierce day that even the warrior would find himself crying out bitterly. The only possible reprieve at Yahweh's court would be found in his merciful intervention on behalf of those who live by faith in him.[175]

The judicial nuances of the various Day of the Lord constructions seem to be substantiated primarily throughout biblical literature. There is evidence, however, in extrabiblical literature that the idiomatic phrase demonstrated a forensic meaning in contexts regarding the fixed day of God's judgment upon his enemies.[176] For instance, in Jdt 16:17, the

---

172. See, for example, Ellingworth, *Epistle to the Hebrews*, 527-30; Moffatt, *Epistle to the Hebrews*, 146-48.

173. BDB, 399; Saebø, "Theological Usage: יום," 26-31; Jenni, "יום," 537-39.

174. King, "Day of the Lord," 26.

175. Ibid. See also Kapelrud, *Prophet Zephaniah*, 28; VanGemeren, *Interpreting the Prophetic Word*, 173-81.

176. See Jdt 16:17; Wis 3:17-19. There are also numerous references in the Pseudepigrapha: *2 Baruch* 30:1-5; *1 Enoch* 22:11, 54:6; *4 Ezra* 7:39-42; *t. Levi* 3:2. It

author gave a stern warning to those nations who rise up against the covenant people of God. Such actions would result in the Lord executing vengeance upon them in the ἡμέρᾳ κρίσεως.

It seems reasonable to consider that Paul used the prepositional phrase ἐν τῇ ἡμέρᾳ to depict both an apocalyptic and forensic tone. In keeping with the judicial aspect of 2 Thess 1, the apostle incorporated the idiom to describe the future establishment of the Lord's divine tribunal. Furthermore, Best has argued that Paul's intended purpose for this idiom was to:

> remind the Thessalonians of Christ's coming, of the judgment that will take place, and of the reversal of earthly values so that the persecutors will be punished and the persecuted will be released to be with the Lord.[177]

4.1.12 μαρτύριον

The final term for discussion in verse 10 is μαρτύριον. The term, along with its numerous constructions, typically denotes "legal connections and can mean to 'testify under oath' in a court of law or to 'adjure' a witness to do so."[178] In the current passage, Paul seems to have reminded the Thessalonian Christians that they believed his μαρτύριον of the gospel message along with his instructions while he ministered among them before being forced out of Thessalonica. When considering that the predominate usage of the μαρτύριον derivatives throughout the Pauline corpus are found in legal contexts, it is most likely that the apostle intended this word to convey a forensic overtone in verse 10 (1 Cor 15:15; 1 Thess 4:6; 1 Tim 5:21).[179]

For example, in 1 Tim 5:19–21 Paul instructed his young delegate regarding elders in the church. In the context, Paul directed Timothy on how he must handle certain situations surrounding an elder, namely when accusations are brought against an elder or when an elder has

---

should also be noted that although Josephus never incorporates any of the "Day of the Lord" idioms, "he does make oblique references . . . to a belief that parallels the Old Testament Day of the Lord." See Lanier, "Day of the Lord," 103–8.

177. Best, *Commentary*, 267.

178. Williams, *Metaphors*, 157–58 n. 51.

179. BDAG, 619; Beutler, "μάρτυς," 393–95; Frame, *Epistles of St. Paul*, 236–38; LSJ, 1082; Spicq, "μάρτυς," 447–52; Strathmann, "μάρτυς, μαρτυρέω, μαρτυρία, μαρτύριον," 474–514; Wanamaker, *Epistles to the Thessalonians*, 232.

sinned. With regard to such charges, Paul reminded Timothy of the criterion found in Deut 17:6 and 19:15, that a matter is to be confirmed only by the testimony of two or three witnesses. Regarding verse 19 Marshall notes that:

> The instruction is addressed to Timothy and the implication is that he has authority to 'hold court;' if he is in charge of a group of churches, presumably he was the 'higher authority' to whom accusations and appeals would be made.[180]

The legal nuance seems probable here, as Paul instructed Timothy that if a public hearing against an elder was necessary there must be at least ἢ δύο τριῶν μαρτύρων. The intent was arguably to guard against false accusations and possible envious motives from those in the church who wished to defame an elder.[181]

The New Testament is also replete with examples of μαρτύριον in various judicial contexts (Matt 10:18; Mark 13:9, 14:63; Acts 6:13). In Acts 7:58 Luke recorded Stephen's defense before the court. His judicial rhetoric recounted God's covenant faithfulness to Israel from Abraham to the completion of the temple by Solomon (verses 2–50). Stephen concluded his appeal with an indictment against the audience, accusing them of the same ignorance of their forefathers. Just as their ancestors had killed the prophets whom God had sent, so also those present at Stephen's trial are accused of murdering the Messiah. Upon the completion of his defense, the ferocity of those present was ignited and the μάρτυρες laid their robes aside and proceeded to stone Stephen. Williams observes the irony of this courtroom scene when he comments that:

> by the time Stephen had finished speaking, the roles of those involved in this trial had effectively been reversed. It was as though the Sanhedrin was on trial and his speech was for the prosecution.[182]

Moreover, with regard to this passage and the numerous trial scenes throughout Acts, Trites has noted that:

---

180. Marshall, *Pastoral Epistles*, 618. See also G. W. Knight, *Pastoral Epistles*, 235.
181. See Mounce, *Pastoral Epistles*, 311–12.
182. Williams, *Acts*, 132. See also Kilgallen, "Function of Stephen's Speech," 173–93; Soards, *Speeches in Acts*, 57–70.

the frequent use of legal language in connection with real courts of law is germane to Luke's presentation and part of his theological intention. The claims of Christ are being debated, and Luke intends by the use of law-court scenes and legal language to draw attention to this fact.[183]

Considering the forensic context of Acts 7, it is probable that Luke, like Paul, also understood μάρτυρες in the typical forensic fashion.

The Old Testament however, seems to be the origin of the New Testament's understanding of μαρτύριον as a judicial term. The Septuagint usually translates μαρτύριον and its synonyms from גמל לבד or ראה, which are terms commonly found in legal contexts (Exod 20:16; Lev 5:1; Num 5:13; Deut 22:14).[184] For instance, Num 5:11–31 relates the proper procedure of a husband suspicious of his wife's unfaithfulness and his desire to bring her to trial. At such a legal proceeding, when the alleged adulteress appears before the court, corroborating μάρτυς must be present. Furthermore, in the context of the passage Knierim and Coats have suggested that:

> the trial is based on her being a suspect, and not on the presumption of either her guilt or her innocence. On the presumption of the suspicion alone, the trial aims at establishing either her guilt or innocence.[185]

As a result, if there is not a μάρτυς, the court would find the wife innocent even if she has defiled herself.

Finally, evidence of μαρτύριον is prevalent in legal contexts throughout extrabiblical literature.[186] In Wis 4:1–6, the author presented a contrast between those who remain pious despite being childless and those who have acted immorally and bore children illicitly. The author reminded his audience that such children would serve as μάρτυρές against their parents. The legal nuance of the context is evident since the author's point

---

183. Trites, "Legal Scenes and Language," 278–84.

184. See Van Leeuwen, "עד," 840, who notes that "the term עד is at home in the legal language of the OT. The עד appears in both civil matters and criminal proceedings." See also Chisholm, "עוד," 335–40.

185. Knierim and Coats, Numbers, 79. See also Harrison, Numbers, 106–121.

186. See CD 9:20–22; 1 Macc 2:37; 1QS 8:6; Philo On Planting 173; On the Special Laws 1.55; Wis 4:6; SIG 799.28, 953.19.

was arguably that when the parents appear for trial at the final assize their illegitimate children would serve as testimony against them.[187]

With regard to 2 Thess 1:10 Morris contends that the apostle used the word μαρτύριον referring to "the essential task carried out by Paul and his companions who had born witness of the saving truths of the gospel [to the Thessalonians]."[188] It is arguable that, in view of the immediate judicial context of verses 5–10, coupled with the fact that μαρτύριον was often used in legal contexts in both biblical and nonbiblical writings, Paul may have utilized this term to express a forensic overtone. He and his associates testified before the Thessalonians the truth of the gospel, and they believed their testimony. However, Paul's testimony was not believed by their oppressors and would therefore testify against those oppressors when they appeared before God's court at the final judgment.

Paul concluded 2 Thess 1 with a prayer for the church in verses 11–12, which seemingly do not contain any judicial terms.[189] Yet it should be noted that κλῆσις is found in legal contexts twice in the New Testament (Acts 4:18, 24:2). There is, however, no evidence of the forensic nature of κλῆσις in the Pauline corpus. The term is overwhelmingly used by the apostle in a theological sense as the technical term for God's calling an individual to salvation or to carry out a task. Conversely, both papyri and classical Greek literature reveal that κλῆσις was used in a variety of judicial contexts, meaning a summons to court.[190] Moreover, Williams writes that κλῆσις can refer to:

> the formal process of laying charges against an individual and both the noun and the verb (cf. Acts 4:18; 24:2) are associated with being cited to appear before a judge in court.[191]

Furthermore, in 2 Thess 1:11, the term εὐδοκία is also found in classical Greek in judicial contexts referring to consent or approval in legal documents but does not appear to be used as a forensic term in the Scriptures.[192]

---

187. See, for example, deSilva, *Apocrypha*, 127–52; Harrington, *Invitation to the Apocrypha*, 55–77; Reider, *Book of Wisdom*, 82–83.

188. Morris, *Thessalonians*, 207.

189. See Wanamaker, *Epistles to the Thessalonians*, 233; Bruce, *Thessalonians*, 156.

190. See, for example, BGU 4.113813; LSJ, 960; P.Hal. 1.1, 1.224; Preisigke, *Wörterbuch*, 1:728; P.Lips. 40.2.9; Demosthenes 19.211; Xenophon *Hellenica* 1.7.13.

191. Williams, *Metaphors*, 157.

192. LSJ, 710.

In the context of Paul's prayer, it seems best not to interpret these terms as denoting a judicial meaning. Paul more than likely used κλῆσις in his standard theological manner to refer both to God calling the Thessalonians to salvation and in an eschatological sense that they would be vindicated at the final assize.[193] Paul used εὐδοκία in reference to God completing every good desire or intention of the Thessalonian believers as they continued to persevere amid a hostile environment.

4.2 CONCLUSION

The above discussion has presented sufficient evidence that Paul, specifically drawing from the Old Testament, intentionally used forensic language in 2 Thess 1:5–10 for a specific purpose. It has been argued that the judicial word clustering of 2 Thess 1 was utilized to communicate to the Thessalonian church a message of encouragement that though persecuted, they were to remain firm in their faith and steadfast in their advancement of the gospel because their vindication would come at God's eschatological court.[194] The belief throughout Judaism that God would return and bring vindication for his covenant people is abundantly clear throughout the Old Testament Scriptures, particularly from the Day of the Lord motif. With regards to 2 Thess 1:5–10 Neil has commented that:

> Paul uses the traditional language of Judaism attached to the Great Deliverance of the Day of the Lord and applies it to the Triumph of Christ. Whether we can read out of it what Paul believed is like asking whether we ourselves use the language of the hymn-book and the psalter to express our theology. . . . There is a popular traditional language of the hymn-book and there is a language of theology.[195]

Therefore, coupled with his knowledge of the Old Testament and his faith in Jesus, Paul arguably understood that the Day of the Lord would find its fulfillment in the parousia of Christ. Although the various judicial terms in 2 Thess 1 are found incorporated throughout ancient literature, this appears to have had little effect on Paul's *theological* concept of the forensic nature of the Lord's return, which is most predomi-

193. See chapter 5 for the theological significance of these verses.

194. G. Green, *Thessalonians*, 293.

195. Neil, *Thessalonians*, 146. See also Prat, *Theology of Saint Paul*, 2:374 n.1; Travis, *Place of Divine Retribution*, 48. Prat provides a very helpful list of all the Old Testament allusions evident in 2 Thess 1:5–10.

nately found throughout the Old Testament. The Thessalonian church was already familiar with Christ's return (2 Thess 2:5), and Paul utilized this knowledge as a reminder to these believers regarding the Day of the Lord (Acts 17). As a result, the apostle borrowed various forensic terms and phrases from the Old Testament to remind the Thessalonians that the Day of the Lord was essentially God's eschatological tribunal where the roles of suffering would be reversed. The Thessalonian Christians who were once persecuted would be vindicated and would witness God pronounce his judicial verdict upon their adversaries, who neither knew God nor obeyed the gospel of the Lord Jesus Christ. And consequently, as the Old Testament prophets had predicted, the Day of the Lord would serve as both a day of punishment and a day of rejoicing.

5

The Theological Significance of Judicial Language in 2 Thess 1:1–12

UNDERSTANDING PAUL'S INTENTIONAL USE of judicial language throughout 2 Thess 1 invites an examination concerning the theological significance that such a forensic word grouping has on the interpretation of the passage. Therefore, the objective of the following discussion is to offer a more accurate interpretation of 2 Thess 1 based on the evidence presented from the previous chapters. It will be argued that Paul used numerous judicial terms and allusions in 2 Thess 1 with the specific intent to encourage the Thessalonian Christians to remain steadfast amid intense persecution. Based on what he had previously taught them regarding the Lord's return, the apostle likely utilized such forensic language and allusions to remind the Thessalonian church that their vindication would come at the Day of the Lord when the righteous Judge would pass his impartial sentence at the final assize.

5.1 THE STRUCTURE OF 2 THESS 1

The structural analysis of 2 Thess 1 varies among scholars.[1] Many divide the chapter into three sections: verses 1–2 consist of the salutation, verses 3–10 are understood as a one-sentence prologue that leads into the letter body, and verses 11–12 conclude the chapter with a prayer for the Thessalonians.[2] While it is certainly advantageous to examine the common rhetorical structures involved in first-century writing, Boers has

---

1. See Dunham, "2 Thess 1:3–10," 39–46; Jewett, *Thessalonian*, 216–25. Jewett provides numerous charts detailing the different possible outlines of chapter 1 held by various scholars.

2. See Jewett, *Thessalonian*, 225; Nicholl, *From Hope to Despair*, 144–56.

noted that "one should be careful not to assume that Paul's letters had to conform to a particular pattern . . . it would be a mistake to assume that his letters had to follow a given pattern."[3] The following discussion, however, will divide the pericope into four sections. The reason for a fourfold division is that it affords a more complete interpretation for Paul's intended meaning. The following divisions are as follows: verses 1–2 contain the salutation, verses 3–4a provide the first thanksgiving, verses 4b–10 explain the reason for the thanksgiving, and verses 11–12 offer a prayer for the Thessalonians.[4]

5.2 2 THESS 1:1-2: THE SALUTATION

Second Thessalonians begins virtually identically to that of First Thessalonians: "παῦλος καὶ Σιλουανὸς καὶ Τιμόθεος τῇ ἐκκλησίᾳ Θεσσαλονικέων." While these missionaries were responsible for establishing the Thessalonian church, it appears that Paul was the primary author of the epistle; however, it is possible that Silas and Timothy may have contributed to the letter in some manner (3:17).[5] Although the introductory greeting is similar to that of First Thessalonians, there are two distinct additions. First, there is the inclusion of the possessive pronoun ἡμῶν after the prepositional phrase ἐν θεῷ πατρί. Paul may have intended the pronoun to denote both a personal and pastoral overtone between the missionaries and the Thessalonian church, revealing that they had a common bond as children of God, that they were united together by their faith, and that they were partners for the advancement of the gospel of the Lord Jesus. Moreover, the prepositional phrase ἐν θεῷ πατρὶ ἡμῶν καὶ κυρίῳ Ἰησοῦ Χριστῷ is noteworthy. Bicknell writes:

> The Greek makes plain that the Father and Christ are one source. It is remarkable that even at this early date, the Son is placed side by side with the Father as the fount of divine grace, without any need of comment.[6]

Referring to God as Father is a common expression throughout the Pauline corpus (Rom 1:7; 1 Cor 1:3; Gal 1:3–4; 1 Thess 1:2). For Paul, the

---

3. Boers, "Form Critical Study," 142.
4. Tomlinson, "Second Thessalonians," 1.
5. See Donfried and Marshall, *Theology*, 84–87; G. Green, *Thessalonians*, 227.
6. Bicknell, *First and Second Epistles*, 66. See also Best, *Commentary*, 247–48; Marshall, *Thessalonians*, 168; Morris, *Thessalonians*, 193.

idea of God as Father seems to have been rooted in his familiarity with the Old Testament's teaching regarding such a concept. Throughout the Old Testament Yahweh took the initiative of calling, nurturing, and loving his chosen people for the sake of his covenant. As Father, Yahweh interacted with his people in both blessing and disciplining them accordingly. In fact, Lowery comments that:

> the concept of God as Father is associated with creation, wisdom, and covenant traditions in the Old Testament. . . . The ideas associated with God as Father include 1) the understanding that a relationship exists which was initiated by God in which he expresses his steadfast love and faithfulness that brings security and protection and discipline. 2) In turn God expects devotion from the covenant partners that expresses itself in trust and obedience.[7]

The inclusion of this phrase would have likely encouraged this church. Being ridiculed and hated by their neighbors, the Thessalonian believers would have welcomed such a statement amidst the hostile environment in which they lived, for such an assertion would have seemingly comforted the church by reminding them of the Father they had in God. Furthermore, Green has argued:

> At the same time, the designation of God as *our* Father draws the Thessalonian believers into one family and joins them together with Paul and his associates, as well as with the church throughout the world. The bedrock of the Christian family and of Christian unity finds its bedrock in this prayer/confession.[8]

Knowing that they were united together with Paul and his fellow companions in the faith as children of the Father probably offered both encouragement and security to the Thessalonian Christians as they continued to persevere amidst great opposition. Paul arguably wanted to remind the Thessalonians that because they belonged to the Father, he not only knew their circumstances but also that he would one day exercise his jurisdiction and righteously judge those who had hurt his children. This idea seems further strengthened with the following phrase, κυρίῳ Ἰησοῦ Χριστῷ, where Christ is understood to be equal with God.[9] The

---

7. Lowery, "God as Father," 68–69.
8. G. Green, *Thessalonians*, 277.
9. See Menken, *Second Thessalonians*, 81.

term κυρίος not only refers to Christ's supreme dominion over the universe but also as the agent who carries out the Father's judicial authority. Furthermore, Menken comments that Jesus can be understood as:

> the exalted Lord, whose divine traits are more and more stressed, and who will return as the eschatological warrior to punish unbelievers (1:7-9) and to annihilate the lawless one (2:8).[10]

Additionally, the immediate context of chapter 1 may support such a possible theological understanding in view of the author's description of the events that transpire before and during the Lord's final court.

The second addition of the salutation is found in verse 2, with the phrase ἀπὸ θεου πατρὸς [ἡμῶν][11] καὶ κυρίου Ἰησοῦ Χριστοῦ, following the nominative absolute χάρις ὑμῖν καὶ εἰρήνη, which is typical Pauline style (Rom 1:7; 1 Cor 1:3; 2 Cor 1:2; Gal 1:3; Eph 1:2; Phil 1:2; Col 1:2). Theologically this is significant because both genitives are governed by the preposition, which simply denotes that God and Christ are the ultimate source of grace and peace for the Thessalonians as they live amid great conflict for their faith.[12]

5.3 2 THESS 1:3-4A: THE FIRST THANKSGIVING

This first thanksgiving, as O'Brien suggests, "has an epistolary, didactic and paraenetic function as well as giving evidence of Paul's pastoral concern."[13] It should not be overlooked that verses 3-10 are one long sentence, which is significant because it seems to emphasize, as Morris suggests, that:

> this is all one complicated piece of Paul's argument. In this section he moves from thanksgiving for the growing faith of the

---

10. Ibid. See also Menken, "Christology," 501-522.

11. See, for example, B. Metzger, *Textual Commentary*, 635. The textual critical evidence is divided regarding the addition of ἡμῶν. Metzger presents a concise explanation for the possible reasons pertaining to both the omission and inclusion of the pronoun.

12. See, for example, Best, *Commentary*, 247-48. Some believe that the differences between the salutations of First and Second Thessalonians prove inauthenticity. The weaknesses of such arguments for inauthenticity were noted in chapter 1. Consequently, this work holds to Pauline authorship of both letters. See Wanamaker, *Epistle to the Thessalonians*, 213-14, who discusses the views of Trilling on this issue.

13. O'Brien, *Thanksgivings*, 168.

Thessalonians to the way they have stood up to persecution and the truth that this shows that God is with them.[14]

Regarding verses 3–10 Ellingworth and Nida have also offered a helpful observation:

> In the original Greek the sentence length is . . . particularly great when Paul's argument or appeal reaches a climax. By far the longest sentence in the whole letter is in this section. It is no coincidence that this is also the passage in which Paul expresses most strongly his affection for the Christians in Thessalonica, and his confidence that, despite all the attacks upon it, their faith will continue to stand firm.[15]

Paul began his thanksgiving in verse 3 with the verb ὀφείλομεν. This verb is never used elsewhere by the apostle in any of his thanksgivings with the exception of here and later in 2:13. Some scholars, such as F. F. Bruce, believe that the Thessalonians had sent a letter to Paul after they received First Thessalonians, asking him not to praise them so highly since they had suffered certain shortcomings (1 Thess 1:3, 3:10).[16] Others contend that the unusual use of this verb proves non-Pauline authorship.[17] However, regarding the context of the passage, it seems best to understand ὀφείλομεν as conveying that the necessary obligation Paul and his companions felt should exist to praise God for what he had accomplished in the lives of the Thessalonian Christians, not the Thessalonians themselves.[18]

Nevertheless, the use of ὀφείλομεν has caused many to speculate about Paul's attitude toward the Thessalonians. As was discussed earlier, some scholars contend that ὀφείλομεν denotes a less personal tone and a more formal attitude toward this church.[19] Such an argument maintains that the use of ὀφείλομεν indicates a feeling of obligation rather than one

---

14. Morris, *Thessalonians*, 192. See also Malherbe, *Thessalonians*, 381–82; Marshall, *Thessalonians*, 169.

15. Ellingworth and Nida, *Thessalonians*, 133.

16. Bruce, *Thessalonians*, 144; Frame, *Epistles of St. Paul*, 221; Morris, *Thessalonians*, 194.

17. See, for example, Bailey, "Who Wrote II Thessalonians?" 134; Bultman, *Theology*, 2:131; Trilling, *Der Zweite Brief*, 43 n. 83.

18. Wanamaker, *Epistles to the Thessalonians*, 216.

19. See, for example, Bailey, "Who Wrote II Thessalonians?" 134; R. F. Collins, *Letters*, 222–23; Trilling, *Der Zweite Brief*, 43–44.

of willingness. Concerning the peculiar use of this verb, Morris has argued that "ὀφείλομεν carries the idea of personal obligation, whereas δεῖ would denote something more in the nature of external compulsion."[20] While it is true that δεῖ may have been more appropriate in the context, ὀφείλομεν in all probability does not indicate a less personal attitude towards the Thessalonian Christians but rather more than likely stresses the *necessity* of thanking God for them. In fact, it has been demonstrated that the expressions Εὐχαριστεῖν ὀφείλομεν along with καθὼς ἄξιόν ἐστιν are often found in both Jewish and Christian writings as liturgical phrases used to convey the necessity and propriety for thanking God in contexts of suffering.[21] Furthermore, Roger Aus has argued that:

> it is precisely in this situation of suffering that the author of Second Thessalonians tells the addressees that he and his fellow Christians ought to give thanks to God as is proper, because the Thessalonians' faith is growing abundantly and their love for one another is increasing; they are steadfast and are demonstrating their faith.[22]

Moreover, none of Paul's letters ever displays an apathetic attitude toward praising God for fellow Christians. The context of Second Thessalonians seems to demand that in no way did Paul use ὀφείλομεν with an uncongenial overtone, for several reasons. First, in the same verse, he referred to the Thessalonians as ἀδελφοί, which is predominately used by the apostle as a term of endearment. In fact, Paul often used ἀδελφοί when addressing the Thessalonians and other fellow churches to express the relationship they shared together in Christ (Rom 1:3, 4:7; 1 Cor 1:10; 2 Cor 1:8; 1 Thess 1:4, 2:1; 2 Thess 2:1, 2:13, 2:15, 3:1). In fact, Burke notes that:

> the term 'brother' is the most frequently occurring expression that the apostle Paul employs in relation to his fellow Christians. It is one of Paul's favorite appellations for believers in his letters.[23]

Second, in 1:4, Paul informed the Thessalonians that he and his companions spoke proudly of them among the other churches. Third, Paul used ὀφείλομεν a second time (2:13), telling the Thessalonians that

---

20. Morris, *Thessalonians*, 193.
21. Aus, "Liturgical," 432–38; Harder, *Paulus*, 62.
22. Aus, "Liturgical," 438.
23. Burke, 165. See also A. Smith, *Comfort One Another*, 104.

he should always give thanks to God for them because they were beloved by the Lord and chosen by God. And finally, to argue that ὀφείλομεν portrays a less personal tone not only goes against what other Pauline epistles reveal about the apostle's attitude towards other Christians (Phil 1:1–7; Col 1:1–12), but it arguably fails to understand the existing context of persecution. Not only were Paul and the Thessalonians united together as children of God but they also had a kindred spirit because they had faced similar persecutions for their faith. Therefore, it was not only proper but also necessary for Paul and his companions to praise God for what he had accomplished in the Thessalonians, and thus it seems reasonable to conclude that the author used ὀφείλομεν for the purpose of "[informing] the Thessalonians that he and his associates offer their thanks to God for them at every opportunity."[24]

Verse 4 begins with an inferential particle, ὥστε, making the reader aware of Paul's intention to state the logical outcome or result.[25] This is strengthened by the use of the infinitive ἐγκαυχᾶσθαι, a *hapax legomenon*, which denotes the idea of boasting concerning someone. Seeing the evidence of God's redeeming work in the Thessalonians' lives, their growing faith, and their love for one another resulted in the missionaries' boasting of this church for its perseverance and faith amidst intense persecution.

The accusative phrase αὐτοὺς ἡμᾶς functions as the subject of the infinitive ἐγκαυχᾶσθαι and is used as an emphatic "we."[26] This is difficult to understand since there are no references to anyone else praising the church in the text. Scholars have espoused numerous conjectures for the purpose of αὐτοὺς ἡμᾶς. For instance, Frame contends that Paul was making a distinction between his boasting and the esteem of the Thessalonian Christians (1 Thess 1:3, 3:10).[27] Morris has argued that while it was common for other churches to boast of one another, it was uncommon for the founders to do so, and yet Paul was emphasizing

---

24. G. Green, *Thessalonians*, 279.

25. See BDF, §§390–91; Porter, *Idioms*, 199; Turner, *Syntax*, 135–36; Wallace, *Greek Grammar*, 590–94. The predominant understanding of ὥστε plus an infinitive can either express purpose or result. In accord with the context, understanding the infinitive in terms of result makes better sense.

26. See Malherbe, *Thessalonians*, 386.

27. Frame, *Epistles of St. Paul*, 223–24.

that he and companions were actually boasting of the Thessalonians.[28] Since Paul did boast of other churches (2 Cor 7:14, 8:24, 9:3), it seems reasonable that the phrase αὐτοὺς ἡμᾶς should be understood as simply emphasizing that while other churches were boasting of them, so also Paul and his associates spoke proudly about the Thessalonians to other churches of God. Their boasting probably hearkens back to 1 Thess 1:8 where he had no need to say anything about this church because their faith was already well known throughout Macedonia, Achaia, and the surrounding districts. Paul and his companions could not refrain from their boasting among the churches with regard to what God had accomplished in the Thessalonian believers as they continued to remain steadfast in the midst of persecution.

5.4 2 THESS 1:4B-10: THE REASON FOR THE THANKSGIVING: THE USE OF JUDICIAL LANGUAGE FOR THE PURPOSE OF ENCOURAGING THE THESSALONIAN CHURCH

In the previous chapter the argument was presented that Paul purposefully used numerous judicial terms and allusions in 2 Thess 1:5-10 to encourage the persecuted Thessalonian Christians that they would be vindicated at God's court in the final assize. He continued his affirmations by reminding them that when the Lord returned, he would not only exonerate them, but he would also punish their persecutors by sentencing them to eternal judgment.

In the second half of verse 4 Paul explained his reason for his thanksgiving to God for what he had accomplished in the Thessalonians. Two terms seem to dictate the reason for his boasting, namely the Thessalonians' ὑπομονή and πίστις. The term ὑπομονή is predominately used in contexts referring to endurance in the midst of difficulty (Luke 21:10-19; Rom 5:3-5; 2 Cor 6:1-10; Jas 1:2-4). It is clear from verse 4, and the rest of Second Thessalonians, that persecution served as the backdrop for the epistle. Certainly after Paul's forced departure from Thessalonica, the unbelievers turned their hostility towards this newly formed church. Nevertheless, the Thessalonian Christians continued to

---

28. Morris, *Thessalonians*, 194.

persevere in the face of the harassment brought on by their unbelieving neighbors.

The second term, πίστις, referred to the Thessalonians' continued trust in God as they endured persecutions and tribulations. Paul's use of πίστις in this particular context is probably best understood as denoting its usual meaning of belief or trust in God.[29] The apostle sent Timothy back to Thessalonica to observe the faith of this church because he feared that they had fallen away due to the intense persecution they were experiencing (1 Thess 3:1–3). Timothy's report, however, was what Paul wanted to hear: their faith in Christ was maturing, which was proven by their endurance in the midst of great suffering. Thus, Paul and his companions could speak proudly among all the churches concerning the Thessalonians' perseverance and faith in Christ.

The perseverance and faith of the Thessalonians was evident through their endurance of persecutions: ἐν πᾶσιν τοῖς διωγμοῖς ὑμῶν καὶ ταῖς θλίψεσιν αἷς ἀνέχεσθε. Life was not easy for this church. Although the text is silent regarding the details of the Thessalonians' afflictions, it is clear that this church suffered much hostility (1 Thess 1:6, 2:14, 3:3–5). The degree of intensity is evident from both First and Second Thessalonians, and persecution may have become accepted as normative for these Christians (1 Thess 2:14). The terms διωγμός and θλῖψις are somewhat synonymous and solicit the question as to why Paul incorporated both terms. Abraham Malherbe has suggested that the difference in the terms is that διωγμός refers more to an external suffering while θλῖψις refers to the internal or psychological anguish the Thessalonians experienced as believers amid a hostile environment.[30] While this is certainly a plausible suggestion, the context of the Thessalonian epistles seems to demand that Paul intended more than just mental anguish with his use of θλῖψις.[31] This is apparent in how Paul used θλῖψις earlier in 1 Thess 1:6 when he referred to the church's imitation of the Lord and how they received the Word ἐν θλίψει πολλῇ. More than likely, he was not reminding the Thessalonian church that they simply received the gospel amidst much psychological turmoil. When considering the conflict they had faced

---

29. See Jewett, "Matrix of Grace," 63–70.

30. Malherbe, *Paul and the Thessalonians*, 48.

31. See Best, *Commentary*, 79; deSilva, "Worthy of His Kingdom," 49–79; Frame, *Epistles of St. Paul*, 83; G. Green, *Thessalonians*, 283; Meeks, *Origins of Christian Morality*, 224 n. 32; Still, *Conflict*, 210–13; Wanamaker, *Epistles to the Thessalonians*, 81.

from their neighbors during Paul's stay and departure, it seems best to understand θλῖψις as a reference to the external tribulations caused by the residents of Thessalonica who opposed the gospel. Similarly, in 1 Thess 2:14, Paul wrote that this church endured the same sufferings τὰ αὐτὰ ἐπά ἐπάθετε as the other churches in Judea. Again, it was their external physical sufferings that were likely in view. Moreover, the imperfective aspect of the verb ἀνέχεσθε stresses that the Thessalonians were in the process of ongoing endurance from their persecutions and afflictions.[32] Certainly the external sufferings of the Thessalonians could contribute to internal anguish, but in the Thessalonian epistles Green notes that:

> *trials* refers exclusively to the hostility they endured as Christians and as such is synonymous with the word *persecutions*. These believers were not simply distressed emotionally but buffeted by great hostility.[33]

Furthermore, Still has argued that "Paul's considerable and continued concern for the spiritual steadfastness of the Thessalonians strongly suggests that they were facing something far more serious than psychological angst."[34] Therefore, διωγμός and θλῖψις are probably best understood as a reference to the afflictions the Thessalonian Christians endured at the hand of their contemporaries.

Paul shifted from boasting in verse 4 to instructing the Thessalonians concerning what would happen to them at the final assize in verses 5–10. Throughout these verses Paul seems to have made it clear that God knew the sufferings the Thessalonian church had endured and that he would repay their persecutors who caused them such turmoil according to his righteous judgment.

While the term ἔνδειγμα in all probability is a forensic term referring to legal evidence, it still presents difficulty in determining with precision as to what the evidence for God's judgment refers to in the immediate context. In fact, Wanamaker argues that "the interpretation of this verse is pivotal for a proper understanding of the whole letter."[35] He has offered three possible solutions for understanding the complexities of this verse. First, he suggests that it may have been the Thessalonians'

---

32. See Porter, *Idioms*, 21.
33. G. Green, *Thessalonians*, 283.
34. Still, *Conflict*, 208–217.
35. Wanamaker, *Epistles to the Thessalonians*, 220.

endurance and faith that comprised the evidence of God's righteous judgment. Second, it may have been their persecutions and sufferings that they experienced that served as evidence for God's judgment. Third, ἔνδειγμα may refer to all of what Paul has previously said: that their endurance and faith amidst intense persecutions and afflictions constituted the judgment of God.[36]

Syntactically ἔνδειγμα can be understood to function either as a nominative, forcing the reader to supply ὅ ἐστιν, or as an accusative in apposition. Nevertheless, despite the syntax, the dilemma as to what actually constitutes the evidence of God's righteous judgment remains an issue. Several scholars have argued that the ἔνδειγμα of God's righteous judgment refers to the entire context of Paul's boast in verse 4, namely that the Thessalonians' perseverance and faith in the midst of persecutions would serve as evidence that they were worthy of God's kingdom.[37] The weakness of this view is that throughout the remainder of the chapter Paul does not mention again the Thessalonians' endurance but rather addresses the fact of their persecutions and eventual vindication.[38] As Ernst von Dobshütz comments:

> Was P. meint, ist kurz gesagt: Zum Endgericht gehört, daß Gott die Christen zur Seligkeit führt, während die Andern der Verdammnis verfallen; dies erweist sich als gerecht, wenn es dem jus talionis entspricht: die Christen haben Drangsal gelitten, die Andern haben sie mit Drangsal gequält; jetzt erfahren die Christen Erfrischung und ihre Bedränger Qual.[39]

In addition, the grammar does not require the reader to understand ἔνδειγμα to be in apposition to the entirety of Paul's boast in verse 4. In fact, it may be more natural to understand ἔνδειγμα in apposition to its immediate antecedent, τοῖς διωγμοῖς ὑμῶν καὶ ταῖς θλίψεσιν αἷς ἀνέχεσθε, which seems to have directed the author's message in the immediate context of verses 5–10 as he focused on the persecutions of these believers, the divine retribution that their oppressors would face, and the Thessalonians' ultimate vindication.[40] It is possible, then,

---

36. Ibid.
37. See Best, *Commentary*, 254–55; Ellicott, *St. Paul's Epistles*, 96–97; Frame, *Epistles of St. Paul*, 226; Morris, *Thessalonians*, 198.
38. Wanamaker, *Epistles to the Thessalonians*, 221.
39. Dobschütz, *Die Thessalonicher-Briefe*, 242.
40. See, for example, Wanamaker, *Epistles to the Thessalonians*, 221, who also notes

that the ἔνδειγμα of God's righteous judgment is not referring to the Thessalonians' perseverance and faith, nor to the whole of Paul's boast in verse 4, but rather it may be that the ἔνδειγμα of God's righteous judgment are the persecutions that the Thessalonians endure.[41] By interpreting ἔνδειγμα in this manner Paul may have been reminding the Thessalonians about the concept of suffering that was often prevalent in both Jewish and Christian theology.[42]

For instance, such a theology is seemingly derived from the Old Testament, which predominately demonstrates that suffering, whether corporate or individual, was typically an effect of sin (Exod 33; Num 14). Nonetheless, there were occasions where suffering was experienced not as a consequence of covenant violation but rather for the sake of God (Ps 44; Jer 15:10–11, 15:15).[43] At times, the people of God suffered as a result of their allegiance to him. Martin has further suggested that in certain contexts, "suffering can be the consequence of faithfulness to God, something one bears 'for the sake of' God and God's service."[44] This type of suffering motif can seemingly be traced back to the Exodus narrative where God delivered his people from affliction in order to reveal his covenant faithfulness. For centuries God's chosen people had innocently suffered under the bondage of slavery from which Yahweh not only redeemed them but also provided them with an inheritance, demonstrating his commitment to the covenant.[45] Another possible example regarding the theology of suffering may be evident throughout the Servant Songs in Isaiah (chapters 51–55), where an echo of the Exodus motif is ostensibly apparent.[46] While in that particular context, Israel's

---

that it is more natural to relate ἔνδειγμα to τοῖς διωγμοῖς ὑμῶν καὶ ταῖς θλίψεσιν αἷς ἀνέχεσθε, "because of the word order in the sentence."

41. See Bassler, "Enigmatic," 496–510; G. Green, *Thessalonians*, 284–86; Rigaux, *Saint Paul*, 620; Dobschütz, *Die Thessalonicher-Briefe*, 242; Wanamaker, *Epistles to the Thessalonians*, 221.

42. See Bassler, "Enigmatic," 496–510, who discusses several examples from Jewish literature of the theology of suffering concept. See also Pss 19:9, 119:137; 1 Pet 4:17–19.

43. See, for example, G. Martin, "Psalm 44," 18–33.

44. Ibid., 31.

45. See, for example, Keesmaat, *Paul and His Story*, 34–53; Rowland, *Christian Origins*, 27.

46. See, for example, Birch, *Singing the Lord's Song*, 54–58; Lindsey, *Servant Songs*, 27.

suffering in exile was certainly a result of the nation's sin, these chapters seem to indicate that God's punishment would soon end and that he would vindicate his name and redeem his people for his sake.[47] It seems reasonable, then, to conclude that such a concept of suffering for God's sake may have greatly influenced Paul's theology, as evident throughout his biblical writings, specifically in Second Thessalonians (Rom 8:14–17; Phil 1:29). The apostle arguably understood that suffering for Christ's sake was in certain contexts parallel to Israel's suffering for Yahweh's sake as they continued through their pilgrimage awaiting their inheritance. From Paul's perspective, it seems that in correlation with Israel's wanderings and subsequent inheritance of the promise land, Christians are likewise sojourners in a foreign land who suffer for Christ's sake, awaiting their eschatological inheritance (Phil 3:14, 20–21; Col 3:24).[48] In fact, Keesmaat argues that from Paul's viewpoint, it seems that:

> the Exodus was still underway, the hope of the inheritance of the new creation remained in the future, and the wilderness continued to press on all sides. But those in the midst of such an Exodus journey knew that God was on the path with them.[49]

Such a concept of suffering was arguably contradictory from the perspective of the citizens of Thessalonica. In the minds of unbelievers, suffering often indicated a punishment for a wrong done or possibly as a result of inner wickedness.[50] From a Christian perspective, however, the cross serves as the model. The Scriptures often teach that believers should count it all joy when suffering because the testing of a Christian's faith produces endurance and proven character, which essentially validates the presence of genuine faith (Jas 1:2–4; 1 Pet 1:5–7). With regard to the theological significance of suffering, particularly in Second Thessalonians, Bassler observes:

> Thus temporal suffering is no longer a sign of rejection by God. In this theological framework it is viewed somewhat paradoxically as a sign of *acceptance* by God insofar as he offers through it an opportunity for his elect to receive in this age punishment for

---

47. See, for example, Wagner, "Heralds of Isaiah," 193–222.
48. See, for example, Denton, "Inheritance," 157–62.
49. Keesmaat, "Empire," 135. See also Davies, "Paul," 443–63; Evans, "Aspects," 316–28; Hafemann, "Paul," 367–71; N. T. Wright, "New Exodus," 26–35.
50. For instance, Polybius 38.3.8–13.

their few sins, thus preserving the full measure of their reward in the age to come.⁵¹

Moreover, Karl Donfried comments that "[the Thessalonians'] steadfastness during these difficulties is a sign that they will be made worthy of the kingdom of God."⁵² This argument seems further strengthened by the infinitive construction εἰς τὸ καταξιωθῆναι, which was likely used to indicate the result of their persecutions and sufferings, if εἰς τὸ refers back to the διωγμοῖς ὑμῶν καὶ ταῖς θλίψεσιν αἷς ἀνέχεσθε in verse 4.⁵³ Furthermore Wanamaker notes that:

> it was not necessary for the readers to suffer in order to be considered worthy of God's dominion, but the writer certainly wished to comfort them with the fact that as a result of their experience of affliction they were considered worthy of it by God.⁵⁴

Certainly the grammar is somewhat vague, and it is syntactically possible that ἔνδειγμα does refer to the entirety of the apostle's boast in verse 4. Nevertheless, because of Paul's dependence upon the Old Testament it seems most plausible to conclude that if ἔνδειγμα is interpreted to be strictly in apposition to the immediate antecedent τοῖς διωγμοῖς ὑμῶν καὶ ταῖς θλίψεσιν αἷς ἀνέχεσθε, then the evidence "does not point to the salvation of the Thessalonians (as it did in Phil 1:27–28) but rather that God's judgment is right."⁵⁵ Paul reminded the Thessalonians that as they suffered for the sake of God that their endurance of persecutions and afflictions would serve as evidence at God's court both to exonerate them by demonstrating that they would be found worthy of God's kingdom and to implicate their oppressors, who would suffer eternal punishment.⁵⁶ Moreover, with regard to the context, it seems best to

---

51. Bassler, "Enigmatic," 502.
52. Donfried, *Paul*, 242.
53. See, for example, Aus, "Comfort in Judgment," 60–64.
54. Wanamaker, *Epistles to the Thessalonians*, 223. However, Bassler, "Enigmatic," 502, contends that the Thessalonian Christians suffered because God was punishing them for their few sins while on the earth so that they would receive their eternal reward. The problem with such an assertion is that throughout the Pauline corpus the apostle never indicates that persecution of Christians is a result of sins. See also Travis, *Retribution*, 47.
55. G. Green, *Thessalonians*, 284. See also Bassler, "Enigmatic," 496–510.
56. See Bassler, "Enigmatic," 496–510; Hughes, *Early Christian Rhetoric*, 53; Krentz, "Lens of Faith," 52–62; Krodel, "Second Thessalonians," 43.

understand ἔνδειγμα as referring to the Thessalonians' persecutions and sufferings, which they were experiencing as evidence that God's judgment is just, since Paul referred strictly to the church's afflictions in the remainder of verses 5–10. Thus, it is reasonable that in the immediate context the righteous judgment of God is based on the application of the *lex talionis* to the oppressors, while those who are afflicted are granted relief without emphasis on their endurance.[57]

Consequently, when Christ returns at the final assize to judge, the Thessalonians would act as "exhibit A" in his court, and their persecutions and afflictions would serve as evidence demonstrating that they were worthy of God's kingdom, for which they had suffered. As a result, the τῆς δικαίας κρίσεως τοῦ θεοῦ would be glorious for the Thessalonian Christians, who would be vindicated, but for their oppressors this final court would prove to be ruinous.[58]

Because of their intense suffering, the Thessalonian Christians believed that they had missed the Lord's return and were concerned whether they would be vindicated (2 Thess 2:1–2). They earnestly longed for the parousia, when their tribulations would end and their enemies would face justice. Paul arguably incorporated various forensic terms and idioms in verses 5–10 to encourage the Thessalonians by reminding them that when Christ's final court convenes he would sentence those who caused this church to suffer by repaying them with affliction (see also 2 Thess 2).

The conditional particle εἴπερ at the beginning of verse 6 assumes the reality of the statement that follows. Wallace notes that the use of εἴπερ is appropriate because the particle "is a spin-off [and a more emphatic form] of εἰ, strengthening the ascensive force."[59] Since εἴπερ

---

57. See G. Green, *Thessalonians*, 284–86; Ellingworth and Nida, *Thessalonians*, 141; Wanamaker, *Epistles to the Thessalonians*, 221.

58. Some scholars, however, contend that the judgment referred to in verse 5 is best understood as present and not future. See, for example, Lenski, *Interpretation*, 382; Marshall, *Thessalonians*, 173, although Marshall does argue that the judgment is both present and future. However, Paul's intent in the immediate context and throughout the entire epistle was to encourage the Thessalonians to remain steadfast until their vindication at the Lord's final court (1:7–10). The church had apparently been disturbed "by a spirit or a message or a letter" (2:2), which caused them to believe that they had missed the Lord's return and their exoneration. Paul, therefore, exhorts the Thessalonian church to continue persevering until the final assize where they would receive their eternal reward. The consensus here is that "God's judgment is working out proleptically in the present" (Malherbe, *Thessalonians*, 395).

59. Wallace, *Greek Grammar*, 694. See also Brooks and Wibery, *Syntax*, 163;

is typically used to imply a true hypothesis (Rom 8:9; 1 Pet 2:3), Paul reminded the Thessalonian church that it was certainly righteous for God to repay their oppressors and thus reassured the Thessalonian believers of their ultimate exoneration. The word ἀνταποδοῦναι has been demonstrated to be a judicial term denoting the idea of the recompense one would receive at court for what one had done, whether positive or negative. In many instances throughout the Septuagint ἀνταποδοῦναι refers to the retribution of Yahweh's judgment (Deut 32:35; Isa 34:8, 35:4, 66:6; Lam 3:64).[60] Moreover, the Scriptures frequently express that God will execute justice for his people.[61] The theological significance of Paul's exhortation in the immediate context, then, was to remind the church that at the Day of the Lord they would find relief. Furthermore, Paul's message of divine retribution in verses 6–12 seems to be an intertextual replication of Isa 66.[62] In fact, Roger Aus has demonstrated that the background for Paul's exhortation in verse 6 seems to have been grounded in Isa 66:4–6, which addresses the fact of Yahweh's divine retribution upon his enemies. In this passage, a judgment theophany is evident, since the prophet expressed that not only would the Lord return but also that he would pour out his vengeance upon his enemies and give repreive to his covenant people.[63] Arguably Paul used Isa 66 as the backdrop for verse 6 (and in all probability for the entirety of chapter 1), as he reminded the Thessalonian Christians that they had not yet missed the Lord's return, for at his parousia he would administer divine vengeance upon their tormentors. Thus, from his extensive knowledge of the Day of the Lord motif found in the Old Testament, particularly in Isa 66, Paul seems to have asserted in verse 6 "that it would be unjust for God to allow the persecutors to escape their deserved judgment."[64]

Legal imagery here is apparent, for at the Day of the Lord the final assize will convene and the Lord Jesus, who has been appropriated as Judge, will pronounce his sentence upon those who had afflicted the

---

Ellingworth and Nida, *Thessalonians*, 143.

60. See, for example, Travis, *Retribution*, 47.

61. Gen 18:28; 1 Kgs 8:31–32; 2 Chr 6:22–23; Pss 7:8–9, 7:11, 9:4, 9:8, 35:25; 2 Tim 4:8; Rev 18:6–7, 19:1–2.

62. Aus, "Relevance," 252–68.

63. Ibid, 266–65.

64. G. Green, *Thessalonians*, 286. See also Pobee, *Persecution and Martyrdom*, 112–13.

Thessalonian church.[65] The Thessalonians could be encouraged, knowing that God not only observes those who cause his children to suffer but also that he would bring them to justice when the Lord Jesus is revealed from heaven.

Not only is it just for God to repay those who have persecuted the Thessalonians, but it is also right for him to give relief to this church, along with Paul and his associates, who had persevered through much suffering at the hands of unbelievers. The controlling verb in verse 7 is the term ἀνταποδοῦναι from the preceding verse.[66] Paul's intent for using one governing verb was arguably to complete his contrast between the fate of the afflicters and the afflicted. Just as it is right for God to repay the oppressors with affliction so also it is right for him to grant rest to the Thessalonians. This is further evident from the term ἄνεσις, which in all likelihood stands in contrast to the θλῖψις in verse 6 and refers to the rest that the Thessalonians and the missionaries would receive when the Lord returns.[67] This motif is arguably parallel with Isa 66:18–24, where the prophet described the final gathering of God's people in Jerusalem at the Day of the Lord when their pilgrimage would be over and they would behold Yahweh's glory.[68] Paul often used ἄνεσις in passages regarding the relief believers would have from suffering (2 Cor 7:5, 8:8–13), and this same concept is seemingly applied here in verse 7 as the apostle encouraged the church with the reminder that God would bless them with eternal relief—a relief found in heaven when the Thessalonians' pilgrimage would be over and they would be separated from their enemies and in the presence of God. It seems that the apostle desired to remind the Thessalonians that though their contemporaries afflicted them, they, along with Paul and his associates, would be found innocent at God's tribunal and would be granted rest, while those who had oppressed them would be found guilty.

Paul then appears to specify in verses 7–10 both when and how the vengeance on their persecutors and relief for the Thessalonians would occur: ἐν τῇ ἀποκαλύψει τοῦ κυρίου Ἰησοῦ ἀπ'οὐρανοῦ μετ'ἀγγέλων δυνάμεως αὐτοῦ ἐν πυρὶ φλογός. His depiction of this event as an ἀποκάλθψις rather than a παρουσία was not only intentional but also ap-

---

65. See, for example, Fee, *Pauline Christology*, 55–83.
66. See, for example, G. Green, *Thessalonians*, 287.
67. See, for example, Aus, "Comfort," 63.
68. Ibid., 64.

propriate for the immediate context. The difference between the terms ἀποκάλθψις and παρουσία is that the former simply denotes a disclosure or revealing of something, such as a secret or the mysteries of God (Rom 16:25; Gal 1:12; Eph 1:17). Furthermore, ἀποκάλθψις is often found in contexts involving both the persecution of believers and the final judgment (1 Cor 1:7–8, 3:13; 1 Pet 1:5–7).[69] The latter term often refers to the arrival or coming of someone (Matt 24:3; 1 Cor 1:8; Phil 1:26). Paul's use of ἀποκάλθψις coincides with the judicial nature of the context because he reminded the Thessalonian Christians that even though it was currently hidden, God's righteous judgment would eventually be revealed upon all people at the final assize. However, certain people and events must precede the Lord's return (2 Thess 2:1–15). For the Thessalonian church, the revealing of the Lord Jesus Christ represented relief from persecution and eternal rewards, while conversely it involved eternal punishment for their oppressors.[70]

Three prepositional phrases describe the revealing of the Lord Jesus, which in all likelihood would have encouraged the Thessalonians regarding their future vindication. The first is ἀπ'οὐρανοῦ, which simply indicates that from the time of his ascension Jesus has dwelt in heaven and that from heaven he would return and carry out the final judgment (see also 1 Thess 4:16).[71] Second, μετ'ἀγγέλων δυνάμεως αὐτοῦ is somewhat more complex and has produced various interpretations. The syntax of the phrase affords a number of possible renderings.[72] The phrase may be understood to mean "his powerful angels," where δυνάμεως functions as an attributive genitive of ἀγγέλων, stressing the quality of the angels. Another option is "his angels of power," which as Frame argues, refers to a specific class of angels.[73] But this seems to miss the overall point of the passage since Paul was not concerned with the angels themselves but rather the preeminence of the Lord's return. The final option is "angels of his power," which seems most plausible in the context for at

---

69. See, for example, Aus, "Comfort," 76; BDAG 112; LSJ 201; Nicholl, *Hope*, 150. In addition, Aus has shown that while ἀποκάλθψις occurs only four times in the Septuagint, the term is found in passages that denote both retribution and comfort in the Day of the Lord (77).

70. See G. Green, *Thessalonians*, 288–89; Marshall, *Thessalonians*, 176.

71. See, for example, Aus, "Comfort," 77; Harris, "ἀπό," 1180.

72. See, for example, Marshall, *Thessalonians*, 176; Wanamaker, *Epistles to the Thessalonians*, 226.

73. See, for example, Frame, *Epistles of St. Paul*, 232.

least two reasons. First, Paul's intent in the context was arguably to stress the magnificence of Christ's return. In fact, Wanamaker comments that "it is best to render the phrase as 'the angels of his power' in order to emphasize the character of the coming Lord, rather than the quality or nature of the angels who will accompany."[74] Second, the phrase is arguably an allusion to the various Old Testament Sinai theophanies where angels accompany Yahweh (Exod 3:2, 19:13, 19:16, 19:19). Likewise, this phrase may also be a possible allusion to passages found throughout the prophetic literature where angels are present with Yahweh at the Day of the Lord (Isa 13; Zech 14:5).[75] Moreover, Kittel notes that Jesus and New Testament authors "ascribe to [angels] the role of accompanying hosts who come with the Judge, who act with Him and for Him, and who are present at the judgment" (Luke 12:8; 1 Thess 4:16).[76] Thus, the prepositional phrase μετ'ἀγγέλων δυνάμεως αὐτοῦ is arguably best understood as emphasizing Christ's power when he is revealed from heaven. The angels, then, are simply "those attendants appropriate to his position and power."[77] Considering the forensic nature of the passage, it seems likely that Paul intended the reference of the accompaniment of angels with the Judge to be a direct allusion to the various judgment theophanies depicted throughout the Old Testament. Regarding Paul's mention of angels, Witherington has concluded that:

> the Day of Yahweh had become the Day of the Lord Jesus in Paul's thought world. Christ is coming with his heavenly retinue—"with angels of his might," which may mean the angels through whom he will exercise his judicial might.[78]

---

74. Wanamaker, *Epistles to the Thessalonians*, 226.

75. See, for example, O. Kaiser, *Isaiah 13–39*, 8–9; Schaefer, "Zechariah 14," 66–91. See also Kurze, *Der Engels*, 18–19, who argues that angels were present at the giving of the Law. He contends that angels sounded the trumpets and announced Yahweh's arrival at the Sinai theophanies.

76. Kittel, "ἄγγελος," 84–85. Kittel also observes the various views regarding the involvement of angels at the final judgment. For instance, rabbinic literature nowhere mentions the cooperation of angels in the judgment, whereas the Apocalypse not only mentions that angels will accompany God at the final judgment, but states they will assist in it. See also Bicknell, *First and Second Epistles*, 69; G. Green, *Thessalonians*, 289; Malherbe, *Thessalonians*, 399.

77. Williams, *Thessalonians*, 114.

78. Witherington, *Thessalonians*, 194–95.

Moreover, Kurze has argued that the mention of angels in the context of verse 7:

> er trägt dazu bei, Christi göttliche Majestät recht hervortreten zu lassen. Paulus nennt die Engel ἀγγέλων δυνάμεως αὐτοῦ, weil sie der Welt die Machtbefehle des Weltenrichters übermitteln.[79]

It seems then, that the apostle continued the legal nature of the passage as he described a courtroom scene to remind the Thessalonians that their vindication would come when the Lord is revealed in all his power to administer the final judgment.[80]

The final prepositional phrase ἐν πυρὶ φλογός begins verse 8 and seemingly illustrates the fierceness of the Lord's wrath as he unleashes his vengeance upon the Thessalonians' oppressors.[81] Two issues of debate center on this phrase. The first is whether ἐν πυρὶ φλογός or the textual variant ἐν φλογὶ πυρός is the original. The latter reading is well attested and corresponds to numerous references in the Septuagint (Ps 28:7; Isa 29:6, 66:15; Dan 7:9). However, the external evidence for ἐν πυρὶ φλογός is also greatly confirmed with the potent combination of the uncials ℵ and A. Furthermore, in accord with the basic rules of textual criticism, the more difficult reading ἐν πυρὶ φλογός should probably be accepted.[82] However, in this instance neither reading affects the interpretation.[83]

The second issue of debate is whether ἐν πυρὶ φλογός should be anaphoric with verse 7 or cataphoric with verse 8. If the prepositional phrase is understood to refer to what precedes in verse 7, then ἐν πυρὶ φλογός would refer to the awesome sight of the Lord when he is revealed. If it is understood to refer to what follows in verse 8, then it is a reference to the fierceness of the Lord's vengeance upon his enemies at the great assize. The context seems to favor this latter option due to Paul's dependence upon the Old Testament, as particularly evident in both the Exodus motif and Isa 66:15–18. For instance, if the interpretation is cor-

---

79. Kurze, *Der Engles*, 19.

80. See, for example, Neil, *Epistle of Paul*, 147.

81. See Frame, *Epistles of St. Paul*, 232; Malherbe, *Thessalonians*, 400, who both argue that ἐν πυρὶ φλογός refers to the awesome sight of the Lord at his revealing. However, as discussed below, ἐν πυρὶ φλογός is not anaphoric to what Paul has said in verse 7 but refers to his judicial punishment on the Thessalonian's enemies.

82. See, for example, Aland and Aland, *Text*, 280–82; Greenlee, *Introduction*, 111–12.

83. See, for example, Wanamaker, *Epistles to the Thessalonians*, 226.

rect that Paul was referring to the fierceness of the Lord's vengeance in judgment against those who persecute his children, it may be reasonable to conclude that Paul was alluding to the Exodus narrative when God poured out his vengeance upon Pharaoh and the Egyptians who had afflicted his covenant people (Exod 14:23–31).[84] Yahweh's judgment of Pharaoh may have been viewed by the apostle as a typological reference to the final assize, where the Lord would unleash his final judgment upon those who persecuted his children.[85] Furthermore, in Isa 66:15–18 the prophet described the Lord coming to judge the nations with fire. Wanamaker contends that Paul was also more than likely paraphrasing Isa 66:15, which is "a text depicting the Lord coming . . . to give out vengeance in wrath and damning in flames of fire; cf. Isa 66:16, which describes the Lord as judging all the earth in fire."[86] Thus, it seems significant that Paul may have used ἐν φλογὶ πυρός in order to enhance the forensic nature of the context of chapter 1, for it arguably reminded the Thessalonians that just as God punished Israel's oppressors, so also at the Lord's return would he pour out his judicial punishment upon those who had afflicted this congregation.[87] Therefore, considering the legal imagery Paul portrayed regarding the Lord's return and the judicial punishment described in verse 8, it seems more appropriate to understand ἐν πυρὶ φλογός as cataphoric.

The three prepositional phrases in verses 7–8 are theologically significant because they enhance the legal imagery regarding the Lord's return at the final assize. Paul wanted to encourage his beloved Thessalonians to remain steadfast as they faced opposition from their neighbors who opposed the gospel. In fact, the unbelieving citizens in Thessalonica had essentially rejected the Lord Jesus, who one day "would come with great authority and judicial power, accompanied by those who would aid in the execution of divine judgment."[88]

---

84. See, for example, Niehaus, *God at Sinai*, 365–37.

85. See, for example, Ninow, *Indicators of Typology*, 153–56.

86. Wanamaker, *Epistles to the Thessalonians*, 227. See also Aus, "Relevance," 266; Katz, "Ἐν πυρὶ φλογός," 133–38; Savran, *Encountering the Divine*, 64–69. Katz does see an allusion to Isa 66; he argues that Paul is using Exod 3:2 as his parallel text.

87. See G. Green, *Thessalonians*, 289; Marshall, *Thessalonians*, 177; Wanamaker, *Epistles to the Thessalonians*, 226–28.

88. G. Green, *Thessalonians*, 289.

In verses 8–9 Paul described the punishment that the Thessalonian persecutors would face at the final assize. Green has noted that this punishment "is the result of a judicial decision and disposition against those who have rejected God and His gospel."[89] The Thessalonians who had suffered at the hands of their contemporaries would seemingly find great comfort from Paul's words that their enemies, all who do not know God or obey the gospel of the Lord Jesus Christ, would have their just retribution.

It has been suggested by several commentators that the repeated use of the plural article τοῖς in verse 8 reveals that Paul was referring to two distinct groups of people: those who do not know God and those who do not obey the gospel of the Lord Jesus.[90] Marshall contends that the first group refers to the Gentiles, who were commonly referred to in the Old Testament as those who do not know God (Ps 79:6; Jer 10:25).[91] He further argues that the second group refers to Jews, who were considered as those who do not obey the gospel of the Lord Jesus Christ (Isa 66:4; Acts 6:7). Marshall is correct in this observation since such an interpretation does in some respects adhere to the immediate context, with regard to the persecutions against the Thessalonian Christians by both Jews and Gentiles. However, this suggestion that Paul had two distinct groups in mind is unconvincing for several reasons. First, the Old Testament contains references to Jews as not knowing God (Jer 4:22, 9:3; Hos 5:4), and similarly the New Testament makes reference to Gentiles as those who do not obey the Gospel (Rom 11:30–32).[92] Second, the context of 2 Thess 1 does not clearly distinguish between two groups. While Paul does make such a distinction in 1 Thess 4:5 that the Gentiles do not know God, he does not do so here.[93] Third, the repetition of τοῖς is likely used syntactically to function as an anaphoric reference to τοῖς θλίβουσιν in verse 6, making the καί epexegetical, with the second parti-

---

89. Ibid., 290.

90. See Frame, *Epistles of St. Paul*, 233; Lünemann, *Handbook to the Epistles*, 193–94; Marshall, *Thessalonians* 178.

91. See, for example, Marshall, *Thessalonians*, 178.

92. This seems to be Paul's argument in the first three chapters of Romans, that *all*, both Jew and Gentile are sinners, and unless they obey the gospel will face God's condemnation (2:11; 3:23). See, for example, Best, *Commentary*, 260; Bruce, *Thessalonians*, 151–52; G. Green, *Thessalonians*, 290; Milligan, *St. Paul's Epistles*, 90; Wanamaker, *Epistles to the Thessalonians*, 227; Witherington, *Thessalonians*, 195.

93. See, for example, Malherbe, *Thessalonians*, 401.

ciple functioning as a particular case of the first.[94] In fact, several scholars contend that in verse 8 Paul utilized the literary style often found in Hebrew poetry of synonymous parallelism, which has led them to discount the perception of two distinct groups.[95]

While the question remains open, it seems that the author's intent in verse 8 was not to distinguish between two groups but rather to remind the Thessalonians that blatant disobedience to the gospel by their oppressors was identical to not knowing God.[96] Furthermore, Menken comments that:

> both indications concern the oppressors mentioned in 1:6; for [the] author . . . considers Jesus as bearing God's name and exercising Gods' functions, rejection of the gospel, the good news of Jesus, is tantamount to a refusal of God himself.[97]

Paul arguably wanted to reassure his audience that their vindication would come, as their oppressors, both Jew and Gentile, would face God's judicial sentence of eternal punishment.[98] Such persons had committed an offense against God and would, therefore, be unable to plead their case before him who serves as the final judge and who will punish them accordingly. Paul continued in verse 9 to elaborate on the fate of God's enemies who must stand trial before him and await his ruling. Those found guilty of disobedience will be sentenced to legal punishment (δίκην τίσουσιν),[99] namely eternal suffering by being cut off from the presence of the Lord and the glory of his power. The phrase ὄλεθρον αἰώνιον ἀπὸ προσώπου τοῦ κυρίου functions in apposition to δίκην and depicts a reality that is often used throughout various New Testament contexts to refer to the eternal punishment that unbelievers face, namely separation from God (Matt 25:41; 1 Thess 5:3; 1 Tim 6:9; Jude 7). With regard to this destruction, Fudge has argued that:

---

94. Williams, *Thessalonians*, 115. See also Aus, "Comfort," 88; Menken, *Second Thessalonians*, 89.

95. Aus, "Comfort," 88; Bruce, *Thessalonians*, 151; Malherbe, *Thessalonians*, 401; Rigaux, *Saint Paul*, 629.

96. See, for example, Krentz, "Through a Lens," 52–62.

97. Menken, *Second Thessalonians*, 89.

98. See, for example, Malherbe, *Thessalonians* 401.

99. See pages 103–6 for the judicial nuance of this idiom. See also BDAG 198, 818; MM 163, 636.

Paul tells the Thessalonians that the wicked will be punished with everlasting destruction. It will proceed from God's glorious, fiery presence. It will also remove the wicked away from his presence forever.[100]

Fudge asserts that in the context of verse 9 the wicked are separated from the Lord (i.e., they are in exile).[101] In this context it may be reasonable to argue that Paul understood the punishment that the oppressors would encounter as a possible allusion to the theme of exile, for it seems that throughout the Old Testament the status of exile refers to separation from God.[102] This is evident throughout Israel's history, where the nation was predominately sent into exile on account of covenant disobedience. For instance, during Israel's Babylonian exile, not only was the nation separated from God but it was even depicted as dead despite their future restoration (Ezek 37).[103] While the nation of Israel was punished for their sins, God remained faithful to his covenant and promised to restore his people. In contrast, however, there are instances where Yahweh declared that those who had afflicted his covenant people would suffer final destruction, being permanently exiled from the glory of the Lord (Jer 46–51; Ezek 25–32). It is conceivable, then, that in view of Paul's dependence upon the Old Testament, his understanding of separation from God may have been derived from the exilic motif prevalent throughout Scripture. The apostle may have recognized that the final destruction that the Thessalonians' oppressors would face was a correlation to exile, where they would be permanently separated from the glory of the Lord (Isa 2:10; Jer 25:31, 46–51; Hag 2:22).[104] Furthermore, this concept may also be evident from the nuance of the preposition ἀπό, which typically denotes the idea of separation.[105] There are, however, a variety of other nuances that ἀπό portrays such as "cause" or "source."[106] If, as Quarles

---

100. See, for example, Fudge, *Fire That Consumes*, 249; M. Green, *Evangelism*, 72–73; J. W. Wenham, "Conditional Immortality," 161–91.

101. See, for example, Fudge, *Fire That Consumes*, 242–43.

102. See, for example, Klingbeil, "Exile," 246–49; Howard, "גלה," 861–64.

103. See, for example, Wendland, "These Bones," 241–72.

104. See, for example, Keesmaat, "Empire," 182–212; R. W. Klein, *Israel in Exile*, 66–67. See also Raitt, *Theology of Exile*, 217–22.

105. See, for example, BDAG, 105; Schneider, "ἀπό," 124–25; Wallace, *Syntax*, 368.

106. See, for example, Harris, "ἀπό," 1180–81; Moule, *Idioms* 71–73; Wallace, *Syntax*, 368.

has suggested, Paul used ἀπό to express "source" in this context, his thought in verse 9 would be that the presence of the Lord is the source from which judgment comes.[107] In fact, the argument is made that Paul likely understood the preposition to denote "source" since the presence of the Lord was often associated with divine judgment throughout the Old Testament and the book of Revelation (Num 16:46; Judg 5:5; Pss 34:16, 96:13; Rev 6:16, 20:11).[108] As Paul noted in verse 7, he certainly understood that judgment would commence at the coming of the Lord. Moreover, he elaborates regarding the judgment the Lord will deliver at his parousia in chapter 2. In the immediate context of verse 9, however, Paul has reminded the Thessalonians that those who have afflicted them will suffer eternal destruction. The prepositional phrases ἀπὸ προσώπου τοῦ κυρίου and ἀπὸ τῆς δόξης τῆς ἰσχύος αὐτοῦ clarify that their eternal destruction consists of being separated from his presence and from the glory of his power.[109] This has led Green to argue that Paul's intent for the prepositional phrases was to express, "not [only] that the disobedient will be excluded from the Lord's presence but that from the Lord's presence the everlasting destruction comes forth."[110] This seems, then, to be the best interpretation, since it allows ἀπό to function with its normal spatial nuance.[111] This interpretation is also reasonable if the καί following ἀπὸ προσώπου τοῦ κυρίου is epexegetical, for this would, arguably, further validate Paul's intent to remind the Thessalonians that the eternal destruction that their oppressors would suffer was separation from the Lord, that is, ἀπὸ τῆς δόξης τῆς ἰσχύος αὐτοῦ.[112]

Regardless of the nuance that ἀπό conveys (i.e., "separation" or "source"); it appears that the objective of the verse in the immediate context was to encourage the Thessalonians concerning their future vindication. As they persevered amidst great opposition, Paul reiterated that their antagonists would inevitably face divine judgment, namely eternal

---

107. See, for example, Quarles, "ΑΠΟ," 201–211.

108. See, for example, Bruce, *Thessalonians*, 152; Quarles, "ΑΠΟ," 203–4.

109. See, for example, Keesmaat, "Empire," 207; Porter, *Idioms*, 139–42; Wanamaker, *Epistles to the Thessalonians*, 259.

110. G. Green, *Thessalonians*, 293.

111. See, for example, Wanamaker, *Epistles to the Thessalonians*, 229.

112. See, for example, G. Green, *Thessalonians*, 293; Malherbe, *Thessalonians*, 403; Wanamaker, *Epistles to the Thessalonians*, 229; who all note the parallelism of 2 Thess 1:9 with Isa 2:10 to depict the Lord's coming in judgment.

exile. Moreover, regarding Paul's intent in verse 9, Neil has offered the following summary:

> Here the emphasis is on the final vindication of goodness and the punishment of evil at the Day of Judgment. When the Lord Jesus is revealed from heaven . . . on that Day . . . it is those who have afflicted the weak and persecuted the righteous—those who refuse obedience to the gospel (v. 8) will suffer the just punishment of God by being destroyed eternally from the presence of the Lord (v. 9).[113]

Thus, in keeping with the judicial nature of the passage it seems that Paul wanted to remind the Thessalonians that their oppressors essentially opposed Christ himself and that at his coming, the final assize would convene, and they would face eternal judgment from the Lord, who would vindicate his people. The Thessalonians would likely be consoled in knowing that their perseverance amidst great suffering was not in vain. Such consolation would escape those who did not know God and disobeyed the gospel at the parousia, and would result in their judgment and eternal separation from the Lord.[114]

Having just described the fate of those who reject God and the gospel in verse 9, namely that the punishment of their adversaries would commence at the Lord's return, Paul continued in verse 10 by reminding the Thessalonian believers that the significance of the parousia would be entirely different for them, since it would indicate that their final justification had come.[115] Menken has argued that Paul's intent in verse 10 was to present a contrast with verse 9, namely that "the fate of the faithful is opposed to the fate of the unbelievers."[116] Thus, the verdict at the final assize is contingent upon knowing God and obeying the gospel.

In keeping with the legal nature of the passage, verse 10 depicts the events that will transpire at God's eschatological court.[117] This seems to fit the context best for several reasons. First, Schneider has noted that the term ἔρχομαι is predominately used in the Pauline epistles in contexts of "eschatological statements [regarding] Christ's coming [for judgment]

113. Neil, *Epistle of Paul*, 145.
114. See, for example, Harris, "ἀπό," 1180–81; Schneider, "ἀπό," 124–25.
115. See, for example, Malherbe, *Thessalonians*, 404.
116. Menken, *Second Thessalonians*, 91.
117. See, for example, G. Green, *Thessalonians*, 294–95; Wanamaker, *Epistles to the Thessalonians*, 230.

(Col 3:6; Eph 5:6; 1 Thess 5:2, 4:2)."[118] Second, the aorist subjunctive ἔλθῃ depicts an indefinite temporal nuance indicating a future contingency.[119] This is further substantiated by the conjunction ὅταν[120] together with the temporal phrase ἐν τῇ ἡμέρᾳ ἐκείνῃ. Third, the prepositional phrase ἐν τῇ ἡμέρᾳ ἐκείνῃ has been shown to be a common judicial idiom throughout the Old Testament, referring to the final judgment, which, as the context appears to demonstrate, is seemingly twofold: for the Lord's enemies it is separation from him but for his covenant people it is the conclusion of their pilgrimage and final vindication (Isa 13:1–10; Ezek 13:5; Joel 1:15; Amos 5:18–20).[121] Thus, it seems probable then, to understand verse 10 forensically, as Paul continued to reference what would transpire at the final assize.

The apostle reminded the Thessalonians of what would take place when the Lord returns, namely ἐνδοξασθῆναι ἐν τοῖς ἁγίοις αὐτοῦ καὶ θαυμασθῆναι ἐν πᾶσιν τοῖς πιστεύσασιν. The two infinitival clauses are seemingly derived from the Septuagint (Pss 88:8, 67:36) and probably function to express the purpose of the Lord's coming.[122] An interpretive issue that surrounds the first clause is the exegesis of the preposition ἐν. Does ἐν denote an instrumental idea, meaning "by his saints"; a causal nuance that he will be glorified "because of his saints"; or a spatial nuance, "among his saints?" While all of these options are viable, it seems that because ἐνδοξασθῆναι ἐν τοῖς ἁγίοις αὐτοῦ is an apparent parallel to Ps 88:8 (LXX), it may be best to understand the prepositional phrase as conveying the idea that the Lord will be glorified in the "company of his saints," since this appears to be the intention of the Psalmist who wrote "ὁ θεὸς ἐνδοξαζόμενος ἐν βουλῇ ἁγίων."[123] In fact, Wanamaker has suggested:

---

118. Schneider, "ἔρχομαι," 674; Schramm, "ἔρχομαι," 55–7; Preuss, "Coming Judgment," 34–37. See also G. Green, *Thessalonians*, 294; Wanamaker, *Epistles to the Thessalonians*, 229–30.

119. Wallace, *Greek Grammar*, 479. See also BDF, §§ 381–82; Turner, *Syntax*, 112–13.

120. Syntactically, ὅταν seems best interpreted as a temporal conjunction meaning that the Lord's coming is certain but the *time* is unknown. See, for example, Morris, *Thessalonians*, 207 n. 34; Porter, *Idioms* 214; Wallace, *Greek Grammar*, 677.

121. See pages 107–10 for a lengthy discussion of this legal idiom.

122. See, for example, Malherbe, *Thessalonians*, 404; Wanamaker, *Epistles to the Thessalonians*, 230–31. Cf. Aus, "Comfort," 99, who views the infinitives as causative.

123. See, for example, Williams, *Thessalonians* 117; Wanamaker, *Epistles to the*

This sense agrees with the meaning of ἐν in Psalm 88:8 (LXX), but more importantly it counterbalances the physical exclusion of the persecutors of the Thessalonian community from the presence of the Lord and His mighty angels when He comes (v. 9) by making clear that the Lord will be present in the midst of the community of His saints and they will share in His glory.[124]

However, in the context of Ps 88:8 βουλῇ ἁγίων is simply "council of holy ones," which some have understood as a reference either to angels or divine beings.[125] Nonetheless, the apostle demonstrates throughout his biblical writings that he understood ἁγίων to refer both to angels and saints (1 Thess 3:13; Rom 1:7; 1 Cor 1:2).[126] Furthermore, Paul arguably understood ἁγίων in verse 10 to denote saints since it is followed by the parallel clause ἐν πᾶσιν τοῖς πιστεύσασιν.[127] It seems then, that Paul makes a distinct contrast between those in verse 10 and those in verses 8-9 who will face God's divine retribution.[128]

The second infinitival clause, θαυμασθῆναι ἐν πᾶσιν τοῖς πιστεύσασιν, arguably refers to a wider group of saints other than the Thessalonians who will similarly glorify the Lord.[129] It is likely that Paul intended to stress that all who have believed will glorify and marvel at the Lord when he returns.[130] The use of the causal ὅτι serves to both encourage and explain to the Thessalonians that they, along with all of God's children, will participate in glorifying the Lord at his return because ἐπιστεύθη τὸ μαρτύριον ἡμῶν ἐφ' ὑμᾶς. Such a concept is arguably parallel to the exilic motif prevalent throughout the Old Testament, where God's covenant people are told that they will be restored to him and will be considered worthy to be in his presence because of what they endured through their

---

Thessalonians, 230-31.

124. Wanamaker, *Epistles to the Thessalonians*, 230-31.

125. See, for example, Bratcher and Reyburn, *Translator's Handbook*, 773-74; Tate, *Psalms 51-100*, 420; Ward, "Literary Form," 321-39.

126. See, for example, Bruce, *Thessalonians*, 152-53; G. Green, *Thessalonians*, 294; Menken, *Second Thessalonians*, 91; Wanamaker, *Epistles to the Thessalonians*, 230.

127. Marshall, *Thessalonians*, 181; Menken, *Second Thessalonians*, 91-92.

128. See, for example, G. Green, *Thessalonians*, 295; Malherbe, *Thessalonians*, 404.

129. See, for example, Williams, *Thessalonians*, 117.

130. The aorist participle πιστεύσασιν is arguably used, rather than the present participle, to stress the completed act of believers coming to faith. See, for example, K. McKay, *New Syntax*, 30-31; Porter, *Idioms*, 21; Wanamaker, *Epistles to the Thessalonians*, 231; Williams, *Thessalonians*, 117.

pilgrimage and its sufferings (Isa 51:3; Jer 24:4-7, 31:31-34).[131] Thus, Paul may have implicitly alluded to the exilic motif in order to encourage the Thessalonian sojourners that they would be delivered from suffering at the Lord's return, when their pilgrimage would be over and they would realize the greatness of their redemption as they entered into their new Exodus.[132]

In verses 5-10, Paul encouraged his Thessalonian believers who faced intense persecutions at the hand of their contemporaries by reminding them of their future vindication at the Day of the Lord, when the final assize convenes. Throughout this section the apostle used numerous judicial terms and idioms to stress that the Thessalonians would be found "not-guilty" at God's eschatological court, while their oppressors would be found "guilty." In fact, with regards to these verses, particularly 7-10, Dibelius has argued that "ist aus jüdischem Material, der Schilderung einer Gerichts theophanie."[133] Both Jews and Greeks, who did not know God or obey the gospel of the Lord Jesus Christ, would face the vengeance of God, who would repay them with his divine sentence of eternal destruction.

5.5 2 THESS 1:11-12: PRAYER FOR THIS PERSECUTED CHURCH

Paul concluded chapter 1 with an intercessory prayer for the Thessalonian Christians. He was pleased that they had remained steadfast amidst a hostile environment and, as in his others epistles, offered a prayer of encouragement on behalf of these converts.

The idiom εἰς ὅ likely functions anaphorically to express the purpose of what Paul had said in the previous section, namely that the believers would be vindicated, while the wicked would be sentenced to eternal punishment.[134] At the beginning of the prayer, he reminded the Thessalonians, as he did earlier in verse 3, that he and his companions always pray for the church. This is followed by a ἵνα ὑμᾶς, which

---

131. See, for example, Hester, *Inheritance*, 43-44; LaRondelle, *Our Creator Redeemer*, 148-49.

132. See, for example, Davies, "New Exodus," 447; Ninow, *Indicators of Typology*, 120; Stock, *Way in the Wilderness*, 14-15.

133. Dibelius, *An die Thessalonicher*, 42.

134. See Malherbe, *Thessalonians*, 409; Wanamaker, *Epistles to the Thessalonians*, 232.

as O'Brien has argued, "introduces the content, not purpose, of Paul's prayer, and the ὑμᾶς, placed first for emphasis, underlines the apostle's special concern for them."[135]

Paul's prayer is seemingly framed with a twofold petition. First, that ὑμᾶς ἀξιώσῃ τῆς κλήσεως ὁ θεὸς ἡμῶν, where the pronoun is placed at the beginning likely to emphasize the Thessalonians and the ἡμῶν indicates the pastoral attitude the missionaries had for these fellow believers.[136] Furthermore, the concern of the prayer was not that the Thessalonians might fall away from being God's chosen, but rather the prayer is focused on the idea that these believers should walk in a manner worthy of God, who has called them to salvation as they endure persecutions, and that they should wait for their final justification. In fact, Marshall has argued that the intent of this prayer "is clearly of living in an appropriate manner by responding to the gracious call and living in accordance with God's standards."[137] In their own strength, the Thessalonians could not sustain this manner, and thus, the prayer offered petitions God to intervene on behalf of these believers, causing them to live worthy of their calling.[138]

The second petition is similar to the first. However, O'Brien notes that:

> the first request is concerned with God's action in relation to *his* calling the Thessalonians. The second petition also refers to God's activity, but this time with reference to the *Thessalonians'* good resolve and work of faith.[139]

The verb πληρώσῃ denotes the idea that God will finish what he started in them. Paul entreated God, the ultimate source of all good, to fulfill in the Thessalonians their desire ἀγαθωσύνης and their ἔργον πίστεως. From the apostle's perspective, all this is achieved by the δύναμις, which only comes from God. Paul realized that the Thessalonian believers were vehemently persecuted, and as they faithfully persevered, he prayed that God would strengthen them and fulfill their desire to do good as well as to continue in their work of faith as he worked in them

---

135. O'Brien, *Thanksgivings*, 178.
136. See, for example Marshall, "Election and Calling," 259–76.
137. Ibid., 272. See also Morris, *Thessalonians*, 209.
138. See, for example, Menken, *Second Thessalonians*, 92–93.
139. O'Brien, *Thanksgivings*, 179.

powerfully. Paul prayed that God would enable the Thessalonians to live how they ought in the midst of a hostile environment so that when the Lord returns at the final judgment he will be able to count them worthy of his kingdom.[140]

The use of ὅπως indicates the reason for Paul's prayer, which was supremely for the glory of the Lord Jesus. Again Paul's personal tone is evident as he explained the reason for his prayer, which was that ἐνδοξασθῇ τὸ ὄναμα τοῦ κυρίου ἡμῶν Ἰησοῦ ἐν ὑμῖν, καὶ ὑμεῖς ἐν αὐτῷ. Moreover, it is likely that Paul's prayer reminded the Thessalonians about the Old Testament motif, where the Day of the Lord is depicted as the vindication of exiled Israel (Isa 51:3; Jer 24:4–7, 31:31–34). In other words, Paul's prayer may have intended to reiterate to the Thessalonians that they had been faithful to God throughout their pilgrimage and that when the righteous Judge returns at the final consummation, "the name of the Lord Jesus will be glorified instead of being despised and rejected as it was in Thessalonica (Acts 17:7)."[141] Furthermore, the Lord Jesus would also be glorified by vindicating the Thessalonians from exile, while his adversaries would be separated from him into the final exile. In summary of Paul's prayer, F. F. Bruce comments that:

> the missionaries' prayer has the Advent in view, but it will be fulfilled when only as their converts are progressively transformed by the Spirit here and now in the image of Christ, "from one degree of glory to another" (2 Cor 3:18).[142]

5.6 CONCLUSION

The theological significance of Paul's use of forensic language throughout 2 Thess 1:1–12 was its use to encourage this church as they endured severe persecution and awaited their redemption at the Day of the Lord. The intense suffering likely influenced every aspect of their lives to the point where they wondered if they had missed the return of the Lord and if he would ever vindicate them. The apostle seemingly understood the Day of the Lord motif as an appointed court day, which is ultimately consummated at Christ's return when he presides as Judge and admin-

---

140. See, for example, Marshall, "Election," 272; Menken, *Second Thessalonians*, 92–93.

141. G. Green, *Thessalonians*, 298.

142. Bruce, *Thessalonians*, 157.

isters justice. Borrowing from the Day of the Lord concept found in the Old Testament, Paul seemingly utilized numerous judicial terms in verses 5–10 to remind the Thessalonian believers that the Lord had counted them worthy of his kingdom and that when he returns at the final judgment he would vindicate them at his eschatological court by finding them "not-guilty," while he would find their persecutors "guilty" and issue them their sentence of eternal separation. Paul concluded chapter 1 with a prayer for the Thessalonian church, requesting that God would work powerfully in them for the glory of the Lord Jesus Christ so that he would find them worthy.

6

The Theological Significance of the Judicial Language in 2 Thess 1 in Relation to the Entire Epistle

THE FOREGOING STUDY HAS attempted to demonstrate that Paul intentionally used judicial language and allusions throughout 2 Thess 1 to encourage the persecuted church to remain steadfast because their vindication would come at God's final court. It was argued that the Old Testament, particularly contexts referring to the Day of Yahweh and other judgment theophanies, served as Paul's primary source for such forensic language. It was further suggested that the apostle understood the Day of Yahweh as an appointed court day when the Lord Jesus, serving as the Father's judicial agent, would carry out his righteous judgment at the final assize. The Thessalonian church longed for this day because it meant that they would be exonerated, while their opponents would be declared guilty and sentenced to eternal punishment. By understanding the intentional use of legal language in 2 Thess 1, the purpose of the following discussion is to explore how such forensic idioms and allusions affect the interpretation of the final chapters of the letter.

6.1 CHAPTER 2 IN RELATION TO CHAPTER 1: THE LETTER BODY

Chapter 2 begins the letter body, where Paul addressed the issue concerning the return of the Lord. Regarding this short chapter, Hiebert has commented that "this paragraph constitutes the very heart of the epistle. It is crucial because of its momentous eschatological import."[1]

---

1. Hiebert, *Thessalonian Epistles*, 299.

It seems that Paul's purpose for writing chapter 2 was to remind the Thessalonian Christians of his previous teaching that the Lord would return, that certain events would precede his coming, and that they should not be disturbed by any alleged Pauline teaching (2:5).[2] In verses 1–2, it is evident that the Thessalonian church had somehow received inaccurate information about the Day of the Lord, either διὰ πνεύματος, μήτε διὰ λόγου, or δἰ ἐπιστολῆς.[3] Paul was unsure of the means by which such false teachings had infiltrated the church at Thessalonica and part of his concern, as Fee suggests, was:

> to deny that he could be held responsible for eschatological teaching that so thoroughly contradicted what he had clearly taught them previously, so much so that he spent the next several sentences reiterating that teaching by way of reminder.[4]

The Thessalonians knew what Paul had taught them concerning the Day of the Lord (2 Thess 2:5), but they had become disturbed that they had somehow missed the Lord's advent. Consequently, the apostle wrote to further explain the events that must precede the Lord's return and their gathering to him, in order to encourage these believers that they had not missed his coming, and that they must continue to persevere, for their vindication was still to come.

The focus of Paul's request in verse 1 regarding the Lord's parousia and their gathering to him has produced an inordinate amount of theological discussion. The debate seems to center on whether Paul was referring to one or two eschatological events. Simply, does the apostle make a distinction between the coming court day of Christ and the gathering together to him or is he referring to the same event? Such a discussion is often prominent among those who are entrenched in the pre-tribulation/post-tribulation debate, where 2 Thess 2:1 is often used as a proof text to support either viewpoint.[5] Several scholars, however,

---

2. See Hughes, *Early Christian Rhetoric*, 102.

3. See Fee, "Pneuma and Eschatology," 299. Fee argues that "when Paul refers to the originating source of something he uses παρά or ἀπό; when he refers to the secondary agent, that through which something has been mediated he uses διά."

4. Ibid., 297.

5. For support of the pre-tribulational view, see, for example, Brindle, "Biblical Evidence," 138–51; Feinberg, "Pretribulation Rapture Position," 47–86; Stanton, *Kept from the Hour*, 21. For support of the post-tribulational view, see, for example, Giblin, 243–44; McClain, "Pretribulation Rapture," 233–45; Williams, *Thessalonians*, 122.

seem to favor that Paul was referring to one event in 2:1, based on the syntax of the prepositional phrase ὑπὲρ τῆς παρουσίας τοῦ κυρίου ἡμῶν Ἰησοῦ Χριστοῦ καὶ ἡμῶν ἐπισυναγωγῆς ἐπ'αὐτόν.[6] The reason that it is often purported to refer to the Day of the Lord and the gathering to him as the same event is that in the context, the Greek article is governing multiple substantives that are connected by καὶ, which typically demonstrates a close association.[7] In fact, Wallace has commented that:

> in Greek, when two nouns are connected by καὶ and the article precedes only the first noun, there is a close connection between the two. That connection always indicates at least some sort of *unity*. At a higher level, it may connote *equality*. At the highest level it may indicate *identity*.[8]

Thus, it is contended that a single event is clearly in view in 2 Thess 2:1, since the two nouns παρουσίας and ἐπισυναγωγῆς, connected by καὶ, are governed by the single article τῆς. Furthermore, Williams has argued that:

> the two nouns, coming and being gathered, are governed by the one article and are thus depicted as one (complex) event. . . . Those who use this verse to make a distinction between the time of the so-called Rapture of the saints and the Parousia, do so in defiance of the syntax. A single event comprises the return of Jesus and the Rapture of the saints.[9]

It is syntactically correct to understand multiple substantives governed by a single article to have the same referent, that is, the second noun provides a further description of the first.[10] However, it has been argued that such constructions are applicable only when the substantives meet three criteria: both are personal, both are singular, and both are non-proper.[11] It seems, then, that the problem with understanding

---

6. See, for example, Bruce, *Thessalonians*, 163; Best, *Commentary*, 274; G. Green, *Thessalonians*, 301; Morris, *Thessalonians*, 214.

7. See Sharp, *Remarks*. See also Porter, *Idioms*, 110–11; Wallace, *Greek Grammar*, 270–90.

8. Wallace, *Greek Grammar*, 270.

9. Williams, *Thessalonians*, 122.

10. See, for example, Sharp, *Remarks*, 3.

11. It should be noted that Sharp restricted this rule to personal singular non-proper substantives and does not mention whether impersonals could be included. It does seem, however, that he believed that *only* such nouns applied to this criterion. See

παρουσίας and ἐπισυναγωγῆς in 2 Thess 2:1 as referring to the same event is that both nouns are *impersonal*. Since both substantives are impersonal it is arguable that "the highest degree of doubt is cast upon the probability of the terms referring to the same event."[12] If this is correct, then what is the proper understanding of the syntax in 2:1, and what was Paul intending to communicate to the Thessalonian church?

Arguably, there are two reasonable options for discerning the syntax of this construction.[13] First, when a single article governs multiple *impersonal* substantives connected by καὶ, those nouns may be understood as distinct though united.[14] In certain contexts the impersonal nouns will demonstrate some sort of unity, but yet they are not identical. For instance, in Luke 21:12 Jesus informed his disciples that when they are persecuted on account of his name, they will be delivered over to τὰς συναγωγὰς καὶ φυλακάς. The syntax seems to suggest that even though synagogues and prisons are distinct places, they are united in that they both represent hostile environments for Christians.[15] It is possible then to interpret παρουσίας and ἐπισυναγωγῆς in 2 Thess 2:1 as distinct yet united events, in that they are both eschatological.

However, understanding παρουσίας and ἐπισυναγωγῆς in this manner has allowed some to view these two events as "thematically united" and that they are possibly separated in time, that is, between the tribulation.[16] Those who adhere to this view argue that Christ must come *for* his saints before he can come *with* his saints.[17] However, the problem with this interpretation is that Paul is silent with regards to whether any time will elapse between the παρουσίας and ἐπισυναγωγῆς. Furthermore, throughout all of chapter 2 the apostle's intent was seemingly to remind

---

Sharp, *Remarks*, 119–20; Wallace, "Article with Multiple Substantives," 47–48. Cf. Rider, "Investigation," 23–25, cited in Wallace, "Semantic Range," 66 n. 12. Rider argues that *impersonal* substantives should be included under the criteria.

12. Wallace, *Greek Grammar*, 290.

13. Ibid., 279–83.

14. See Wallace, "Article," 172, who notes that the semantic possibilities for impersonal nouns are the same as personal plural substantives. See also Porter, *Idioms*, 111; Robertson, *Grammar*, 787; Turner, *Syntax*, 181; Wallace, *Greek Grammar*, 279.

15. See, for example, Marshall, *Gospel of Luke*, 767; Nolland, *Luke: 18:35–24:53*, 995–96.

16. See, for example, Feinberg, "Pre-tribulation Rapture Position," 84–85; Wallace, "Article," 202.

17. See, for example, Feinberg, "Pre-tribulation Rapture Position," 84–85.

the Thessalonian church that they had not missed the Day of the Lord and that they must continue to remain faithful, awaiting his return, through their pilgrimage.[18] In fact, even though the syntax demonstrates that παρουσίας and ἐπισυναγωγῆς are not identical, it certainly does not negate that these events could happen simultaneously.[19]

The second option for discerning this construction in 2 Thess 2:1 is that syntactically the article may reveal that the second noun (ἐπισυναγωγῆς) is a subset of the first (παρουσίας).[20] For instance, in Matt 24:36 Jesus revealed that he did not know the time of his return. He even informed his disciples that he did not know τῆς ἡμέρας ἐκείνης καὶ ὥρας. If the intention in the current example was to demonstrate that the second substantive functions as a subset of the first, then Jesus essentially told his disciples that he did not know the day, *particularly the hour of his return*.[21] Furthermore, the Septuagint often utilizes the cognate συναγωγή in an eschatological sense, where Yahweh's covenant people will one day be released from exile and be gathered to him at the Day of the Lord (Isa 52:12, 56:8, 66:18–24; Ezek 37:10; Zech 9:12).[22] It may be reasonable to conclude that in the context of 2 Thess 2 the syntax coupled with the Old Testament motif of the eschatological gathering of God's people may indicate that from Paul's perspective, the ἐπισυναγωγῆς of God's elect would transpire at the Lord's παρουσίας and arguably make these distinct events simultaneous. In fact, Morris suggests that "the coming of the Lord and the gathering of the saints are regarded as closely connected, as the use of the single article shows. They are two parts of one great event."[23] Thus, the apostle may have understood the ἐπισυναγωγῆς as part of the παρουσίας since his intent throughout chapter 2 was ostensibly to encourage the Thessalonians to persevere because certain events would transpire before their vindication at the Day of the Lord when they would be gathered to him.[24]

---

18. See, for example, Moo, "Christology," 184–85.

19. See Wallace, *Greek Grammar*, 290.

20. See Porter, *Idioms*, 110–11; Wallace, *Greek Grammar*, 280–81.

21. Davies and Allison, *Gospel according to Matthew*, 3:377–78; Sim, *Apocalyptic Eschatology*, 150–55.

22. See, for example, Burkeen, "Parousia of Christ ," 368–72; Schrage, "συναγωγή," 802–5.

23. Morris, *Thessalonians*, 214.

24. See, for example, Pohill, "Hope in the Lord," 22–44.

At the outset of chapter 2 Paul exhorted the Thessalonians that they had previously received the correct instruction pertaining to the parousia, and thus were to disregard the false doctrine that had infiltrated the church and caused them to become concerned as to whether they had missed the Day of the Lord. Since the Thessalonians experienced Jesus' teachings firsthand regarding the hatred and persecution his followers would face (Matt 24:9), they longed for their exoneration. However, they needed to understand that certain events would precede their vindication at the Lord's coming, and therefore, Paul encouraged them to remain steadfast through their pilgrimage so that the righteous Judge would count them worthy at the final assize.

Throughout 2:3–8 Paul seems to have offered two reasons that validated the fact that the Judge had not yet returned and that the Thessalonians' acquittal still awaited them, namely the apostasy and the revealing of the man of lawlessness.[25] Paul began by reminding the Thessalonians that the rebellion and the revealing of the man of lawlessness are directly related and that they both must first occur before the Lord's advent.[26]

Initially, in verse 3 Paul reaffirmed to the church that the Day of the Lord would not come until after the apostasy.[27] The term ἀποστασία denotes a defiance or rebellion against established authority, whether political, judicial, or religious.[28] Paul's understanding of apostasy was most plausibly derived from the Old Testament, where the term often referred to the religious aspect of those who were rebellious against God (Josh 22:22; 2 Chr 29:19; Jer 2:19). As with those throughout the Old Testament who rebelled against God, it appears that Paul understood

---

25. See, for example, G. Green, *Thessalonians*, 307; Wanamaker, *Epistles to the Thessalonians*, 242–43.

26. While the temporal adverb πρῶτον may suggest that the rebellion must come first, followed by the revealing of the man of lawlessness, it seems more probable, as Wanamaker contends, that "the absence of ἔπειτα with ἀποκαλυφθῇ it is more likely that the temporal adverb includes all of the protasis," 243. See also Malherbe, *Thessalonians*, 418; Marshall, *Thessalonians*, 188; Menken, *Second Thessalonians*, 102; Wanamaker, *Epistles to the Thessalonians*, 243.

27. See Giblin, *Threat to Faith*, 122–39, who disagrees with the predominant understanding that this ellipsis refers to the previous contexts but argues that it should be applied to what follows. Cf. Best, *Commentary*, 280–81; Frame, *Epistle of Paul*, 250; G. Green, *Thessalonians*, 306–7; Marshall, *Thessalonians*, 188; Milligan, *St. Paul's Epistles*, 98; Morris, *Thessalonians*, 218; Wanamaker, *Epistles to the Thessalonians*, 243–45.

28. See, for example, Balz, "ἀφίστημι," 183; Schlier, "ἀποστασία," 512–14.

there to be a correlation: namely that those who rebel against the gospel would suffer similar consequences.[29] Even early Jewish eschatology understood that before the final return of God there would be great rebellion (*Jubilees* 23:14–23; *1 Enoch* 90:26, 91:5–8).[30] Likewise, in the New Testament, ἀποστασία and its cognate ἀφίσταναι predominately denote a religious connotation, specifically of those who are insurgent towards God (Luke 8:13; Heb 3:12).

While the use of ἀποστασία in verse 3 should in all likelihood be understood in a religious sense, the term has curiously produced an interpretive issue regarding the identity of those directly related with the apostasy.[31] For instance, some have suggested that Paul was strictly referring to an apostasy of the Jews.[32] Wanamaker has proposed that:

> the reference to the temple in verse 4 suggests that [Paul] is working with a traditional apocalyptic understanding in which it was maintained that many of the people of God, that is the Jews, would rebel against God and the Law at the time of the end.[33]

Certainly Jews would be involved in the coming apostasy that Paul was referring to, but nothing in the context indicates that only Jews were to be understood as the subject of the apostasy. Throughout the entire letter Paul never specifically distinguished the Jews or even remarked about their involvement in the coming eschatological events. Conversely, Marshall has commented that there is "an emphatic contrast drawn between such unbelievers and those beloved by God who were chosen for salvation and believed in the truth."[34] In all likelihood, Paul's intent may have been to remind the Thessalonian church that all of their opponents,

---

29. See, for example, Oropeza, "Apostasy," 69–86; T. A. Wilson, "Wilderness Apostasy," 550–71.

30. See, for example, LaRondelle, "Paul's Prophetic Outline," 61–69; Scott, "Paul," 133–43.

31. The intent here is *not* to embark on a comprehensive theological discussion regarding the doctrines of assurance or perseverance of the saints. Rather, the goal is to determine the theological significance of "the apostasy" as it pertains to the overall theme of Second Thessalonians.

32. See, for example, Denney, *Thessalonians*, 309; H. A. A. Kennedy, *St. Paul's Conception*, 218; Lightfoot, *Notes*, 111; Wanamaker, *Epistles to the Thessalonians*, 244. Lightfoot does argue that the term may include Christians but states that it cannot refer to Gentiles.

33. Wanamaker, *Epistles to the Thessalonians*, 244.

34. Marshall, *Kept*, 99.

whether Jew or Gentile, were culpable for their rebellion and disobedience and would be sentenced to eternal punishment. Furthermore, the problem with understanding that the rebellion only refers to Jews is that it fails to consider Paul's own sentiments for his Jewish brethren, which are particularly evident throughout Rom 9–11, where he clearly demonstrates his desire to see the salvation of his kinsmen (Rom 9:3–4).[35] Regarding Paul's perspective on the eschatological future of Israel, Bruce notes that "there is no word of an end-time rebellion but of a present partial insensitiveness to be followed by a future restoration."[36] In the context of Second Thessalonians, it seems most probable that Paul was not strictly identifying Jews with the coming apostasy but rather with all who disobey God (2 Thess 2:8–12).

Another suggestion promulgated concerning whom the apostasy refers to in verse 3 is Christians.[37] Those who adhere to such a view argue that Paul was reminding the Thessalonians that some Christians would defect before the Lord's return. In fact, Green has argued that:

> we should recognize that in the face of the great persecution the church endured in the first century and the temptations their former life presented, not a few people abandoned the faith, and their apostasy became a paradigm for what was expected in the last times. The hope of the apostle is that the church in Thessalonica would in no way participate in the apostasy.[38]

But interpreting Christians as the subject of the apostasy may impose too much onto the context since Paul never gave the impression in Second Thessalonians that the elect would be involved in the final rebellion before the Lord returns.[39] Moreover, the entire Pauline corpus seemingly never indicates that Christians would in the end rebel but rather that they would persevere (Rom 5:3–5; 1 Thess 1:3–10).[40] Best has argued that "the NT gives the impression that the elect will not fail (Matt

---

35. See, for example, Abasciano, *Paul's Use*, 27–44; Best, *Commentary*, 282; Campbell, *Paul*, 127–29; Kim, *God, Israel*, 95–114.

36. Bruce, *Thessalonians*, 167. See also, Davies, "People of Israel," 4–39.

37. G. Green, *Thessalonians*, 307; Malherbe, *Thessalonians*, 418; Menken, *Second Thessalonians*, 103.

38. G. Green, *Thessalonians*, 307.

39. Oropeza, *Paul and Apostasy*, 219.

40. Oropeza, *Paul and Apostasy*, 218–20; Schreiner and Caneday, *Race Set before Us*, 260–67; Gundry Volf, *Paul and Perseverance*, 70–74.

16:16); certainly there is nothing in the genuine Pauline letters to suggest that he expected the church to apostatize."[41] Furthermore, throughout the Thessalonian correspondence the apostle praised the genuine faith and perseverance of the Thessalonians amidst a hostile environment, encouraged the congregation that God had chosen them, and assured them that they would gain the glory of Christ at the final assize (1 Thess 1:2–10, 3:6–13, 4:17; 2 Thess 1:4, 1:11, 2:13–14).[42] This has led Marshall to conclude that:

> it is quite clear that what Paul is describing here has nothing to do with believers. The rebellion or apostasy led by the man of lawlessness takes place in the non-Christian world among those who did not believe the truth but had pleasure in unrighteousness.[43]

Understanding Christians as the subject of the apostasy is seemingly improbable since it impresses too much into the context of Second Thessalonians and also misinterprets the Pauline theology of election and perseverance.[44]

Since Paul does not identify the subject of ἡ ἀποστασία it seems that a likely interpretation could be that the apostasy refers to a time of pervasive rebellion about which the Thessalonians had already been instructed and would be able to discern.[45] This is strengthened by the use of the definite article, which indicates that this is the rebellion par excellence.[46] Neil has suggested that the apostasy in the context of 2:3 refers to "a widespread and violent defiance of the authority of God."[47] More than likely, Paul understood the apostasy to be an extensive, blatant revolt against God, which would directly affect his covenant people. Furthermore, Williams has argued that apostasy in the context of Second Thessalonians "expresses not so much apathy as deliberate opposition, and it is better to see this as a reference to events outside the

---

41. Best, *Commentary*, 282.

42. See, for example, Best, *Commentary*, 282; Frame, *Epistle of Paul*, 251; Gundry Volf, *Paul and Perserverance*, 15–20.

43. Marshall, *Kept*, 99.

44. See, for example, W. W. Klein, "Semantic Analysis," 388–91; Roetzel, "Election/Calling," 552–69; Westblade, "Divine Election," 63–87.

45. See, for example, Best, *Commentary*, 283; Eadie, *Epistles of Paul*, 266; Frame, *Epistle of Paul*, 250–51.

46. See, for example, Bruce, *Thessalonians*, 167; Wallace, *Syntax*, 99.

47. Neil, *Epistle of Paul*, 160. See also Witherington, *Thessalonians*, 216.

church, which, however, will profoundly affect the church."[48] Simply put, ἡ ἀποστασία in the context of Second Thessalonians more than likely denotes the "rebellion of the creature against the Creator."[49]

Conjectures that attempt to pinpoint the subject of the apostasy arguably misunderstand Paul's intended meaning for the Thessalonian church. The concept of the coming apostasy was not foreign to the Thessalonians, who had likely received instruction from Paul regarding this matter (2 Thess 2:5). The apostle simply wanted to encourage these believers that certain events must take place before their vindication would come at the Day of the Lord. By reminding the Thessalonians of his previous instructions, Paul not only comforted them regarding their situation, but, as Menken suggests, the apostle also:

> saw the congregation as standing on the threshold of the event of the end: what they experienced at the present was not yet the great oppression and apostasy of the end, but it constituted, so to say, the preamble of these events.[50]

The Thessalonians would be encouraged to stand firm because their situation would only grow more difficult; however, they could be assured that they would eventually be exonerated at God's final court.

The second event that must occur before the return of the Lord is that the man of lawlessness would be revealed (verses 3–4).[51] This individual should most likely be seen against the background of the great rebellion Paul had just described, for he signifies the epitome of rebellion by exalting himself above every so-called god and displays himself to be God.[52]

The most arduous question surrounding the man of lawlessness is his identity. Throughout the entire letter Paul never specifically identified the man of lawlessness but only qualified that he is destined for destruction (verse 4). Nevertheless, several conjectures regarding this

---

48. Williams, *Thessalonians*, 124. See also Best, *Commentary*, 283; Frame, *Epistle of Paul*, 251; Morris, *Thessalonians*, 219; Dobschütz, *Die Thessalonicher-Briefe*, 270.

49. Morris, *Thessalonians*, 219 n. 12.

50. Menken, *Second Thessalonians*, 103.

51. Concerning the textual critical evidence for the translation "man of sin" or "man of lawlessness," see B. Metzger, *Textual Commentary*, 635. Metzger contends that the copyists altered the original reading ἀνομίας, a word rarely used by Paul, replacing it with the more common term ἁμαρτίας.

52. See Morris, *Thessalonians*, 220–21.

lawless one's identity have included the Roman emperor, the imperial power of Rome, and, during the time of the Reformation, the papacy.[53] A lengthy discussion of this issue is contrary to the purpose of this chapter. However, two observations are noteworthy. First, the man of lawlessness in all probability is not to be identified as Satan since in the context he is distinguished from him in verse 9.[54] Rather it seems that the man of lawlessness is merely an instrument of Satan.[55] Second, the man of lawlessness is more than likely not an authoritative figure in power at the time of the letter's writing.[56] This seems most probable due to the eschatological tone of Second Thessalonians, coupled with Paul's dependence upon the apocalyptic teachings from both the Old Testament and Jesus.[57]

It is often argued that the apostle's reference to the man of lawlessness in verses 3–4 is parallel to certain Old Testament prophecies (Isa 14:13–14; Ezek 28:8–9). Furthermore, some scholars have suggested that Paul's use of the man of lawlessness is to be understood as a direct allusion to Daniel's prophecy regarding Antiochus Epiphanes and his devastating exploits from 175 to 164 BC (Dan 11:31, 11:36–37).[58] The atrocities committed under Antiochus were likely etched in the minds of the Jewish nation, which has further led to conjectures that Paul may have alluded to these events as a way to illustrate to the Thessalonian church that the coming of the man of lawlessness could in some way be compared with the evil deeds committed by Antiochus.[59] Steinmann has even suggested that "the [man of lawlessness] will be like Antiochus IV, who foreshadowed him."[60] But Paul's understanding of the coming-

---

53. For a survey of the views regarding the identity of the man of lawlessness, see Riddlebarger, *Man of Sin*, 15.

54. See, for example, Weima, "Slaying of Satan's Superman," 67–88; Williams, *Thessalonians*, 124.

55. See, for example, Riddlebarger, *Man of Sin*, 134; Williams, *Thessalonians*, 124.

56. See, for example, H. Koester, "Paul's Eschatology," 441–58; Beasley-Murray, *Jesus and the Future*, 232–33; D. Wenham, *Rediscovery*, 176–80; Waterman, "Sources of Paul's Teaching," 105–113; Weima, "Slaying of Satan's Superman," 80.

57. Cf. H. Koester, "Paul's Eschatology," 441–58.

58. See, for example, Beale, *1-2 Thessalonians*, 206–7; Hartman, "Eschatology," 480; Lebram, "König Antiochus," 737–72; Reddit, "Daniel 11," 463–74; VanGemeren, *Interpreting*, 346–47. Cf. Steinmann, "Antichrist in Daniel 11," 195–209, who interprets the king in Dan 11:36–45 as an eschatological ruler foreshadowed by Antiochus.

59. See, for example, G. Holland, *Tradition*, 107–8; Steinmann, "Antichrist in Daniel 11," 208–9; Weima, "Slaying of Satan's Superman," 80–81.

60. Steinmann, "Antichrist in Daniel 11," 208.

man of lawlessness is also markedly parallel to Jesus' own apocalyptic teachings regarding those who would oppose him prior to his advent (Matt 24:4–15; Mark 13:5–27).[61] In fact, Wenham has observed that the apostle's dependence on Jesus' instruction concerning eschatological events is particularly noticeable:

> Not only do Paul and the synoptists agree that one horrible event must precede the end, but they also agree that in some sense the horrible event will lead to the coming of Christ.[62]

Moreover, both Jesus and Paul had to address similar problems regarding end-time events. Jesus warned his followers that various individuals would come declaring to be Christ, which would not only lead many astray but would promote a false Day of the Lord.[63] Paul encountered a similar situation with the Thessalonians who had heard distorted information that led to their concern that they had missed the Lord's advent. Thus, by appealing to Jesus' own teachings, the apostle reassured the Thessalonian church that their vindication was still to come and certain events would precede the Lord's return, which had yet to transpire. While there are certainly different emphases between Jesus' eschatological teachings found in the Synoptics (i.e., wars, earthquakes, and famines) to that of Second Thessalonians, where Paul needed to alleviate a misconception in order to encourage the church to persevere, the general similarities arguably remain.[64] In all likelihood, then, it seems that a proper interpretation of 2 Thess 2:3–4 may be as Zahn suggests, "mit ist ohne einen starken Anhalt in der Weissagung Jesu geschichtlich unbegreiflich."[65]

The identity of the man of lawlessness is in all probability impossible to ascertain. Whether Paul identified the man of lawlessness during his prior instruction to the Thessalonians is uncertain. Nevertheless, in the context of Second Thessalonians Paul was likely unconcerned with the identity of this instrument of Satan. Rather, he simply reiterated mo-

---

61. See, for example, Beasley-Murray, *Jesus and the Future*, 232–33; D. Wenham, *Rediscovery*, 176–80; Waterman, "Sources of Paul's Teaching," 105–113; Weima, "Slaying of Satan's Superman," 80.

62. D. Wenham, *Rediscovery*, 177.

63. Ibid., 176.

64. Ibid., 177.

65. Zahn, *Das Evangelium des Matthäus*, 653 n. 1. See also H. A. A. Kennedy, *St. Paul's Conception*, 166–68.

tifs found in both the Old Testament and Jesus' teachings concerning the events leading up to the Lord's return in order to encourage this persecuted church to remain steadfast, for their vindication would come. The eschatological tone of the epistle coupled with the apparent parallels found in both the Old Testament and the Synoptics concerning such end-time events more than likely served as the background for Paul's understanding of the man of lawlessness. Consequently, regarding the identity of the man of lawlessness, Weima has suggested that:

> the striking parallels between 2 Thessalonians 2 and eschatological teachings of Jesus as recorded in the synoptic gospels suggest that the apostle is more than likely drawing from traditional material of early Christian eschatology that was based on the teaching of Jesus, who in turn [may have] incorporated the prophecy of Daniel in expounding his own views of the end times.[66]

The identity of the man of lawlessness was arguably not crucial for Paul's purpose in chapter 2. He simply wanted to remind the Thessalonians that the coming of the man of lawlessness would precede the Day of the Lord. Sequentially, since the man of lawlessness would be in direct contradiction and rebellion against the Lord, he would be destined for destruction.

Paul continued to remind the Thessalonians about the man of lawlessness and the actions he would take during his brief reign, namely that he would exalt himself above every god and object of worship by taking his seat in the temple of God, parading himself out to be God. The phrase τὸν ναὸν τοῦ θεοῦ has caused some discussion regarding the identification of the temple.[67] Paul does not elaborate concerning the identity of the temple because the Thessalonians would have likely understood what he meant from their prior instruction. While certainty over this issue is unattainable, the most widely held view is that Paul was referring to the temple located in Jerusalem.[68] This seems most plausible since ναὸν

---

66. Weima, "Slaying of Satan's Superman," 81. See also D. Ford, *Abomination of Desolation*, 198; Hartman, *Prophecy Interpreted*, 195–205.

67. For a description of the views, see Bruce, *Thessalonians*, 168–69; Donfried, "Cults," 336–56; Frame, *Epistle of Paul*, 75; G. Green, *Thessalonians*, 312–13; Malherbe, *Thessalonians*, 420–21; Marshall, *1 and 2 Thessalonians*, 190–92; Wanamaker, *Epistles to the Thessalonians*, 247–49.

68. See, for example, Bruce, *Thessalonians*, 169; G. Green, *Thessalonians*, 312–13; Malherbe, *Thessalonians*, 421; Menken, *Second Thessalonians*, 105; Williams, *Thessalonians*, 125. Cf. Beale, *1–2 Thessalonians*, 207–8; and Giblin, *Threat to Faith*,

τοῦ θεοῦ is used in the Septuagint to refer to the Jerusalem temple (Dan 5:3; Jdt 4:2, 5:18).[69] Several scholars have even suggested that this phrase may correlate with a possible allusion to the Old Testament prophecy of Dan 11 regarding Antiochus IV and his defiant acts towards God by desecrating the temple.[70] Furthermore, understanding ναὸν τοῦ θεοῦ as a reference to the temple in Jerusalem coincides with Jesus' instruction regarding the profaning of the temple, which would occur prior to his return (Matt 24:15; Mark 13:14–27).[71] Regardless of the location of the temple, Malherbe has suggested that Paul's intent was to remind the Thessalonians that:

> the usurpation of the temple of God as the locus for [the man of lawlessness] claiming himself to be God symbolizes the gravest act of defiance imaginable, and to express that is Paul's intention as he writes in starkly apocalyptic language.[72]

Thus, in keeping with the seemingly judicial nature of the epistle, Paul encouraged the Thessalonians to remain steadfast amidst persecution, for they had not missed the final assize and their ultimate justification at God's court was yet to come.

76–80, who both argue that ναὸν τοῦ θεοῦ is best understood metaphorically as the church.

69. The phrase ναὸν τοῦ θεοῦ is found only a few times throughout the Septuagint; however, the idiom οἶκος τοῦ θεοῦ, which also refers to the temple in Jerusalem is more frequent (1 Chr 28:12, 29:2; 2 Chr 3:3, 4:11, 5:14; Ezra 1:14).

70. Antiochus did not exalt himself in the temple but rather desecrated it by sacrificing swine on the altar to Zeus. Moreover, while Antiochus's deeds were certainly etched in the minds of God's people, other rulers, such as Caligula, attempted to defame the temple by erecting his statue in it, which would have certainly been viewed as an act of insolence against God. Thus, it seems that Paul may have used the incident of Antiochus (and possibly other rulers), as a prototype to reference the tremendous defiance of the man of lawlessness. See also Whitehorne, "Antiochus IV Epiphanes," 270–71; *OCD*, 79–80.

71. Scholars are divided regarding Jesus' prophetic instructions concerning the desecration of the temple. Some understand the prophecy to have been strictly fulfilled in AD 70 with the destruction of the temple. See, for example, Dyer, *Prophecy*, 269–72; France, *Gospel of Mark*, 519–26; Donahue and Harrington, *Mark*, 371–72. Others argue that there is a "dual focus," namely that prophecy points toward the destruction of the temple, which signifies eschatological events and Jesus' final intervention. See, for example, A. Y. Collins, *Beginning*, 77; Geddert, *Watchwords*, 231–39; D. Wenham, *Rediscovery*, 294.

72. Malherbe, *Thessalonians*, 421.

In verses 6–7 Paul continued to remind the Thessalonians that the Day of the Lord had yet to occur because the man of lawlessness had not been revealed and was being restrained. However, despite the fact that the man of lawlessness was being held back, the mystery of lawlessness was already at work (verse 7). The term μυστήριον in the New Testament does not normally refer to something that is secret, rather it typically denotes that which was previously hidden but is now made known for the purposes of God (Mark 4:11; Rom 11:25; 1 Cor 4:1; Eph 3:4–7).[73] It seems reasonable, then, that Paul's use of μυστήριον in the immediate context may have been to reiterate to the Thessalonian church that while there were certain characteristics of the end already at work, the final consummation was still a future event.[74]

The *crux interpretum*, however, surrounding verses 6–7 concerns the participles τὸ κατέχον and ὁ κατέχων. The difficulty resides in the change of gender from the neuter to the masculine, which does not afford any certainty regarding identity. Various suggestions have been offered, such as a supernatural being (an angel, the Holy Spirit)[75] and those pertaining to the *Sitz im Leben* of the Thessalonian church (the Roman Empire or emperor).[76] However, because of the author's heavy dependence upon the Old Testament evident throughout Second Thessalonians, it seems most plausible that the κατέχειν motif may be best understood as an allusion from the Septuagint.

Several scholars have offered an interesting suggestion regarding the identity of τὸ κατέχον and ὁ κατέχων strictly based upon the apparent Old Testament parallels found throughout Second Thessalonians.[77] According to Roger Aus, Isa 66 had significantly influenced Paul's background for the content of his message in 2 Thess 1 and the description of the final judgment theophany of the Lord. Aus has suggested

---

73. See, for example, R. E. Brown, *Semitic Background*, 38–40; Carson, "Mystery and Fulfillment," 413–25; Ahn, "Parousia," 234.

74. See, for example, G. Green, *Thessalonians*, 314.

75. See, for example, Dixon, "Evil Restraint," 445–49; Farrow, "Showdown," 23–26; Nicholl, "Michael," 27–53; C. E. Powell, "Identity," 320–32.

76. See, for example, Krodel, "'Religious Power,'" 440–46; P. Metzger, *Katechon*, 293–95; Milligan, *St. Paul's Epistles*, 101; Wanamaker, *Epistles to the Thessalonians*, 256–57.

77. See, for example, Aus, "God's Plan," 537–53; S. G. Brown, "Intertextuality," 254–77; Hannah, *Michael and Christ*, 132–34; Nicholl, "Michael," 27–53; C. E. Powell, "Identity," 320–32; Ahn, "Parousia," 237–38.

that throughout Isa 66, the prophet depicted the fate of those nations who had defied God and slandered his covenant people. The outcome would result in the punishment of Yahweh's enemies and comfort for his people (verses 15–17).[78] If Paul was heavily dependant upon Isa 66 for his instruction in 2 Thess 1, he may have further used the prophet as a template for his understanding of the restraining factor, τὸ κατέχον. Furthermore, Aus has commented that subsequent to the judicial punishment described in Isa 66, the Lord would arrive and gather the survivors who would then come to Jerusalem and see his glory (verses 18–21). Consequently, the Lord would send those survivors to various nations who had not seen or heard of his fame or glory and from those nations God's children would worship him (verse 23).[79] Specifically, Aus contends that Paul may have drawn his understanding of the κατέχειν idea from Isa 66:19, which reads, ἐξαποστελῶ ἐξ αὐτῶν σεσωσμένους εἰς τὰ ἔθνη.[80] His argument, which is also promulgated by others, is that Paul viewed verse 19 from a Christian perspective, and thus interpreted the saved as those who had found salvation in Jesus and had become missionaries to the nations (1 Cor 1:18; 2 Cor 2:15).[81] According to Isaiah, God would send people to declare his glory to those nations who had not heard, which would result in the remnant of his people worshiping him. It is suggested that Paul may have understood there to be a correlation between the mission's activity in Isa 66 to that of the gospel mission of which he and the Thessalonians were involved. Regarding such a parallel Westermann has also argued that:

> Hier ist zum erstenmal ganz eindeutig von Mission in unserem Sinne die Rede: Sendung einzelner Menschen zu den fernen Völkern, um dort die Herrlichkeit Gottes zu verkündigen. Es entspricht genau der apostolischen Mission am Anfang der christlichen Kirche.[82]

Scholars who adhere to such an interpretation contend that if Paul understood the Christian mission to be a direct parallel to Isaiah's

78. Aus, "God's Plan," 538; Aus, "Relevance," 264 n. 52.
79. See, for example, Aus, "God's Plan," 537–53; Tiemeyer, *Priestly Rites*, 281–86.
80. Aus, "God's Plan," 540.
81. See, for example, Achtemeier, *Community and Message*, 148; Aus, "God's Plan," 540; Herbert, *Book*, 196–97; Wodecki, "SLH," 482–87.
82. Westermann, *Das Buch Jesaja*, 337. See also Blenkinsopp, *Opening the Sealed Book*, 133.

prophecy, then τὸ κατέχον in 2 Thess 2:6 may be a reference to the preaching of the gospel.[83] Aus contends that "it is God's will or plan that the gospel first be carried to all men before the Day of the Lord arrives."[84] Furthermore, Aus has advocated that if Paul understood τὸ κατέχον in 2 Thess 2:6 as God's plan, namely the gospel mission, then the identity of the masculine ὁ κατέχων more than likely refers to God himself.[85] Such a proposal is based upon the context of Paul's argument in 2 Thess 2:8–12 where the Lord is described as having sovereign control over the events described; namely, he slays the man of lawlessness, he permits deluding influences, and he carries out final judgment. But not only is God shown to be in control over the events that pertain to the man of lawlessness and those who perish; he is also grammatically the subject of verses 13–14, for he has chosen the Thessalonians for salvation, calling them through the gospel.[86]

The above argument, however, is not without weaknesses. For instance, it is obscure as to why Paul would refer to God's plan and even God himself in such vague terms. In fact, Krodel has argued that "there would be no reason to avoid saying that it is God who is restraining the lawless one or delaying his appearance."[87] However, the argument could be made that according to 2 Thess 2:5, the church was already familiar with Paul's instruction, and thus it is possible that he had previously explained to them God's role as the restrainer prior to his advent and felt it unnecessary to elaborate on this issue.[88] In addition, Paul's intent throughout Second Thessalonians was not to revisit his prior instructions regarding eschatological events, but arguably to encourage the Thessalonian church that they had not missed the Day of the Lord and to persevere as they await their exoneration at the final assize.

Another possible weakness of the above argument is related to the idiom ἕως ἐκ μέσου γένηται. Specifically, those who argue that ὁ κατέχων should be recognized as referring to God have difficulty reconciling how the syntax of ὁ κατέχων functions as the subject of the temporal

---

83. See, for example, Aus, "God's Plan," 540; Beale, *1–2 Thessalonians*, 215–17; C. E. Powell, "Identity," 329; Ahn, "Parousia," 237.

84. Aus, "God's Plan," 540.

85. Ibid., 541–53. See also C. E. Powell, "Identity," 332; Ahn, "Parousia," 237–38.

86. Aus, "God's Plan," 550.

87. Krodel, "Katechon," 443 n.12.

88. Ahn, "Parousia," 238.

clause. Simply put, if ὁ κατέχων is identified as God, then how can God be removed?[89] Consequently, this has led some scholars to conclude that ὁ κατέχων refers to an angel, particularly Michael, who functions as the restrainer until God removes him.[90]

The identity of τὸ κατέχον and ὁ κατέχων is elusive. However, some scholars have offered three arguments, which they contend may help explain Paul's perspective of τὸ κατέχον as referring to God's plan, namely the gospel mission, and that ὁ κατέχων may refer to an agent of God who restrains the lawless one until he is removed.[91] First, it is argued that Paul seemingly interpreted Isa 66:18–21, especially verse 19, as a possible correlation to the gospel mission. This seems conceivable since both the New Testament and the Pauline corpus demonstrate that the gospel would be preached to all nations before the Day of the Lord arrives (Matt 24:14; Acts 1:8; Rom 15:21).[92] Second, the identity of ὁ κατέχων as an agent of God may fit the immediate context of 2 Thess 2:1–7 where Paul possibly made allusions to Dan 10–12, where Michael is depicted as a restrainer.[93] For instance, in Dan 10:13–21, Michael was responsible for "restraining" the princes of Persia and Greece so that the individual dressed in linen could deliver the revelation to Daniel. In the context, it seems that Michael's act of restraining was not only to ensure that Daniel received the message but to further demonstrate that God's sovereign plan could not be hindered.[94] Consequently, it is argued that Michael's role as God's restraining agent throughout Dan 10–12 may have led Paul to understand ὁ κατέχων as Michael.[95] Third, in both

---

89. See Aus, "God's Plan," 551, who argues that the subject of γένηται is μυστήριον τῆς ἀνομίας and admits that the author should have been more careful with his grammar.

90. See, for example, Goulder, "Silas in Thessalonica," 87–106; Hannah, *Michael and Christ*, 132–34; Nicholl, "Michael," 27–53. Cf. Verhoef, "Delay," 36–44, who notes that Ezek 11:23 states that the ἀνέβη ἡ δόξα κυρίου ἐκ μέσης τῆς πόλεως.

91. See, for example, Goulder, "Silas in Thessalonica," 98–100; Hannah, *Michael and Christ*, 132–34; Nicholl, "Michael," 35–53l.

92. See Aus, "God's Plan," 540 n. 20, who notes that several of the church fathers likewise understood this.

93. See Nicholl, "Michael," 38 n. 41, who also notes that in Jewish apocalyptic literature angels were often described as executing a binding function (e.g., *1 Enoch* 10:4–22, 18:12–16, 21:1–10; *t. Levi* 18:12).

94. See, for example, Doukhan, *Daniel*, 75; Goldingay, *Daniel*, 292–93; Hannah, *Michael and Christ*, 133; Meadowcroft, "Princes of Persia," 99–113; Nicholl, "Michael," 36–37.

95. See, for example, Hannah, *Michael and Christ*, 133; Nicholl, "Michael," 36–37.

Jewish and Christian literature Michael was a prominent figure, particularly with regards to eschatological events.[96] Michael is often depicted as blowing the trumpet at the final assize (1 Thess 4:16) as well as the primary opponent of Satan (Jude 9; Rev 12:7–9).[97] Regarding Michael's eschatological role, R. H. Charles has suggested that "as the end draws nigh the strife grows fiercer, and Michael, Israel's angelic guardian, becomes the great hero of the last days."[98] Furthermore, the proposal that Michael functions as God's restraining agent may be the most plausible explanation regarding the temporal clause ἕως ἐκ μέσου γένηται, since God cannot be removed.

To be sure, 2 Thess 2:6–7 remains a notable *crux interpretum* that does not afford any dogmatic understanding. The cryptic references of τὸ κατέχον and ὁ κατέχων do not offer any certainty regarding the identity of what or whom Paul may have been reminding the Thessalonians. However, the apostle's probable reliance upon both the Old Testament and Jesus' apocalyptic teachings perhaps leads to the view that Paul previously taught the Thessalonian congregation that once the "restraining activity" (possibly the preaching of the gospel to all nations) was fulfilled, God would remove his "restraining agent." This event would usher in the epitome of lawlessness, where those who had not believed and took pleasure in wickedness would believe counterfeit signs and wonders, which would serve as evidence against them at the final assize (2 Thess 2:9–12).[99]

In verses 9–12 Paul elaborated for the Thessalonians regarding the activity of the coming lawless one. Essentially, he contrasted the parousia of the lawless one to that of the parousia of Christ.[100] Once God removed his restrainer, the lawlessness one would come, only to be destroyed by the coming Judge. It is the lawless one who in accordance with Satan will perform various counterfeit miracles, signs, and wonders to further deceive those who have rejected God. The result of such rejection is that

---

96. For example, Dan 12:1; 1 Thess 4:16; Rev 12:7–9; 1QM 9:14–16; 4Q285:10; *t. Levi* 5:5–6. See also *PGM* 4.2770, which reads: Μιξαὴλ . . . κατέχων ὅν καλέυσι δράκοντα μέγαν. Although this is extremely late (fourth century), it nevertheless demonstrates that Michael was understood as a restrainer.

97. Nicholl, "Michael," 34.

98. R. H. Charles, "Michael," 362–63.

99. See, for example, Hannah, *Michael and Christ*, 134; Nicholl, "Michael," 52–53.

100. Williams, *Thessalonians*, 129.

in a judicial act, God will begin to implement judgment on the unbelievers by sending them a deluding influence so that they will not believe (verses 11-12).[101] It seems, then, that the purpose of their unbelief was to serve as indicting evidence against them at God's court, which would ultimately lead to their judgment.[102] In contrast to the coming of the lawless one is the coming of the righteous Judge, the Lord himself, who will slay the lawless one and assemble his final court in order to judge those who did not believe (verses 8, 11-12).[103] The Thessalonians, however, could be encouraged, for those events had yet to occur, and therefore they had not missed their vindication.

The adversative δέ, which begins verse 13, seemingly depicts a direct contrast between those whom the Lord will judge at his final court (verses 8-12) and those of the Thessalonian church who would be exonerated (verses 13-15).[104] Throughout this summary, thanksgiving was offered to God for these believers, as the author gave two reminders for this persecuted church. First, he reminded them of their eternal reward as God's beloved children. When the Lord chose them, they embraced the gospel, which resulted in greater faith and love as they continued through their pilgrimage in the midst of a hostile environment (verses 13-14). Second, Paul encouraged them that as they suffered opposition they were not to be deterred by false teachings, but rather they were to stand firm, adhering to the traditions they had previously learned under his tutelage regarding the Day of the Lord and their future absolution at God's court (verse 15). Paul concluded chapter 2 with a prayer for the Thessalonians that God would encourage and strengthen them as they persevere awaiting their vindication at the Day of the Lord.[105]

101. G. Green, *Thessalonians*, 323; Ahn, "Parousia," 240.

102. See Ahn, "Parousia," 240, who suggests that it may even be plausible that Paul understood such incriminating evidence and the final judgment of God's enemies as an allusion to Yahweh's dealings with Pharaoh and Egypt (v. 12). Furthermore, this idea also seems reasonable from the use of κριθῶσιν, which is often used as a forensic term referring to the conviction of a legal sentence (Jer 1:14-19; Hos 4:1; 2 Cor 5:10; Rev 20:11-15). See also Büchsel, "κρίνω," 921-41; Rissi, "κρίσις," 318-21.

103. The term καταργήσει is often used in the Pauline corpus in contexts referring to the final judgment (1 Cor 15:24, 15:26; 2 Tim 1:10).

104. See Rigaux, *Saint Paul*, 681, who has noted that "Le ἡμεῖς δέ en tête de la péricope est emphatique. Il introduit un contraste entre le sort des incroyants, des impies dont les versets 8 à 12 ont parlé et l'élection des Thessaloniciens." See also G. Green, *Thessalonians*, 325; Marshall, *Thessalonians*, 206.

105. The prayer in verse 16 is addressed to αὐτὸς δὲ ὁ κύριος ἡμῶν Ἰησοῦς Χριστὸς

6.2 CONCLUSION: THE EFFECTS OF LEGAL LANGUAGE IN 2 THESS 1 UPON 2 THESS 2: THE LETTER BODY

What relevance does the above discussion have regarding the proposed judicial language of 2 Thess 1? It seems reasonable to suggest that the description of the final court day of the Lord found in chapter 1 is further elaborated in chapter 2 as evident in the portrayal of the events leading to the final assize. From the outset of the epistle, Paul arguably intended to encourage the Thessalonians to remain steadfast amidst persecution because the righteous Judge would exonerate them at the Day of the Lord. In fact, the author has praised the Thessalonian church for their perseverance and faith amidst great difficulty (1:3–4). Such perseverance and faith would serve as evidence at God's eschatological court that this faithful church was worthy of his kingdom, while their opponents would be incriminated. Knowing the final outcome, the Thessalonians greatly longed for their day at court where their justification would become publicly evident and the Judge would reward them for their faithful pilgrimage (1:5–10).[106] However, the Thessalonians' anticipation was disturbed as they had received false information (perhaps from their antagonists) that the final assize had already occurred. As a result, Paul reassured the church that certain events would precede the Day of the Lord, and therefore, the Thessalonian congregation could be confident that justice would be done and that they would be vindicated. Although persecution would intensify as a consequence of the revealing of the man of lawlessness, the author exhorted the Thessalonian church to persevere and to trust that the Lord would take vengeance by executing righteous judgment. In fact, Krentz has argued that the judicial theme in chapter 1 finds direct correlation in chapter 2 where there is "a similar picture of Jesus as the avenging Judge."[107] Moreover, in chapter 2 the author continued to depict Christ as the righteous Judge who would administer impartial judgment at the Day of the Lord for both the Thessalonians and their

---

καὶ ὁ θεὸς ὁ πατὴρ ἡμῶν. Here Christ appears before the Father, which deviates from the typical Paul's style of written prayers. This order, however, is apparent in several other Pauline texts (Rom 1:7; 1 Cor 1:3; 2 Cor 1:2; Eph 1:2; Gal 1:1; 2 Thess 1:2). It is likely that the apostle used such word order because he understood that God and Christ are both on an equal level. For further discussion see Bauckham, *God Crucified*, 1–79; Harris, *Jesus as God*, 269–99.

106. See Krentz, "Through a Lens," 58, who argues that God's judgment will be a public demonstration.

107. Ibid., 55.

oppressors (2:12, 2:14). Analogous with chapter 1, the apostle further reiterated for the Thessalonians that "[Jesus'] parousia will also be his revelation as Lord, their benefactor and vindicator."[108] It seems possible, then, that the forensic nature of chapter 1 has affected Paul's purpose for chapter 2, which was arguably to further encourage the Thessalonian church to persevere as they anticipated their future vindication at Lord's eschatological court where he would render perfect justice.

6.3 2 THESS 1 IN RELATION TO 2 THESS 3: THE LETTER CLOSING

The first five verses of this final chapter continue the author's prayer, which had begun in 2:16–17.[109] There seems to be a twofold request for the Thessalonians as they continue to pray for Paul and his associates. First, the church was instructed to pray that the word of the Lord would spread rapidly through the missionaries as they continued to advance the gospel. Second, he requested the Thessalonians to pray that they would be rescued from ἀτόπων and πονηρῶν men. In the context, it seems that these two adjectives refer to those who vehemently oppose the message of the gospel and want to detain its progress. Regarding these terms Bruce has argued that:

> the reference here is not restricted to Jews or Gentiles, to those in authority or the "rascal multitude" [in Thessalonica]; it applies to all whose policy or activity hindered the spread of the saving message and worked to the detriment of the messengers.[110]

Like the Thessalonians, Paul himself suffered many afflictions from those who opposed his message (2 Cor 6:3–13), but he understood that the Lord would work through the prayers of his children and would enable the missionaries to persevere in the spreading of the gospel for the glory of God. Before Paul concluded the prayer, he addressed the Thessalonians and their current situation, reminding them that the Lord would strengthen and protect them from the evil one (verses 3–5). The apostle was confident that despite the Thessalonians' difficult circumstances they would

---

108. Ibid., 57.
109. See Dewailly, "Course et Glorie," 25–41.
110. Bruce, *Thessalonians*, 198.

continue to follow the missionaries' commands and that the Lord would cause them to be steadfast until the final court day.[111]

Paul encouraged the Thessalonians to be involved in prayer for him as they partnered together for the advancement of the gospel, even while they experienced intense persecution from those who did not belong to the Lord Jesus. He further prayed that the Thessalonians would have the steadfastness of Christ as they endured much suffering from their unbelieving neighbors, while they awaited their vindication from the Lord when he would return at the final assize.

The remainder of the chapter has been the focus of much debate (verses 6–15). Scholars are divided on how to interpret this section regarding Paul's warning against idleness and why some in the church were conducting themselves ἀτάκτως.[112] The discussions seem to hinge on two possibilities. The first option is based upon an eschatological perspective.[113] Those in support of this position argue that because the Thessalonian church believed that they had missed the Day of the Lord, several within the congregation discontinued their daily responsibilities. Judy Skeen has argued that the Thessalonians were "so intent on awaiting Christ's return that [some] were neglecting their own daily responsibilities to get back to work and carry their own share of the work load."[114] Certainly the Thessalonians greatly anticipated the Day of the Lord, when their persecutions would end and they would finally be exonerated. Thus, it may be reasonable to understand that those within the Thessalonian church who were guilty of idleness may have been so because they believed that if the Day of the Lord had already occurred

---

111. There is some debate concerning whether τὴν ἀγάπην τοῦ θεοῦ is a subjective or objective genitive. However, when referring to the love of God, Paul typically employs the subjective genitive (Rom 5:5, 8:39; 2 Cor 13:13). See also Best, *Commentary*, 330; Bruce, *Thessalonians*, 202; Frame, *Epistle of Paul*, 296; G. Green, *Thessalonians*, 340; Milligan, *St. Paul's Epistles*, 112; Malherbe, *Thessalonians*, 447, who argue that τὴν ἀγάπην τοῦ θεοῦ is subjective genitive. Cf. Lambrecht, "Loving God," 435–41, who argues for objective genitive. Marshall, *Thessalonians*, 217, however, argues that the phrase can be seen as either subjective or objective.

112. See, for example, Burkeen, "Parousia," 368–72; H. Koester, "Schemata," 455–57; Mearns, "Early," 137–57; Menken, "Paradise Regained," 271–289; Russell, "Idle," 105–119; Schmithals, "Historical Situation," 198–99; Winter "If a Man," 303–315.

113. See, for example, Burkeen, "Parousia," 368–72; H. Koester, "Schemata," 455–57; Mearns, "Early," 137–57; Menken, "Paradise Regained," 271–289; Schmithals, "Historical Situation," 198–99; de Villiers, "Life Worthy of God," 343–44.

114. Skeen, "Not as Enemies," 289.

then their daily responsibilities would be futile. In fact, Russell has further suggested that:

> the Thessalonians' belief that Christ would soon return led them to abandon ordinary earthly pursuits such as working for a living so that they could give full attention to spiritual preparation, prayer, and eschatological discussion."[115]

Paul referred to such individuals as undisciplined busybodies who refused to work, and, therefore, were forced to rely on the support of others because they had been misled to believe the false teachings that circulated, espousing that the Day of the Lord had occurred. Some of the members had possibly quit their jobs and stopped providing for themselves because they knew that if the Day of the Lord had transpired, then life as they knew it would radically change, for all hope was gone.[116] Adherents to this eschatological perspective contend that the individuals in the congregation whom Paul referred to as the ἄτακτος likely believed that:

> the restoration of Paradise and the annulment of the curse of Genesis 3:17–19 are being realized or going to be very soon; therefore, there is no need to stick any longer to the order, imposed by God after the Fall, of having to work hard before enjoying food, because this order has or is being annulled.[117]

Paul previously corrected this thinking in chapter 2 by explaining the events that would precede the Lord's return. He further provided a personal illustration of how they ought to live, namely to imitate his example of working, which the church observed when he and associates ministered among them. Therefore, those who had quit work were to be admonished into taking care of everyday responsibilities.

The second option supported by scholars is that the problems Paul addressed in this section were sociological.[118] The basis of this view is stated by Russell:

---

115. Russell, "Idle," 105.

116. See Menken, "Paradise Regained," 271–289; Jewett, *Thessalonian Correspondence*, 104–5.

117. Menken, "Paradise Regained," 287.

118. See G. Green, *Thessalonians*, 342; Russell, "Idle," 105–119; Wanamaker, *Epistles to the Thessalonians*, 282; Winter, *Welfare*, 41–60; Winter, "If a Man," 303–315.

> Paul's converts included the urban poor, and some may have been unemployed or may have formed a client relationship and obligation to a benefactor. Once brought into the circle of Christian love, they could have appeared to outsiders to be idle beggars who exploited the generosity of the Christian community without any sense of reciprocal response to their benefactors. . . . As the idle were caught up in new beliefs and practices, they rejected the idea of work to enjoy their understanding of brotherly love and to propagate their opinions and religious ideas.[119]

Members of the churches Paul had established came from various different social classes. There were certainly believers within the Thessalonian congregation who represented the different societal arenas: the urban poor, the manual labor groups, as well as those who were wealthy.[120] Furthermore, Winter has argued that the issue surrounding idleness in the Thessalonian church may pertain to the patron–client relationship.[121] Winter contends that those who served as benefactors to the less fortunate would have likely continued such a relationship within the Christian community.[122] Moreover, if the client became part of the church at Thessalonica, they would have likely been inundated with love from fellow members as they shared all things in common. Consequently, these clients, instead of continuing to work, would have become undisciplined and accustomed to having the church serve as their benefactor. Paul, however, does not want Christians to be obligated to anyone (1 Thess 4:11–12), just as he was not dependent upon the Thessalonians but labored with his own hands (2 Thess 3:8–9). With this view, it seems that the apostle wanted those who were idle to work, not only to support themselves, but also to be respected by their fellow citizens as self-supporting and be able to benefit others who truly had a need.[123] Thus, Russell concludes that "Paul urges these idle poor, caught up in beneficiaries of Christian love, to work, being self-sufficient and constructive in their relationships with others."[124] This is what Paul taught them not only by word but also by example.

---

119. Russell, "Idle," 113.
120. See Winter, "If a Man," 307.
121. Ibid., 305. See also Lampe, "Paul, Patrons, and Clients," 488–523.
122. Winter, "If a Man," 312.
123. Ibid., 314.
124. Russell, "Idle," 113.

Both arguments seemingly provide valid points. It seems reasonable, however, that the first option regarding the eschatological outlook may be most viable, for such an argument best fits the immediate context of the apostle's instruction regarding the Day of the Lord. Being assured that they had not missed the Lord's return, Paul reminded the Thessalonians of the example that he left them, namely that he did not lead an undisciplined life but labored among them even though he received a gift from the Philippian church (Phil 4:16). Furthermore, Paul had reminded the Thessalonians of the importance of "working with their hands" in his previous letter as the church awaited the Lord's return (1 Thess 4:11-12, 5:12-14). Therefore, prior to writing Second Thessalonians, it had likely come to Paul's attention that some in the church had not heeded his instruction regarding daily work because of the misconception that they had missed the parousia, which forced the apostle to remind them again that "if anyone is not willing to work, then he is not to eat, either."[125]

Paul concluded this section in verse 13 with an exhortation to those conducting themselves accordingly not to grow weary of doing good. He exhorted the Thessalonians to continually do good to those who were in genuine need but not for those who did not obey his instructions, namely, the undisciplined busybodies. Paul understood the danger in continual handouts and therefore commanded the Thessalonians not to συναναμίγνυσθαι with such individuals. This verb is often used in contexts where God's covenant people are not to associate with those who are morally or cultically defiled (Ezek 20:18; Hos 7:8).[126] The infinitive was used to stress the intended result of putting them to shame, namely so that they would realize their foolishness and conduct themselves appropriately.[127] Nevertheless, they were not to regard them as enemies, which Paul no doubt understood would have been detrimental to the lives of these members. Instead of treating them as such, Paul exhorted the church to admonish them, in hopes that they would change their behavior.[128]

Paul concluded the chapter with a benediction for the Thessalonians that in the midst of their persecutions, and until the Lord's return, he would grant them peace in all the circumstances they encountered

---

125. G. Green, *Thessalonians*, 341. See also Jewett, "Tenement," 23–43.

126. See, for example, G. Green, *Thessalonians*, 354; Greeven, "συναναμείγνυμι," 852–55.

127. See Brug, "Exegetical Brief," 208–217.

128. See Skeen, "Not as Enemies," 293.

from their hostile neighbors, their combating of false teaching, and their admonishing the undisciplined as they continued to advance the gospel.[129]

6.4 CONCLUSION: THE EFFECTS OF LEGAL LANGUAGE IN 2 THESS 1 UPON 2 THESS 3: THE LETTER CLOSING

Although Paul's use of judicial language for the purpose of encouraging this church in the midst of persecution may not be as apparent in the closing of 2 Thess 3, the effects can arguably be seen. Not only did this church suffer greatly at the hands of their pagan neighbors, but Paul and his associates themselves faced great opposition from those who did not belong to God. Thus, Paul coveted the prayers of this congregation as he and his associates patiently endured hostility until the Day of the Lord. He also prayed that the Lord would strengthen and protect the Thessalonian church from the evil one who was the architect behind their sufferings. He further addressed the problem of those who were living an undisciplined life because they had been misled to believe that the return of the Lord had already transpired. Paul exhorted the church to not associate with them, while at the same time admonish them so they would understand that they had not missed the coming of the Lord and, therefore, ought to conduct themselves in accordance with the example he and his associates had taught them by word and deed.

The forensic nature of the epistle arguably affected the final benediction, where Paul petitioned the Lord to grant this faithful church, which had remained steadfast in their pilgrimage despite severe persecution, peace in all their endeavors as they continued to advance the gospel among those who opposed them while awaiting the Day of the Lord, when their exile would be over and their vindication wholly realized at the final assize.

---

129. See Jewett, "Form and Function," 24.

7

Conclusion

THE PRIMARY AIM OF this original study was to argue that Paul intentionally used forensic language, allusions, and idioms throughout 2 Thess 1 to encourage the persecuted church to remain steadfast, for their vindication would come at the final assize. It was suggested that understanding the inclusion of such legal language would allow the reader a better understanding of the author's original intent for the epistle. In order to support this thesis it was proposed that such judicial language originated from the Day of Yahweh concept found throughout the Old Testament. It was argued that this motif was likely understood as referring to a court day where the Lord would return to render righteous verdicts upon those who had both obeyed and disobeyed him. By utilizing such a theological theme throughout this letter, Paul would have encouraged the Thessalonian church as they awaited their ultimate justification at God's eschatological tribunal. The following, therefore, offers a brief summary of the findings presented in this work that have led to such a conclusion.

At the outset, this study analyzed various preliminary issues regarding the historical, cultural, and contextual background surrounding the Thessalonian correspondence. It was suggested that such an examination of those subjects was necessary because it arguably promoted a more thorough understanding of those events that impacted the author's rationale for composing Second Thessalonians. Initially, the historical background pertaining to the city of Thessalonica and the issue of authenticity of Second Thessalonians were examined. It was proposed that an understanding of these subjects afforded a more accurate interpretation as to what may have prompted the author to compose the epistle. Regarding the historical background it was established that

Thessalonica was a favored city of Rome, and as a result enjoyed numerous freedoms because of that status. Consequently, the citizens of Thessalonica wanted to remain loyal to the empire since defiance would have resulted in the loss of such a privileged position. It was further argued that such allegiance to Rome had a significant impact on Paul's ministry in Thessalonica and in all probability was a catalyst that led to his early departure and kept him from returning to the city.

Following the brief discussion of Thessalonica's history, the issue of authenticity surrounding Second Thessalonians was examined. While scholarship remains divided regarding the authorship of the epistle it was suggested that the primary arguments proposed for the pseudonymity of the letter may not be as substantial as once thought and that it is therefore reasonable to suppose that Second Thessalonians is authentic. This led to the conclusion that if Paul authored the epistle, then his familiarity with the Old Testament's Day of the Lord motif likely served as an intertextual parallel for his use of forensic language found in 2 Thess 1. Such an understanding would arguably provide credence not only for the theological basis of the judicial language but would also provide a more precise interpretation of the author's original intent.

Subsequently, the argument was made that a proper understanding of Paul begins with his Jewish heritage. The evidence regarding the apostle's background established that as a devout Jew, Paul was extremely dependant upon the Old Testament. Such reliance upon the Old Testament ostensibly demonstrated a twofold conclusion. First, after his conversion Paul remained a faithful Jew who had come to the realization that Jesus was the promised Messiah, the fulfillment of the "law and the prophets," who would one day return for his remnant. Second, the apostle gleaned his theology primarily from the Old Testament, which he understood to be culminated in Christ. This led to the conclusion that the Old Testament served as Paul's theological foundation for his instruction to the Thessalonian church, which was comprised of both Jews and God-fearing Gentiles who would have been familiar with the Scriptures. As a result, it was deduced that what the apostle had instructed the Thessalonian church was in all probability an intertextual parallel based on the Day of the Lord theology prevalent throughout the Old Testament. Therefore, it was suggested that this newly formed congregation would have not only been familiar with the Old Testament and the Day of the Lord motif but also that such a concept would have arguably encouraged them amidst the hostile environment in which they lived, knowing that they would be vindicated at the final assize.

The final preliminary issue examined was the account of Paul's ministry in Thessalonica as recorded in Acts 17. While the book of Acts is often considered to be unreliable, several arguments were presented that suggested that Acts could be considered historically reliable and that it could, therefore, may serve as a viable source of information regarding Paul's ministry in Thessalonica.

If Acts can be considered dependable, then the information that the book provides regarding Paul's tenure in Thessalonica seems to offer two insights, which arguably impact the interpretation of Second Thessalonians. First, the unbelieving Jews in Thessalonica likely opposed Paul from a religious perspective. In other words, Paul and the Thessalonian church seemingly posed a threat to synagogue life. Wanting to dispose of Paul, the nonbelieving Jews instigated a riot and accused the missionaries and some of the brethren to be conspirators against the empire in order to involve the Roman authorities and force them to take action against them. Second, upon hearing the charges brought against the missionaries, it seems that the citizens of Thessalonica may have been politically motivated to take action. Fearing that their privileged status with Rome was in jeopardy because of Paul's message, coupled with the accusation of insurrection, the citizens of Thessalonica erupted and demanded legal action from the city's magistrates. As a result, Paul and Silas were banished from Thessalonica and the newly formed church became the object of persecution from both unbelieving Jews and Gentiles.

The intent of the discussion on these preliminary matters was to gather insight from the various historical, cultural, contextual, and theological issues surrounding the Thessalonian correspondence. Knowledge of such issues not only provided a more complete understanding of the background that may have prompted the writing of Second Thessalonians, but also they seemingly assisted in the facilitation of a more precise interpretation of the epistle.

Following the initial discussions, an examination of all the possible forensic language throughout 2 Thess 1 was investigated. The objective for this was to discover if the author actually incorporated forensic language throughout 2 Thess 1 and to determine whether such language was essentially borrowed from the Old Testament. By examining numerous terms, allusions, and idioms as they appear in specific contexts, mainly throughout the biblical writings, the evidence demonstrated that Paul, primarily drawing from the Old Testament, intentionally used judicial language in 2 Thess 1:5–10 for a specific purpose. It was further argued that the rationale for such a forensic word clustering in 2 Thess 1 was to communicate to the Thessalonian church a message of encouragement, that though persecuted, they were to remain firm in their faith and steadfast in their advancement of the gospel because their vindication would come at God's eschatological court. As a result, the apostle apparently borrowed various judicial terms and phrases from the Day of the Lord motif in the Old Testament to remind the Thessalonians that the parousia of Christ was essentially God's eschatological tribunal where the roles of suffering would be reversed. The Thessalonian Christians, who were once persecuted, would now be vindicated, as they would witness God pronounce his judicial verdict upon their adversaries who neither knew God nor obeyed the gospel of the Lord Jesus Christ, which was what the Old Testament prophets had predicted, namely, that the Day of the Lord would serve as both a day of punishment and a day of rejoicing.

Knowing that Paul intentionally utilized various judicial terms and phrases throughout 2 Thess 1, the ensuing discussions focused on the theological significance that such forensic language had on the interpretation of the entire letter.

In chapter 5, the objective was to explore 2 Thess 1 and determine what theological effect legal language had on its interpretation. It was proposed that Paul's use of forensic motif throughout 2 Thess 1:1–12 was used to encourage the Thessalonian church to remain steadfast as they endured severe persecution awaiting their redemption at the Day of the Lord. The intense suffering the congregation experienced likely influenced every aspect of their lives to the point where they wondered if they had missed the return of the Lord and if he would ever vindicate them. The apostle seemingly utilized numerous judicial terms in verses 5–10 to remind the Thessalonian believers that God had counted them worthy of his kingdom and when he returns at the judgment he would vindicate them at his final court by finding them "not-guilty" of being enemies of God while finding their persecutors "guilty." It was concluded, then, that the forensic language in 2 Thess 1 served to encourage the Thessalonian believers to continue persevering so that at the parousia of Christ they would be found worthy of their reward.

In chapter 6, the aim was to discover how the legal language of 2 Thess 1 affected the interpretation of the remainder of the epistle. It was argued that in 2 Thess 2 it seemed reasonable to suggest that the description of the final court day of the Lord found in 2 Thess 1 was further elaborated upon in 2 Thess 2 as evident in the description of the events leading to the final assize and the church's exoneration. As a result, it was suggested that Paul reassured the Thessalonian church that while certain events would precede the Day of the Lord, they could be confident that justice would be achieved.

It was concluded that legal motifs found in 2 Thess 1 had a significant effect upon 2 Thess 2, for there the author reassured the church that they had not missed the Day of the Lord and that they could be confident knowing that they would be justified. Although persecution would likely intensify, the author exhorted the Thessalonian church to persevere. Furthermore, it was suggested that the author continued the judicial theme by describing Christ as the righteous Judge who would slay his enemies and administer both final and impartial judgment at his parousia for both the Thessalonians and their oppressors. Thus the evidence seemed to establish that the forensic nature of 2 Thess 1 likely affected Paul's purpose in 2 Thess 2, which was to further encourage the Thessalonian church to persevere as they anticipated their future vindication at Lord's court where he would render perfect justice.

The final discussion centered on the theological significance that the forensic language of 2 Thess 1 had upon the final chapter of the letter. It was argued that the effects of the judicial language for the purpose of encouraging this church in the midst of persecution were evident. Throughout this final chapter, not only did the reality of this church's suffering continue to be addressed, but Paul also reminded them that he and his associates themselves faced great opposition from those not belonging to God. As a result, the apostle requested prayer from the Thessalonians as he and his associates patiently endured similar hostility until the Day of the Lord.

Also in the final chapter, the issue was addressed concerning the problem of those who were living an undisciplined life because they had been misled to believe that the return of the Lord had already transpired. The author exhorted the church not to associate with such individuals and at the same time admonished them, so they would understand that they had not missed the coming of the Lord and, therefore, ought to conduct themselves in accordance with the example Paul and his associates had taught them by word and deed until their exoneration at the Day of the Lord.

It was also apparent that the forensic nature of the epistle affected the final benediction, where the apostle petitioned the Lord to grant the faithful church peace in all their endeavors and to support them in advancing the gospel, despite the opposition, until the Day of the Lord.

The purpose of this study was to demonstrate that Paul intentionally used forensic language, allusions, and idioms in 2 Thess 1 for the specific purpose of encouraging the persecuted church to remain faithful because they would be vindicated at the parousia. The original contribution of the this work has demonstrated that a deliberate forensic word grouping is not only evident throughout 2 Thess 1 but was derived from the theology of the Day of the Lord motif found throughout the Old Testament, rather than first-century Hellenistic culture. It has been established that the apostle understood the Day of the Lord concept as a court day, which would be consummated at Christ's parousia. Furthermore, it was proposed that the legal language incorporated in 2 Thess 1 not only accentuates Paul's hermeneutic that the Old Testament understood the Day of the Lord as an appointed judicial day but that such judicial idioms were used to encourage the Thessalonian Christians to persevere, for they had not missed their day at court where their vindication awaited.

Moreover, the judicial terminology incorporated by Paul was not Hellenized by the apostle to communicate Christ's return to a predominately Gentile congregation. Rather, the forensic language served a theological purpose, which emphasized that the Old Testament's theology regarding the Day of the Lord corresponded to the final eschatological court that will convene at Christ's return. Much like the prophets in the Old Testament who referred to the Day of Yahweh in a judicial sense, Paul seemingly understood the parousia of Jesus to be a direct parallel. In other words, the judicial language in 2 Thess 1 served to emphasize that Christ's return will be the eschatological Day of the Lord where, as the righteous Judge, he will render the final verdict. The apostle, therefore, used this forensic motif to encourage the Thessalonian church to remain steadfast through their pilgrimage, for the Lord would soon come to vindicate them at the final assize.

Thus, the Thessalonian correspondence offers hope and encouragement for modern Christians enduring persecution in a culture that is adamantly opposed to the gospel message. As the author of Second Thessalonians sought to incorporate forensic language in order to encourage this first-century church regarding God's righteous judgment, so also does this message continue to be relevant for Christians in the modern era, who proclaim the exclusive message of Christ and await vindication at the Day of the Lord.

Bibliography

Abasciano, Brian J. *Paul's Use of the Old Testament in Romans 9:1-9: An Intertextual and Theological Exegesis*. LNTS 301. London: T&T Clark, 2005.
Achtemeier, Elizabeth. *The Community and Message of Isaiah 56-66*. Minneapolis: Augsburg, 1982.
Aegyptische Urkunden aus den Königlichen Staatlichen Museen zu Berlin: Griechische Urkunden. 15 vols. Berlin: Weidmannsche Buchhandlung, 1895-2000.
Ahn, Yong-Sik Joseph. "The Parousia in Paul's Letters to the Thessalonians, the Corinthians, and the Romans, in Relation to its Old Testament-Judaic Background." PhD diss., Fuller Theological Seminary, 1989.
Aland, Kurt, and Barbara Aland. *The Text of the New Testament: An Introduction to the Critical Editions and to the Theory and Practice of Modern Textual Criticism*. 2nd ed. Grand Rapids, MI: Eerdmans, 1995.
Alexander, Desmond T., and David W. Baker, eds. *Dictionary of the Old Testament: Pentateuch*. Downers Grove, IL: InterVarsity Press, 2003.
Alexander, Loveday. "Fact, Fiction and the Genre of Acts." *NTS* 44 (1998) 380-99.
The Ante-Nicene Fathers. Edited by A. Roberts and J. Donaldson. 10 vols. 1885-87. Reprint, Peabody, MA: Hendrickson, 1994.
Apostolic Fathers. Translated by Kirsopp Lake et al. 2 vols. Loeb Classical Library. Cambridge, MA: Harvard University Press, 1952.
Appian. *Appian's Roman History*. Translated by H. White. 4 vols. Loeb Classical Library. Cambridge, MA: Harvard University Press, 1964.
Applebaum, Shimon. "The Legal Status of Jewish Communities in the Diaspora." In *The Jewish People in the First Century: Historical Geography, Political History, Social, Cultural, and Religious Life, and Institutions*, edited by S. Safrai and M. Stern, 420-63. Vol. 1 of *Compendia Rerum Iudaicarum ad Novum Testamentum*, edited by W. J. Burgers and H. E. Gaylord. Assen: Van Gorcum, 1974.
Arichea, Daniel C., and Howard A. Hanton. *A Handbook on Paul's Letters to Timothy and Titus*. New York: United Bible Societies, 1995.
Aristophanes. *The Frogs*. Translated by B. Bickley. 3 vols. Loeb Classical Library. Cambridge, MA: Harvard University, 1979-82.
Auld, A. Graeme. *Joshua: Jesus Son of Nauē in Codex Vaticanus*. SCS. Leiden: Brill, 2005.
Aus, Roger D. "Comfort in Judgment: The Use of the Day of the Lord and Theophany Traditions in Second Thessalonians 1." PhD diss., Yale University, 1971.
———. "God's Plan and God's Power: Isaiah 66 and the Restraining Factors of 2 Thess 2:6-7." *JBL* 96 (1977) 537-53.
———. "The Liturgical Background of the Necessity and Propriety of Giving Thanks according to 2 Thess 1:3," *JBL* 92 (1973) 432-38.

———. "The Relevance of Isaiah 66:7 to Revelation 12 and 2 Thessalonians 1." *ZNW* 67 (1976) 252–68.
Avishur, Yitshak. *Stylistic Studies of Word Pairs in Biblical and Ancient Semitic Literatures.* AOAT 210. Neukirchen-Vluyn: Neukirchener Verlag, 1984.
Bailey, John A. "Who Wrote II Thessalonians?" *NTS* 25 (Jan 1979) 131–45.
Balz, H. "ἀνατρέφω." In *EDNT* 1:94
———. "ἀφίστημι." In *EDNT* 1:183.
———. "δῆμος." In *EDNT* 1:296.
———. "σέβομαι." In *EDNT* 3:236.
Balz, H. R., and Schneider, G., eds. *Exegetical Dictionary of the New Testament.* 3 vols. Grand Rapids, MI: Eerdmans, 1990–93.
Banker, John. *A Semantic and Structural Analysis of Philippians.* Dallas: Summer Institute of Linguistics, 1996.
Barclay, John M. G. "Conflict in Thessalonica." *CBQ* 55 (1993) 512–30.
———. *Jews in the Mediterranean Diaspora: From Alexander to Trajan (323 BCE–117 CE).* Edinburgh: T&T Clark, 1996.
Barram, Michael. "Romans 12:9–21." *Int* 57 (2003) 423–26.
Barrett, C. K. *The Acts of the Apostles.* ICC. 2 vols. Edinburgh: T&T Clark, 1994/1998.
———. *A Commentary on the Epistle to the Romans.* BNTC. London: Adam & Charles Black, 1957.
———. "The Historicity of Acts." *JTS* 50 (1999) 515–34.
———. *Luke the Historian in Recent Study.* London: Epworth, 1961.
Barton, John, and John Muddiman, eds. *The Oxford Bible Commentary.* Oxford: Oxford University Press, 2001.
Bassler, Jouette. "Divine Impartiality in Paul's Letter to the Romans." *NovT* 26 (1984) 43–58.
———. "The Enigmatic Sign: 2 Thessalonians 1:5." *CBQ* 46 (1984) 496–510.
Bauckham, Richard, ed. *The Book of Acts in its Palestinian Setting.* Vol. 4 of *The Book of Acts in Its First Century Setting.* Edited by B. W. Winter. Grand Rapids, MI: Eerdmans, 1995.
———. *God Crucified: Monotheism and Christology in the New Testament.* Grand Rapids, MI: Eerdmans, 1999.
———. *Jude, 2 Peter.* WBC 50. Waco, TX: Word Books, 1983.
Bauer, Walter. *A Greek-English Lexicon of the New Testament and Other Early Christian Literature.* Translated by William F. Arndt and F. Wilbur Gingrich. 3rd ed., edited by Frederick William Danker. Chicago: University of Chicago Press, 2000.
Bauman, R. A. *The Crimen Maiestatis in the Roman Republic and Augustan Principate.* Johannesburg: Witwatersrand University Press, 1967.
Baur, F. C. *Paulus, der Apostel Jesu Christi.* Leipzig: Fue's, 1866. Microfiche.
Beale, Gregory K. *The Book of Revelation: A Commentary on the Greek Text.* NIGTC. Grand Rapids, MI: Eerdmans, 1999.
———. *1–2 Thessalonians.* Downers Grove, IL: InterVarsity Press, 2003.
Beale, G. K., and D. A. Carson, eds. *Commentary on the New Testament Use of the Old Testament.* Grand Rapids, MI: Baker Academic, 2007.
Beare, Francis W. *A Commentary on the Epistle to the Philippians.* BNTC. London: Adams & Charles Black, 1959.

Beasley-Murray, George. *Jesus and the Future: An Examination of the Criticism of the Eschatological Discourse, Mark 13 with Special Reference to the Little Apocalypse Theory.* London: Macmillan, 1954.

Beker, J. C. *Heirs of Paul: Paul's Legacy in the New Testament and in the Church Today.* Minneapolis: Fortress, 1991.

———. "The Faithfulness of God and the Priority of Israel in Paul's Letter to the Romans," *HTR* 79 (1986) 10–16.

Becker, Jürgen. *Paul: Apostle to the Gentiles.* Translated by O. C. Dean. Louisville: Westminster John Knox, 1993.

Beckwith, Roger. *The Old Testament Canon of the New Testament Church and Its Background in Early Judaism.* Grand Rapids, MI: Eerdmans, 1985.

Beker, Johan and C. Benoit, P. "L'Inscription Grecque du Tombeau de Jason," *IEJ* 17 (1967) 112–13.

Bertram, G. "παιδεύω." In *TDNT* 5:595–625.

Best, Ernest. *A Commentary on the First and Second Epistles to the Thessalonians.* Harper's New Testament Commentaries. New York: Harper & Row, 1972.

Betz, Hans D. "Zum Problem des religionsgeschichtlichen Verständnisses der Apokalyptik." *ZTK* 63 (1966) 391–409.

Beutler, Johannes. "μάρτυς." In *EDNT* 2:393–95.

Bicknell, E. J. *The First and Second Epistles to the Thessalonians.* Westminster Commentaries. London: Methuen, 1932.

Birch, Bruce C. *Singing the Lord's Song: A Study of Isaiah 40–55.* Nashville: Abingdon, 1981.

Black, Mark. "Paul and Roman Law in Acts," *ResQ* 24, no. 4 (1981) 209–218.

Blass, F., and A. Debrunner. *A Greek Grammar of the New Testament and Other Early Christian Literature.* Chicago: University of Chicago Press, 1961.

Blenkinsopp, Joseph. *Opening the Sealed Book: Interpretations of the Book of Isaiah in Late Antiquity.* Grand Rapids, MI: Eerdmans, 2006.

Bloesch, Donald G. *The Last Things: Resurrection, Judgment, Glory.* Downers Grove, IL: InterVarsity Press, 2004.

Blomberg, Craig. *From Pentecost to Patmos: An Introduction to Acts through Revelation.* Nottingham: Apollos, 2006.

Bock, Darrell L. *Luke: Volume 2; 9:51–24:53.* BECNT. Grand Rapids, MI: Baker Books, 1996.

Boecker Hans J. *Recht und Gesetz im Alten Testament und im Alten Orient.* Neukirchen-Vluyn: Neukirchner Verlag, 1984.

———. *Redeformen des Rechtslebens im Alten Testament.* WMANT 14. 2nd ed. Neukirchen-Vluyn: Neukirchener Verlag, 1970.

Boeckh, A., J. Franz, E. Curtius, A. Kirchhoff, and H. Roehl, eds. *CIG.* Berolini: Ex Officina Academica: Vendit G. Reimeri Libraria, 1828–77.

Boers, Hendrikus. "The Form Critical Study of Paul's Letters: 1 Thessalonians as a Case Study." *NTS* 22 (1976) 140–58.

Bornemann, Wilhelm. *Die Thessalonicherbriefe.* Göttingen: Vandenhoeck und Ruprecht, 1894.

Bornkam, Günther *Paul/Paulus.* Translated by D. M. Stalker. New York: Harper & Row, 1971.

Botterweck, G. J., and H. Ringgren, eds. *Theological Dictionary of the Old Testament.* Translated by J. Willis. 15 vols. Grand Rapids, MI: Eerdmans, 1974–2006.

Bovati, Pietro. *Re-Establishing Justice: Legal Terms, Concepts, and Procedures in the Hebrew Bible.* JSOTSup 105. Translated by M. J. Smith. Sheffield: Sheffield Academic Press, 1994.

Bovon-Thurneysen, Annegreth. "Ethik und Eschatologie im Philipperbrief des Polycarp von Smyrna." *TZ* 29 (1973) 242.

Bratcher, Robert G., and William D. Reyburn. *A Translator's Handbook on the Book of Psalms.* New York: United Bible Societies, 1991.

Brin, Gershon. *Studies in Biblical Law: From the Hebrew Bible to the Dead Sea Scrolls.* JSOTSup 176. Translated by J. Chipman. Sheffield: Sheffield Academic Press, 1994.

Brindle, Wayne A. "Biblical Evidence for the Imminence of the Raputre." *BSac* 158 (2001) 138–51.

Brocke, Christoph von. *Thessaloniki: Stadt des Kassander und Gemeinde des Paulus.* WUNT 125. Tübingen: Mohr Siebeck, 2001.

Brooks, James A., and Carlton L. Wibery. *Syntax of New Testament Greek.* Washington DC: University Press of America, 1979.

Brown, Colin. "δίακαιοσύνη." In *NIDNTT* 3:352–77.

———, ed. *The New International Dictionary of New Testament Theology.* Edited by C. Brown. 4 vols. Grand Rapids, MI: Regency Reference Library, 1975–78.

Brown, F., S. R. Driver, and C. A. Briggs, eds. *The Brown-Driver-Briggs Hebrew and English Lexicon: With an Appendix Containing the Biblical Aramaic; Coded with the Numbering System from Strong's Exhaustive Concordance of the Bible.* Peabody, MA: Hendrickson Publishers, 1996. Reprint, 2004.

Brown, Raymond E. *The Semitic Background of the Term Mystery in the New Testament.* Philadelphia: Fortress, 1968.

Brown, Stephen G. "The Intertextuality of Isaiah 66:17 and 2 Thessalonians 2:7: A Solution for the 'Restrainer' Problem." In *Paul and the Scriptures of Israel,* edited by C. A. Evans and J. A. Sanders, 254–77. JSNTSup 83. Sheffield: JSOT, 1993.

Bruce, F. F. *1 and 2 Thessalonians.* WBC vol. 45. Waco, TX: Word Books, 1982.

———. *The Acts of the Apostles: The Greek Text with Introduction and Commentary.* 3rd ed. Grand Rapids, MI: Eerdmans, 1990.

———, ed. *The Book of Acts.* NICNT. Grand Rapids, MI: Eerdmans, 1979.

———. *The Epistle to the Hebrews.* NICNT. Grand Rapids, MI: Eerdmans, 1964. Reprint, 1981.

———. "Macedonia." In *ABD* 4:454–57.

———. *Paul: Apostle of the Heart Set Free.* Exeter: Paternoster, 1977. Reprint, Grand Rapids, MI: Eerdmans, 1999.

Brug, John F. "Exegetical Brief: 2 Thessalonians 3:6, 14, 15; Admonish Him as a Brother." *WLC* 96 (1999) 208–217.

Büchsel, Friedrich. "κρίνω." In *TDNT* 3:921–43.

———. "The OT Term שפט." In *TDNT* 3:923.

Bultmann, R. *Primitive Christianity in Its Contemporary Setting.* Translated by R. H. Fuller. London: Thames & Hudson, 1956.

———. *Theology of the New Testament.* Translated by Kendrick Grobel. 2nd ed. Vol. 2. New York: Scribner, 1955.

———. *Theology of the New Testament: Complete in One Volume.* Translated by K. Grobel. New York: Scribner, 1970.

Burkeen, W. H. "The Parousia of Christ in the Thessalonians Correspondence." PhD diss., University of Aberdeen, 1979.

Burton, E. D. "The Politarchs." *AJT* 2 (1898) 598–632. Ann Arbor, MI: University Microfilms, a Xerox Company, 1973, microfilm.

Burtt, Edwin A. *Types of Religious Philosophy*. Rev. ed. New York: Harper, 1951.

Cadbury, H. J. *The Book of Acts in History*. London: Black, 1955.

Cadbury, H. J., F. J. F. Jackson, and K. Lake. "The Greek and Jewish Traditions of Writing History." In *Prolegomena II: Criticism*, edited by F. J. F. Jackson and K. Lake, 7–29. Vol. 2 of *The Beginning of Christianity: The Acts of the Apostles*, edited by F. J. F. Jackson and K. Lake. Grand Rapids, MI: Baker Book House, 1979.

Campbell, William S. *Paul and the Creation of Christian Identity*. LNTS 322. London: T&T Clark, 2006.

Cambier, J. M. "Le Jugement de tous les homes par Dieu seul, selon la vérité, dans Rom 2:1–3:20." *ZNW* 67 (1976) 187–213.

Carpenter, E. "גמל." In *NIDOTTE* 1:871–73.

Carroll, John T. "Present and Future in Fourth Gospel Eschatology." *Biblical Theology Bulletin* 19 (1989) 63–69.

Carson, D. A. *Divine Sovereignty and Human Responsibility: Biblical Perspectives in Tension*. Atlanta: John Knox, 1981.

———. "Matthew." In *Matthew, Mark, Luke*, edited by Frank E. Gaebelein. Vol. 8 of *The Expositor's Bible Commentary*. Grand Rapids, MI: Zondervan, 1984.

———. "Mystery and Fulfillment: Toward a More Comprehensive Paradigm of Paul's Understanding of the Old and New." In *Justification and Variegated Nomism Volume II: The Paradoxes of Paul*, edited by D. A. Carson, P. T. O'Brien, and M. A. Seifrid, 413–25. WUNT 181. Tübingen: Mohr Siebeck, 2004.

Carson, D. A., Douglas J. Moo, and Leon Morris. *An Introduction to the New Testament*. Grand Rapids, MI: Zondervan, 1992.

Cassidy, Richard J. *Jesus, Politics, and Society: A Study of Luke's Gospel*. Maryknoll, NY: Orbis Books, 1978.

———. *Society and Politics in the Acts of the Apostles*. New York: Orbis Books, 1987.

Černy, Ladislav. *The Day of Yahweh and Some Relevant Problems*. Prague: Nakladem Filosoficke Fakulty University Karlovy, 1948.

Chae, Young S. *Jesus as the Eschatological Davidic Shepherd: Studies in the Old Testament, Second Temple Judaism, and the Gospel of Matthew*. WUNT 216. Tübingen: Mohr Siebeck, 2006.

Charles, J. Daryl. *Literary Strategy in the Epistle of Jude*. Scranton, PA: University of Scranton Press, 1993.

———. *Virtue amidst Vice: The Catalog of Virtues in 2 Peter 1*. JSNTSup 150. Sheffield: Sheffield Academic Press, 1997.

Charles, R. H. "Michael." In *HBD* 3:362–63.

Charlesworth, James H., ed. *The Old Testament Pseudepigrapha*. 2 vols. New York: Doubleday, 1985.

Childs, Brevard S. *The Book of Exodus: A Critical, Theological Commentary*. Philadelphia: Westminster, 1974.

Chilton, Bruce, and Jacob Neusner. *Judaism in the New Testament*. London: Routledge, 1995.

Chilton, David. *The Days of Vengeance: An Exposition of the Book of Revelation*. Fort Worth, TX: Dominion, 1987.

Chisholm, Robert B. "עוד." In *NIDOTTE* 3:335–40.

Clement. *The Epistle of Barnabas*. In *The Apostolic Fathers: Greek Texts and Translations*, edited by M. W. Holmes, 270–327. Grand Rapids, MI: Baker Books, 1999.

———. *The Stromata*. Vol. 2 of the *Ante-Nicene Fathers*, edited by A. Roberts and J. Donaldson. 5th ed. 10 vols. Grand Rapids, MI: Eerdmans, 1979–83.

———. *Stromateis: Books One to Three*. Vol. 85 of *Fathers of the Church*. Translated by J. Ferguson. Washington, DC: Catholic University of America Press, 1991.

Clements, R. E. "Achan's Sin: Warfare and Holiness." In *Shall Not the Judge of All the Earth Do What Is Right*, edited by D. Penchansky and P. L. Redditt, 113–26. Winona Lake, IN: Eisenbrauns, 2000.

Clines, David J. A. *Job 1–20*. WBC 17. Dallas: Word Books, 1989.

Collange, Jean Francois. *The Epistle of Saint Paul to the Philippians*. Translated by A. W. Heathcote. London: Epworth, 1979.

Collins, Adela Y. *The Beginning of the Gospel: Probings of Mark in Context*. Minneapolis: Fortress, 1992.

Collins, Raymond, F. *Letters That Paul Did Not Write: The Epistle to the Hebrews and the Pauline Pseudepigrapha*. GNS 28. Wilmington, DE: Michael Glazier, 1988.

———. *The Thessalonian Correspondence*. Leuven: Leuven University Press, 1991.

Coppes, L. J. "קרב." In *TWOT* 2:811–13.

Court, J. M. "Right and Left: The Implications for Matthew 5:31–46." *NTS* 31 (1985) 223–33.

Cranfield, C. E. B. *The Epistle to the Romans*. ICC 2. Edinburgh: T&T Clark, 1979.

Culy, Martin M., and Mikeal C. Parsons. *Acts: A Handbook to the Greek Text*. Waco, TX: Baylor University Press, 2003.

Curkpatrick, Stephen. "Dissonance in Luke 18:1–8." *JBL* 121 (2002) 107–121.

Dana, H. E., and J. R. Mantey. *A Manual Grammar of the Greek New Testament*. New York: Macmillan, 1927.

Danby, H., ed. *The Mishnah*. London: Oxford University Press, 1950.

Davis, James F. *Lex Talionis in Early Judaism and the Exhortation of Jesus in Matthew 5.38–42*. JSNTSup 281. London: T&T Clark International, 2005.

Davies, W. D. *The Gospel and the Land: Early Christianity and Jewish Territorial Doctrine*. Berkeley and Los Angeles: University of California Press, 1974. Reprint, Sheffield: Sheffield Academic Press, 1994), 234.

———. "Paul and the New Exodus." In *The Quest for Context and Meaning: Studies in Biblical Intertextuality in Honor of James A. Sanders*, edited by C. A. Evans and S. Talmon, 443–63. Leiden: Brill, 1997.

———. "Paul and the People of Israel." *NTS* 24 (1977) 4–39.

———. *Paul and Rabbinic Judaism: Some Rabbinic Elements in Pauline Theology*. London: SPCK, 1955.

Davies, W. D., and D. C. Allison. *The Gospel according to Matthew: XIX–XXVIII*. ICC. 3 vols. Edinburgh: T&T Clark, 1997.

Day, John N. "Coals of Fire in Romans 12:19–20." *BSac* 160 (2003) 414–20.

Day, Peggy L. "Adulterous Jerusalem's Imagined Demise: Death of a Metaphor in Ezekiel 16." *VT* 50 (2000) 285–309.

de Boer, Martinus C. "God-Fearers in Luke-Acts." In *Luke's Literary Achievement*, edited by C. M. Tuckett, 50–71. JSNTSup 116. Sheffield: Sheffield Academic Press, 1995.

Deissmann, Adolf. *Paul: A Study in Social and Religious History*. Translated by W. Wilson. 2nd ed. New York: Doran, 1926.

Delling, Gerhard. "NT Usage: ἡμέρα." In *TDNT*, 2:948–53.

Demosthenes. Translated by C. A. Vince, J. H. Vince, A. T. Murray, N. W. DeWitt, and N. J. DeWitt. 7 vols. Loeb Classical Library. Cambridge, MA: Harvard University Press, 1962–84.

den Heyer, C. J. *Paul: A Man of Two Worlds.* Translated by J. Bowden. Harrisburg, PA: Trinity, 2000.

Denney, James. *The Epistles to the Thessalonians.* 3rd ed. New York: Armstrong, 1899.

Denton, D. R. "Inheritance in Paul and Ephesians." *EvQ* 54 (1982) 157–62.

deSilva, David. *Introduction to the Apocrypha: Message, Context, and Significance.* Grand Rapids, MI: Baker Academic, 2002.

———. "Worthy of His Kingdom: Honor Discourse and Social Engineering in 1 Thessalonians." *JSNT* 64 (1996) 49–79.

de Villiers, Pieter G. R. "A Life Worthy of God: Identity and Ethics in the Thessalonian Correspondence." In *Identity, Ethics, and Ethos in the New Testament,* edited by J. G. van der Watt, 335–55, BZNW 141. Berlin: de Gruyter, 2006.

Dewailly, L. M. "Course et Glorie de la Parole: 2 Thess. 3:1." *RB* 71 (1964) 25–41.

Dibelius, Martin. *An Die Thessalonicher I, II an die Philipper.* HNT 11. Tübingen: Mohr Siebeck, 1937.

———. *Paul.* Edited by W. G. Kümmel. Translated by F. Clarke. London: Longmans, Green, 1953.

Dio Cassius. *Roman History.* Translated by E. Cary. 9 vols. Loeb Classical Library. Cambridge, MA: Harvard University, 1914–27.

Diodorus Siculus. Translated by C. H. Oldfather and F. R. Walton. 12 vols. Loeb Classical Library. Cambridge, MA: Harvard University Press, 1961–83.

Diogenes. *The Lives of Eminent Philosophers.* Translated by R. D. Hicks. 2 vols. Loeb Classical Library. Cambridge, MA: Harvard University Press, 1950.

Dionysius. *Roman Antiquities.* Translated by E. Cary. 7 vols. Loeb Classical Library. Cambridge, MA: Harvard University Press, 1937–50.

Dittenberger, W., ed. *Orientis graeci inscriptiones selectae.* 2 vols. Hildesheim: G. Olms, 1960.

———, ed. *Sylloge Inscriptionum Graecarum.* 3rd ed. 4 vols. Leipzig: S. Hirzel, 1915–24.

Dittenberger, W., K. Otto, H. von Gaertringen, and F. Freiherr, eds. *Inscriptiones Graecae.* Berolini: apud G. Reimerum, 1897–1908.

Dixon, Paul S. "The Evil Restraint in 2 Thess 2:6." *JETS* 33 (1990) 445–49.

Dobschütz, Ernst von. *Die Thessalonicher-Briefe.* Göttingen: Vandenhoeck & Ruprecht, 1974.

Dodd, C. H. *According to the Scriptures: The Sub-Structure of New Testament Theology.* New York: Scribner, 1953.

Donahue, John R., and Daniel J. Harrington. *Mark.* SP 2. Collegeville, MN: Liturgical Press, 2002.

Donfried, Karl P. "The Cults of Thessalonica and the Thessalonian Correspondence." *NTS* 31 (1985) 336–56.

———. *Paul, Thessalonica, and Early Christianity.* Grand Rapids, MI: Eerdmans, 2002.

Donfried, Karl P., and I. H. Marshall. *The Theology of the Shorter Pauline Epistles.* Cambridge: Cambridge University Press, 1993.

Doukhan, Jacques B. *Daniel: The Vision of the End.* Berrien Springs, MI: Andrews University Press, 1987.

Dunham, Duane A. "2 Thessalonians 1:3–10: A Study in Sentence Structure." *JETS* 24 (1981) 39–46.

Dunn, James D. G. *The Acts of the Apostles*. Narrative Commentaries. Edited by I. H. Jones. Valley Forge, PA: Trinity, 1996.
———. *The Epistles to the Colossians and to Philemon*. NIGTC. Grand Rapids, MI: Eerdmans, 1996.
———. "Jesus the Judge: Further Thoughts of Paul's Christology and Soteriology." In *The New Perspective on Paul*, 398–405. WUNT 185. Tübingen: Mohr Siebeck, 2006.
———. *Romans 1–8*. WBC 38. Dallas: Word Books, 1988.
———. *The Theology of Paul the Apostle*. Grand Rapids, MI: Eerdmans, 1998.
———. *The Theology of Paul's Letter to the Galatians*. Cambridge: Cambridge University Press, 1993.
———. *Unity and Diversity in the New Testament: An Inquiry into the Character of Earliest Christianity*. 2nd ed. Harrisburg, PA: Trinity, 1990.
Dyer, Keith D. *The Prophecy on the Mount: Mark 13 and the Gathering of the New Community*. ITS 2. Bern: Peter Lang, 1998.
Eadie, John. *Epistles of Paul to the Thessalonians*. London: Macmillan, 1877. Reprint, Grand Rapids, MI: Baker Book House, 1979.
Edson, Charles. "Cults of Thessalonica." *HTR* 41 (1948) 153–204.
Ehrenberg, Victor, and A. H. M. Jones. *Documents Illustrating the Reigns of Augustus and Tiberius*. 2nd ed. Oxford: Clarendon, 1979.
Ehrensperger, Kathy. *That We May Be Mutually Encouraged: Feminism and the New Perspective in Pauline Studies*. New York: T&T Clark, 2004.
Ellicott, Charles J. *St. Paul's Epistles to the Thessalonians: A Critical and Grammatical Commentary*. London: Longmans, Green, 1866.
Ellingworth, Paul. *The Epistle to the Hebrews*. NIGTC. Grand Rapids, MI: Eerdmans, 1993.
Ellingworth, Paul, and Eugene A. Nida. *A Translator's Handbook on Paul's Letter to the Thessalonians*. New York: United Bible Societies, 1976.
Ellis E. Earle. *Paul's Use of the Old Testament*. Edinburgh: Oliver & Boyd, 1957.
Engberg-Pedersen, Troels, ed. "Stoicism in Philippians." In *Paul in His Hellenistic Context*, 256–90. Edinburgh: T&T Clark, 1994.
Eusebius. *Historia Ecclesiastica*. Translated by K. Lake. 2 vols. Loeb Classical Library. Cambridge, MA: Harvard University Press, 1926–38.
Evans, Craig A. "Aspects of Exile and Restoration in the Proclamation of Jesus and the Gospels." In *Exile: Old Testament, Jewish, and Christian Conceptions*, edited by J. M. Scott, 299–328. JSJSup 56, edited by J. J. Collins. Leiden: Brill, 1997.
Evans C. A., and S. E. Porter, eds. *Dictionary of New Testament Background*. Downers Grove, IL: InterVarsity Press, 2000.
Farrow, Douglas. "Showdown: The Message of Second Thessalonians 2:1–12 and the Riddle of the 'Restrainer.'" *Crux* 25 (1989) 23–26.
Fee, Gordon D. *1 and 2 Timothy and Titus*. NIBCNT. Rev. ed. Peabody, MA: Hendrickson, 1988.
———. *The First Epistle to the Corinthians*. NICNT. Grand Rapids, MI: Eerdmans, 1987.
———. *New Testament Exegesis: A Handbook for Students and Pastors*. 3rd ed. Louisville: John Knox, 2002.
———. *Pauline Christology: An Exegetical-Theological Study*. Peabody, MA: Hendrickson, 2007.
———. *Paul's Letter to the Philippians*. NICNT. Grand Rapids, MI: Eerdmans, 1995.

———. "Pneuma and Eschatology in 2 Thessalonians 2:1–12: A Proposal about 'Testing the Prophets' and the Purpose of 2 Thessalonians." In *To What End Exegesis?* 290–308. Grand Rapids, MI: Eerdmans, 2001.
Feinberg, Paul D. "The Case for the Pretribulation Rapture Position." In *The Rapture: Pre-, Mid-, or Post-Tribulational?* edited by Gleason L. Archer Jr., 47–86. Grand Rapids, MI: Zondervan, 1984.
Fekkes, Jan. *Isaiah and Prophetic Traditions in the Book of Revelation: Visionary Antecedents and Their Development*. JSNTSup 93. Sheffield: Sheffield Academic Press, 1994.
Feldman, L. H. "Proselytes and 'Sympathizers' in Light of the New Inscriptions from Aphrodisias." *REJ* 148 (1989) 265–305.
Ferguson, Everett. *Backgrounds of Early Christianity*. 2nd ed. Grand Rapids, MI: Eerdmans, 1993.
Ferguson, William D. *The Legal Terms Common to the Macedonian Inscriptions and the New Testament*. Chicago: University of Chicago Press, 1913.
Field, D. H. "ἀγοράζω." In *NIDNTT* 1:267–68.
Fields, Weston W. *Sodom and Gomorrah: History and Motif in Biblical Narrative*. JSOTSup 231. Sheffield: Sheffield Academic Press, 1997.
Findlay, G. G., ed. *The Epistles of Paul the Apostle to the Thessalonians*. CGTC. Cambridge: Cambridge University Press, 1911.
Fiore, Benjamin. *The Function of Personal Example in the Socratic and Pastoral Epistles*. AnBib 105. Rome: Biblical Institute Press, 1986.
Fitzmyer, Joseph A. "The Language of Palestine in the First-Century A. D." *CBQ* 32 (1970) 501–531.
———. *Romans*. AB 33. New York: Doubleday, 1993.
Fletcher-Louis, Crispin H. T. *Luke-Acts: Angels, Christology, and Soteriology*. WUNT 94. Tübingen: Mohr Siebeck, 1997.
Ford, Desmond. *The Abomination of Desolation in Biblical Eschatology*. Washington DC: University Press of America, 1979.
Ford, J. M. "The Structure and Meaning of Revelation 16." *ExpTim* 98 (1987) 327–31.
Forester, W. "σέβομαι." In *TDNT* 7:169–72.
Frame, James E. *A Critical and Exegetical Commentary on the Epistles of St. Paul to the Thessalonians*. ICC 30. New York: Scribner, 1912.
France, R. T. *The Gospel of Mark*. NIGTC. Grand Rapids, MI: Eerdmans, 2002.
———. *Jesus and the Old Testament: His Application of Old Testament Passages to Himself and His Mission*. London: Tyndale; Downers Grove, IL: Intervarsity Press, 1971.
Freed, Edwin D. *The Apostle Paul, Christian Jew: Faithfulness and Law*. Lanham, MD: University Press of America, 1994.
Freedman, David N., ed. *The Anchor Bible Dictionary*. 6 vols. New York: Doubleday, 1992.
Fudge, Edward. "The Final End of the Wicked." *JETS* 27 (1984) 325–34.
———. *The Fire That Consumes: A Biblical and Historical Study of Final Punishment*. Houston: Providential Press, 1982.
Fuhs, H. F. "ראה." In *TDOT* 13:208–242.
Fuks, G. "Where Have all the Freedmen Gone? On an Anomaly in the Jewish Grave-Inscriptions from Rome." *JJS* 36 (1985) 26–32.
Fung, Ronald Y. K. *The Epistle to the Galatians*. NICNT. Grand Rapids, MI: Eerdmans, 1988.

Fürst, D. "παιδεύω." In *NIDNTT* 3:775–81.
Gager, John G. "Jews, Gentiles, and Synagogues in the Book of Acts." *HTR* 79 (1986) 91–99.
Gane, R. E., and J. Milgrom. "קרב." In *TDOT* 13:135–48.
Garlington, Don. "Role Reversal and Paul's Use of Scripture in Galatians 3:10–13." *JSNT* 65 (1997) 85–121.
Gasque, W. Ward. "Tarsus." In *ABD* 6:333–34.
Gaventa, Beverly H. *First and Second Thessalonians*. Louisville: John Knox, 1998.
Geddert, Timothy J. *Watchwords: Mark 13 in the Markan Eschatology*. JSNTSup 26. Sheffield: JSOT, 1989.
Giblin, Charles. *The Threat to Faith: An Exegetical and Theological Re-Examination of 2 Thessalonians 2*. Rome: Pontifical Biblical Institute, 1967.
Gill, David W. J., and Conrad Gempf, eds. *The Book of Acts in Its Graeco-Roman Setting*. Vol. 2 of *The Book of Acts in Its First Century Setting*, edited by Bruce W. Winter. Grand Rapids, MI: Eerdmans, 1994.
Gillman-Morgan, F. "Jason of Thessalonica (Acts 17:5–9)." In R. F. Collins, *Thessalonian Correspondence*, 39–49.
Glasson, T. Francis. *The Second Advent: The Origin of the New Testament Doctrine*. 2nd ed. London: Epworth, 1947.
———. "Theophany and Parousia." *NTS* 34 (1988) 259–70.
Goguel, Maurice. *Introduction au Nouveau Testament*. Paris: Éditioins Ernest Leroux, 1925.
Goldingay, John E. *Daniel*. WBC 30. Dallas: Word Books, 1989.
Goldstein, Horst. "ἔκδικος." In *EDNT* 1:408.
Goulder, Michael D. "Silas in Thessalonica." *JSNT* 48 (1992) 87–106.
Grech, P. "The 'Testomonia,' and Modern Hermeneutics." *NTS* 19 (1972–73) 318–24.
Green, Gene L. *The Letters to the Thessalonians*. PNTC, edited by D. A. Carson. Grand Rapids, MI: Eerdmans, 2002.
Green, Michael. *Evangelism through the Local Church*. Nashville: Thomas Nelson, 1992.
Greenberg, Moshe. *Ezekiel 1–20*. AB 22. Garden City, NY: Doubleday, 1983.
Greenlee, J. Harold. *Introduction to New Testament Textual Criticism*. 2nd ed. Peabody, MA: Hendrickson, 1999.
Greeven, H. "συναναμείγνυμι." In *TDNT* 7:852–55.
Grenfell, B. P., A. S. Hunt, G. Turner, and M. T. Lenger, eds. *The Hibeh Papyri*. 2 vols. London: Egypt Exploration Fund, 1906–1955.
Gschnitzer, Fritz. "Politarches." *Paulys Realencyclopädie der classischen Altertumswissenschaft Supplement* 13 (1973) col. 491.
Gundry Volf, Judith M. *Paul and Perseverance: Staying in and Falling Away*. Louisville: Westminster John Knox, 1990.
Gunther, John J. *St. Paul's Opponents and Their Background: A Study of Apocalyptic and Jewish Sectarian Teachings*. NovTSup 35. Leiden: Brill, 1973.
Günther, W. "σέβομαι." In *NIDNTT* 2:91–95.
Haacker, Klaus. "Gallio." In *ABD* 2:901–3.
Habel, Norman C. *The Book of Job*. OTL. Philadelphia: Westminster, 1985.
Haenchen, Ernst. *The Acts of the Apostles: A Commentary*. Translated by B. Noble and G. Shinn. Philadelphia: Westminster, 1971.

Hafemann, Scott J. "Paul and the Exile in Galatians 3-4." In *Exile: Old Testament, Jewish, and Christian Conceptions*, edited by J. M. Scott, 329-71. JSJSup 56, edited by J. J. Collins. Leiden: Brill, 1997.
Hahn, H. C. "ζῆλος." In *NIDNTT* 3:1166-68.
Hamilton, Victor P. "אִישׁ." In *TWOT* 1:76-77.
Hammond, Nicholas G. "Macedonia." In *OCD* 904-5.
———. "The Western Part of the Via Egnatia." *JRS* 64 (1974) 185-94.
Hamp, Vinzenz. "Fire in Connection with God." In *TDOT* 425-28.
Hannah, Darrell D. *Michael and Christ: Michael Traditions and Angel Christology in Early Christianity*. Tübingen: Mohr Siebeck, 1999.
Harder, Günther. *Paulus und das Gebet*. Gütersloh: Bertelsmann, 1936.
Harrington, Daniel J. *Invitation to the Apocrypha*. Grand Rapids, MI: Eerdmans, 1999.
———. *Jude, 2 Peter*. SP 15. Collegeville, MN: Liturgical Press, 2003.
Harnack, Adolf von. *Die Mission Und Ausbreitung Des Christentums In Den Ersten Drei Jahrhunderten*. Leipzig: Hinrichs'sche Buchhandlung, 1924.
Harris, Murray J. "ἀπό." In *NIDNTT* 3:1180-81.
———. *Colossians and Philemon*. Grand Rapids, MI: Eerdmans, 1991.
———. *Jesus as God: The New Testament Use of Theos in Reference to Jesus*. Grand Rapids, MI: Baker Book House, 1992.
———. "παρά." In *NIDNTT* 3:1201-3.
———. "Prepositions and Theology in the Greek New Testament." In *NIDNTT* 3:1171-1215.
Harris, R. L., and G. L. Archer, eds. *Theological Workbook of the Old Testament*. 2 vols. Chicago: Moody Press, 1980.
Harrison, R. K. *Numbers*. WEC. Chicago: Moody Press, 1990.
Hartman, Lars. "The Eschatology of 2 Thessalonians as Included in a Communication." In R. F. Collins, *Thessalonian Correspondence*, 470-85.
———. *Prophecy Interpreted: The Formation of Some Jewish Apocalyptic Texts and the Eschatological Discourse Mark 13*. Translated by N. Tomkinson. Gleerup: Almqvist & Wiksells, 1966.
Hastings, James., ed. *A Dictionary of the Bible: Dealing with Its Language, Literature, and Contents, including the Biblical Theology*. 5 vols. New York: Scribner, 1911-12.
Hatzopoulos, M. B. "Greek International Scholarship on Ancient Macedonia: Some Recent Developments." In *Macedonian Hellenism*, edited by A. M. Tamis, 109-115. Melbourne: River Seine Press, 1990.
Hawthorne, Gerald F. "The Interpretation and Translation of Philippians 128b." *ExpTim* 95 (1983) 80-81.
Hawthorne G. F., R. P. Martin, and D. G. Reid, eds. *The Dictionary of Paul and His Letters*. Downers Grove, IL: InterVarsity Press, 1993.
Hays, Richard B. *Echoes of Scripture in the Letters of Paul*. New Haven, CT: Yale University Press, 1989.
———. *The Faith of Jesus Christ: The Narrative Substructure of Galatians 3:1-4:11*. Grand Rapids, MI: Eerdmans, 2002.
Heil, John P. "The Double Meaning of the Narrative of Universal Judgment in Matthew 25:31-46." *JSNT* 69 (1998) 3-14.
———. "Ezekiel 34 and the Narrative of the Shepherd and Sheep Metaphor in Matthew." *CBQ* 55 (1993) 698-708.

Hemer, Colin J. *The Book of Acts in the Setting of Hellenistic History*. WUNT 49. Tübingen: Mohr, 1989.

———. "Luke the Historian." *BJRL* 60 (1977) 28–52.

Hendrix, Holland L. "Thessalonica." In *ABD* 6:523–27.

———. "Thessalonica, Thessalonians." In *Encyclopedia of Early Christianity*, edited by Everett Ferguson, 2:1125–27. New York: Garland, 1997.

———. "Thessalonicans Honor Romans." ThD diss., Harvard Divinity School, 1984.

Hengel, Martin. *Acts and the History of Earliest Christianity*. Translated by J. Bowden. Philadelphia: Fortress, 1980.

———. *The Pre-Christian Paul*. Translated by J. Bowden. London: SCM Press, 1991.

Hengel, Martin, and Anna Maria Schwemer. *Paul between Damascus and Antioch: The Unknown Years*. Translated by J. Bowden. Louisville: Westminster John Knox, 1997.

Herbert, A. S. *The Book of the Prophet Isaiah: Chapters 40–66*. Cambridge: Cambridge University Press, 1975.

Herodotus. Translated by A. D. Godley. 4 vols. Loeb Classical Library. Cambridge, MA: Harvard University, 1969–82.

Hester, James D. *Paul's Concept of Inheritance: A Contribution to the Understanding of the Heilsgeschichte*. Edinburgh: Oliver & Boyd, 1968.

Hickling, C. J. A. "The Portrait of Paul in Acts 26." In *Les Actes des Apôtres: Traditions, Rédaction, Théologie*, 499–503. BETL 48. Gembloux: Leuven University Press, 1979.

Hiebert, D. Edmond. *The Thessalonian Epistles: A Call to Readiness*. 4th ed. Chicago: Moody Press, 1977.

Hill, David. *Greek Words and Hebrew Meanings: Studies in the Semantics of Soteriological Terms*. SNTSMS 5. Cambridge: Cambridge University Press, 1967.

Hill, Judith L. "Establishing the Church in Thessalonica." PhD diss., Duke University, 1990.

Hock, Ronald F. "Paul's Tentmaking and the Problem of His Social Class." *JBL* 97 (1978) 555–64.

Holland, Glenn. "Let No One Deceive You in Any Way: 2 Thessalonians as a Reformulation of the Apocalyptic Tradition." *SBLSP* 24:327–41. Atlanta: Scholars Press, 1985.

———. *The Tradition That You Received from Us: 2 Thessalonians in the Pauline Tradition*. Tübingen: Mohr Siebeck, 1988.

Holland, Tom. *Contours of Pauline Theology: A Radical New Survey of the Influences on Paul's Biblical Writings*. Scotland: Mentor Imprint, 2004.

Holley, George H. *Greek Thought in the New Testament*. New York: MacMillan, 1928.

Hornblower, S., and A. Spawforth, eds. *The Oxford Classical Dictionary*. Oxford: Oxford University Press, 1996.

Horsley, G. H. R. "The Politarchs." In *The Book of Acts in Its Graeco-Roman Setting*, edited by David W. J. Gill and Conrad Gempf, pages 419–31. Vol. 2 of *The Book of Acts in Its First Century Setting*, edited by Bruce W. Winter. Grand Rapids, MI: Eerdmans, 1993.

Horsley, G. H. R., S. R. Llewelyn, R. A. Kearsley, and M. Harding, eds. *New Documents Illustrating Early Christianity*. North Ryde, NSW: Ancient History Documentary Research Centre, Macquarie University, 1981–.

Howard, D. M. "נהל." In *NIDOTTE* 1:861–64.

Hubbard, D. A. "Hope in the Old Testament." *TynBul* 34 (1983) 33–59.

Hubbard, Robert L. "Dynamistic and Legal Language in Complaint Psalms." PhD diss., Claremont Graduate School, 1980.
Hughes, Frank W. *Early Christian Rhetoric and 2 Thessalonians*. JSNTSup 30. Sheffield: JSOT Press, 1989.
Hunt, A. S., J. de M. Johnson, V. Martin, C. H. Roberts, and E. G. Turner, eds. *Catalogue of the Greek and Latin Papyri in the John Rylands Library, Manchester*. 4 vols. Manchester: Manchester University Press, 1911–52.
Ignatius. *The Letter to the Ephesians*. In *The Apostolic Fathers*, translated by K. Lake. 2 vols. Loeb Classical Library. Cambridge, MA: Harvard University, 1912–13.
Irenaeus. *Against Heresies*. Vol. 55 of *Ancient Christian Writers*, edited by W. J. Burghardt, T. C. Lawler, and J. J. Dillon. New York: Paulist Press, 1992.
Isocrates. Translated by L. Van Hook and G. Norlin. 3 vols. Loeb Classical Library. Cambridge: Harvard University, 1968–80.
Jenni, Ernst. "יום." In *TLOT* 2:526–40.
Jenni, E., and C. Westermann, eds. *Theological Lexicon of the Old Testament*. Translated by M. E. Biddle. 3 vols. Peabody, MA: Hendrickson, 1997.
Jerome. *Commentariorum Epistolam Ad Philemonem*. Edited by J. P. Migne. *Patrologiae latinae 26*. 217 vols. Paris: Garnier, 1844–64.
Jervell, Jacob. *The Unknown Paul: Essays on Luke-Acts and Early Christian History*. Minneapolis: Augsburg, 1984.
Jewett, Robert. "The Agitators and the Galatian Congregation." *NTS* 17 (1971) 198–212.
———. *A Chronology of Paul's Life*. Philadelphia: Fortress, 1979.
———. "The Form and Function of the Homiletic Benediction." *AThR* 51 (1969) 18–34.
———. "The Law and the Coexistence of Jews and Gentiles in Romans." *Int* 39 (1985) 341–56.
———. "A Matrix of Grace: The Theology of 2 Thessalonians as a Pauline Letter." In *Thessalonians, Philippians, Galatians, Philemon*, 63–70. Vol. 1 of *Pauline Theology*, edited by J. Bassler. Minneapolis: Fortress, 1991.
———. "Tenement Churches and Communal Meals in the Early Church: The Implications of Form-Critical Analysis of 2 Thessalonians 3:10." *BR* 38 (1993) 23–43.
———. *The Thessalonian Correspondence: Pauline Rhetoric and Millenarian Piety*. Philadelphia: Fortress, 1986.
Johnson, Luke T. *The Acts of the Apostles*. SP 5. Collegeville, MN: Liturgical Press, 1992.
———. *The First and Second Letters to Timothy*. AB 35a. New York: Doubleday, 2001.
Johnson, S. Lewis. "God Gave Them Up: A Study in Divine Retribution." *BSac* 129 (1972) 124–33.
Johnson, Sherman E. "The Apostle Paul in Macedonia." *LTQ* 18, no. 3 (1983) 75–83.
Jones, A. H. M. *The Greek City from Alexander to Justinian*. Oxford: Clarendon, 1940. Reprint, Oxford: Oxford University Press, 1960.
Josephus. Translated by H. St. J. Thackeray. 10 vols. Loeb Classical Library. Cambridge, MA: Harvard University, 1926–65.
Joubert, Stephan J. "Persuasion in the Letter of Jude." *JSNT* (1995) 75–87.
Judge, E. A. "The Decrees of Caesar at Thessalonica." *RTR* 30 (Jan–Apr, 1971) 1–7.
———. *The Social Pattern of Christian Groups in the First Century*. London: Tyndale, 1960.
Kaiser, Otto. *Isaiah 13–39*. OTL. Philadelphia: Westminster, 1974.
Kaiser, W. "לכד." In *TWOT* 1:479–80.

Kapelrud, Arvid S. *The Message of the Prophet Zephaniah: Morphology and Ideas.* Oslo: Universitetsforlaget, 1975.

Käsemann, Ernst. *An die Römer.* HNT 8a. Tübingen: Mohr Siebeck, 1974.

Katz, Peter. "Εν πυρί φλογός." *ZNW* 46 (1955) 133–38.

Kaye, B. N. "Acts' Portrait of Silas." *NovT* 21 (1979) 13–26.

Kennedy, H. A. A. "The Epistle of Paul to the Philippians." In *The Expositor's Greek Testament*, edited by W. R. Nicoll, 3:399–473. Grand Rapids, MI: Eerdmans, 1983.

———. *St. Paul's Conception of the Last Things.* London: Hodder & Stoughton, 1904.

Keener, Craig S. *Matthew.* IVP New Testament Commentary Series 1. Downers Grove, IL: InterVarsity Press, 1997.

Keesmaat, Sylvia C. "In the Face of the Empire: Paul's Use of Scripture in the Shorter Epistles." In *Hearing the Old Testament in the New Testament*, edited by S. E. Porter, 182–212. Grand Rapids, MI: Eerdmans, 2006.

———. *Paul and His Story: (Re)Interpreting the Exodus Tradition.* JSNTSup 181. Sheffield: Sheffield Academic Press, 1999.

Kilgallen, John J. "The Function of Stephen's Speech (Acts 2–53)." *Bib* 70 (1989) 173–93.

Kim, Johann D. *God, Israel, and the Gentiles: Rhetoric and Situation in Romans 9–11.* SBLDS 176. Atlanta: Society of Biblical Literature, 2000.

King, Greg A. "The Day of the Lord in Zephaniah." *BSac* 152 (1995) 16–32.

Kittel, Gerhard. "ἄγγελος in the NT." In *TDNT* 1:74–87.

Kittel, G., and G. Friedrich, eds. *Theological Dictionary of the New Testament.* Translated and edited by Geoffrey W. Bromiley. Grand Rapids, MI: Eerdmans, 1964–76.

Klassen, William. "Coals of Fire: Sign of Repentance or Revenge?" *NTS* 9 (1962) 337–50.

Klein, Ralph W. *Israel in Exile: A Theological Interpretation.* Philadelphia: Fortress, 1979.

Klein, Robert W. "The Day of the Lord." *Concordia Theological Monthly* 39 (1968) 517–25.

Klein, William W. "A Semantic Analysis of Paul's Election Vocabulary." PhD diss., University of Aberdeen, 1977.

Klingbeil, M. G. "Exile." In *DOTP* 246–49.

Knierim, Rolf P., and George W. Coats. *Numbers.* FOTL 4. Grand Rapids, MI: Eerdmans, 2005.

Knight, George W. *The Pastoral Epistles.* NIGTC. Grand Rapids, MI: Eerdmans, 1992.

Knight, Jonathon. *2 Peter and Jude.* NTG. Sheffield: Sheffield Academic Press, 1995.

Koester, Craig. *Hebrews.* AB 36. New York: Doubleday, 2001.

Koester, Helmut. "From Paul's Eschatology to the Apocalyptic Schemata of 2 Thessalonians." In R. F. Collins, *Thessalonian Correspondence*, 441–48.

———. *History and Literature of Early Christianity.* Vol. 2 of *Introduction to the New Testament*, edited by R. F. Funk. Philadelphia: Fortress, 1982.

———. *Paul and His World: Interpreting the New Testament in Its Context.* Minneapolis: Fortress, 2007.

Köhler, Wilhem. "παρά." In *EDNT* 3:12–13.

Konkel, A. H. "לבד." In *NIDOTTE* 2:800–1.

Krentz, Edgar. "Through a Lens of Faith: Theology and Fidelity in 2 Thessalonians." In *Thessalonians, Philippians, Galatians, Philemon*, edited by J. Bassler, 52–62. Vol. 1 of *Pauline Theology*, edited by J. Bassler. Minneapolis: Fortress, 1991.

Krodel, Gerhard. "2 Thessalonians." In *The Deutero-Pauline Letters: Ephesians, Colossians, 2 Thessalonians, 1-2 Timothy, Titus*, edited by G. Krodel. Rev. ed. Minneapolis: Fortress, 1993.

———. "The 'Religious Power of Lawlessness' (*Katechon*) as Precursor of the 'Lawless One' (*Anomos*) 2 Thess 2:6-7." *CurTM* 17 (1990) 440-46.

Kühlewein, J. "קרב." In *TLOT* 3:1164-69.

Kurze, Georg. *Der Engels: Und Teufelsglaube des Apostels Paulus*. Freiburg im Breisgau: Herdersche, 1915.

Lake, K. "Proselytes and God-Fearers." In *Additional Notes to the Commentary*, edited by K. Lake and H. J. Cadbury, 74-96. Vol. 5 of *The Beginning of Christianity: The Acts of the Apostles*, edited by F. J. F. Jackson and K. Lake. Grand Rapids, MI: Baker Book House, 1966.

Lambrecht, Jan. "Loving God and Steadfastly Awaiting Christ: 2 Thessalonians 3:5." *ETL* 76 (2000) 435-41.

Lamp, Jeffrey S. "Paul, the Law, Jews, and Gentiles." *JETS* 42 (1999) 37-51.

Lampe, Peter. "Paul, Patrons, and Clients." In *Paul in the Greco Roman World*, edited by J. P. Sampley, 488-532. Harrisburg: Trinity, 2003.

Lang, F. "Fire as a Means of Divine Judgment." In *TDNT* 6:934-47.

———. "Fire in the Greek and Hellenistic World." In *TDNT* 6:928-33.

Lanier, David E. "The Day of the Lord in the New Testament: A Historical and Exegetical Analysis of Its Background and Usage." PhD diss., Southwestern Baptist Theological Seminary, 1988.

LaRondelle, Hans K. *Our Creator Redeemer: An Introduction to Biblical Covenant Theology*. Berrien Springs, MI: Andrews University Press, 2005.

———. "Paul's Prophetic Outline in 2 Thessalonians 2." *AUSS* 21 (1983) 61-69.

Le Tellier, Robert I. *Day in Mamre Night in Sodom: Abraham and Lot in Genesis 18 and 19*. BIS 10. Leiden: Brill, 1995.

Lebram, J. C. H. "König Antiochus Im Buch Daniel." *VT* 25 (1975) 737-72.

Leclerc, Thomas L. *Yahweh Is Exalted in Justice: Solidarity and Conflict in Isaiah*. Minneapolis: Fortress, 2001.

Lenski, R. C. H. *The Interpretation of St. Paul's Epistles to the Colossians, to the Thessalonians, and to Timothy, to Titus and to Philemon*. Columbus: Wartburg Press, 1946.

Levinskaya, Irina. *The Book of Acts in Its Diaspora Setting*. Vol. 5 of *The Book of Acts in Its First Century Setting*, edited by Bruce W. Winter. Grand Rapids, MI: Eerdmans, 1996.

Levinsohn, Stephen H. *Textual Connections in Acts*. SBLMS 31. Atlanta: Scholars Press, 1987.

Lewis, J. P. "נמל." In *TWOT* 1:166-67.

Liddell, Henry George, and Robert Scott. *A Greek-English Lexicon*, 9th ed. Revised by Henry Stuart Jones and Roderick McKenzie. Oxford: Clarendon, 1940; Supplement, 1996.

Liedke, G. "שפט." In *TLOT* 3:1392-99.

Lightfoot, J. B. "The Church of Thessalonica." In *Biblical Essays*, 253-69. London: Macmillan, 1893. Reprint, Grand Rapids, MI: Baker Book House, 1979.

———. *Notes of the Epistles of St. Paul: 1 and 2 Thessalonians, 1 Corinthians 1-7, Romans 1-7, and Ephesians 1:1-14*. Grand Rapids, MI: Zondervan, 1957.

Lillie, William. "The Pauline House-tables." *ExpTim* 86 (1974-75) 179-83.

Lindars, Barnabas. "The Place of the Old Testament in the Formation of New Testament Theology." *NTS* 23 (1975–77) 59–66.

———. "Re-Enter the Apocalyptic Son of Man." *NTS* 22 (1976) 52–72.

Lindsey, F. Duane. *The Servant Songs: A Study in Isaiah*. Chicago: Moody Press, 1985.

Lipinvski, E. "The Obligation to Take Vengeance." In *DOTP* 10:3–9.

Livy. Translated by B. O. Foster, E. T. Sage, and A. C. Schlesinger. 14 vols. Loeb Classical Library. Cambridge, MA: Harvard University, 1966–84.

Loh, I-Jin, and Eugene A. Nida. *A Translators Handbook on Paul's Letter to the Philippians*. Stuttgart: United Bible Societies, 1977.

Longenecker, Richard. *The Origin and Nature of Paul's Christianity: Paul, Apostle of Liberty*. New York: Harper & Row, 1964. Reprint, Grand Rapids, MI: Baker Book House, 1976.

———. "Paul's Early Eschatology." *NTS* 31 (1985) 85–95.

Longman, Tremper. "The Divine Warrior: The New Testament Use of an Old Testament Motif." *WTJ* (1982) 290–307.

Longman, Tremper, and Daniel G. Reid. *God Is a Warrior*. Grand Rapids, MI: Zondervan, 1995.

Louw, J. P., and E. A. Nida. *Greek-English Lexicon of the New Testament: Based on Semantic Domains*. 2nd ed. New York: United Bible Societies, 1989.

Lowery, David K. "God as Father with Special Reference to Matthew's Gospel." PhD diss., University of Aberdeen, 1987.

Lucian. Translated by A. M. Harmon, K. Kilburn, and M. D. Macleod. 8 vols. Loeb Classical Library. Cambridge, MA: Harvard University Press, 1961–79.

Lührman, Dieter. "The Beginnings of the Church at Thessalonica." In *Greeks, Romans, and Christians*, edited by D. L. Balch, E. Ferguson, and W. A. Meeks, 237–49. Minneapolis: Fortress, 1990.

Lünemann, Gottlieb. *The Epistles to the Thessalonians. Critical and Exegetical Commentary on the New Testament*. Edited by Heinrich August Wilhelm Meyer. Translated from German by Paton J. Gloag. 3rd ed. Edinburgh: T&T Clark, 1880.

Lust, J., E. Eynikel, and K. Hauspie, eds. *A Greek-English Lexicon of the Septuagint*. 2 vols. Stuttgart: Deutsche Bibelgesellschaft, 1992.

Lyall, Francis. *Slaves, Citizens, Sons: Legal Metaphors in the Epistles*. Grand Rapids, MI: Zondervan, 1984.

Lysias. Translated by W. R. M. Lamb. Loeb Classical Library. Cambridge, MA: Harvard University, 1976.

Maccoby, Hyam. *The Mythmaker: Paul and the Invention of Christianity*. New York: Harper & Row, 1986.

———. *Paul and Hellenism*. London: SCM Press, 1991.

Magdalene, F. Rachel. "On the Scales of Righteousness: Law and Story in the Book of Job." PhD diss., Iliff School of Theology, 2003.

Malherbe, Abraham. "The Inhospitality of Diotrephes." In *God's Christ and His People*, edited by J. Jervell and W. A. Meeks, 223–26. Oslo: Universitetsforlaget, 1977.

———. *The Letters to the Thessalonians*. AB. New York: Doubleday, 2000.

———. *Paul and the Thessalonians: The Philosophic Tradition of Pastoral Care*. Philadelphia: Fortress, 1987.

Malul, Meir. "Adoption of Foundlings in the Bible and Mesopotamian Documents: A Study of Some Legal Metaphors in Ezekiel 16:1–7." *JSOT* 46 (1990) 97–126.

Manson, Thomas W. *The Sayings of Jesus*. London: SCM Press, 1950.

———. "St. Paul in Greece." *BJRL* 35 (1952–53) 428–47.

———. *Studies in the Gospels and Epistles*. Edited by Matthew Black. Philadelphia: Westminster, 1962.

Manus, C. U. "Luke's Account of Paul in Thessalonica." In R. F. Collins, *Thessalonian Correspondence*, 27–38.

Marguerat, Daniel. *Le Jugement dans l'Évangile de Matthieu*. Genève: Labor et Fides, 1981.

———. *The First Christian Historian: Writing the Acts of the Apostles*. Translated by K. McKinney, G. J. Laughery, and R. Bauckham. SNTSMS 121. Cambridge: Cambridge University Press, 2002.

Marshall, I. Howard. *1 and 2 Thessalonians*. NCBC. Grand Rapids, MI: Eerdmans, 1983.

———. *Commentary on Luke*. NIGTC 3. Grand Rapids, MI: Eerdmans, 1978.

———. "Election and Calling to Salvation in 1 and 2 Thessalonians." In R. F. Collins, *Thessalonian Correspondence*, 259–76.

———. *The Gospel of Luke*. NIGTC 3. Grand Rapids, MI: Eerdmans, 1978.

———. *Kept by the Power of God: A Study of Perseverance and Falling Away*. London: Epworth, 1969.

———. *Luke: Historian and Theologian*. 3rd rev. ed. Downers Grove, IL: InterVarsity Press, 1998.

———. *Pastoral Epistles*. ICC. Edinburgh: T&T Clark, 1999.

Martin, George. "Psalm 44: Suffering for the Sake of God." In *The Bible on Suffering: Social and Political Implications*, edited by A. J. Tambasco, 18–33. New York: Paulist Press, 2001.

Marxsen, Willi. *Introduction to the New Testament*. Philadelphia: Fortress, 1970.

McClain, T. Van. "The Pretribulation Rapture: A Doubtful Doctrine." In *Looking into the Future: Evangelical Studies in Eschatology*, edited by D. W. Baker, 233–45. Grand Rapids, MI: Baker Academic, 2001.

McDonald, Lee M., and Stanley Porter. *Early Christianity and Its Sacred Literature*. Peabody, MA: Hendrickson, 2000.

McGaughy, Lane C. *Toward a Descriptive Analysis of Εἶναι as a Linking Verb in the Greek New Testament*. Missoula, MT: Society of Biblical Literature, 1972.

McKay, John. *Paul: His Life and Teaching*. Grand Rapids, MI: Baker Academic, 2003.

McKay, Kenneth L. *A New Syntax of the Verb in New Testament Greek: An Aspectual Approach*. New York: Peter Lang, 1994.

McRay, J. P. "Thessalonica." In *DNTB* 1231–33.

Meadowcroft, Tim. "Who Are the Princes of Persia and Greece (Daniel 10)? Pointers Towards the Danielic Vision of Earth ad Heaven." *JSOT* 29 (2004) 99–113.

Mealy, J. Webb. *After the Thousand Years: Resurrection and Judgment in Revelation 20*. JSNTSup 70. Sheffield: Sheffield Academic Press, 1992.

Mearns, C. L. "Early Eschatological Development in Paul: The Evidence of I and II Thessalonians." *NTS* 27 (1981) 137–57.

———. "The Son of Man Trajectory and Eschatological Development." *ExpTim* 97 (1985) 8–12.

Meeks, Wayne A. *The First Urban Christians: The Social World of the Apostle Paul*. New Haven, CT: Yale University Press, 1983.

———. *The Origins of Christian Morality: The First Two Centuries*. New Haven, CT: Yale University Press, 1993.

Menken, Maarten J. J. *2 Thessalonians*. London: Routledge, 1994.

———. "Christology in 2 Thessalonians: A Transformation of Pauline Tradition." *EstBib* 54 (1996) 501–522.

———. "Paradise Regained or Still Lost? Eschatology and Disorderly Behavior in 2 Thessalonians." *NTS* 38 (April 1992) 271–89.

Metzger, Bruce. *A Textual Commentary on the Greek New Testament*. London: United Bible Societies, 1975.

Metzger, Bruce M., and Roland E. Murphy, eds. *The New Oxford Annotated Bible with the Apocryphal and Deuterocanonical Books*. New York: Oxford University Press, 1991.

Metzger, Paul. *Katechon: II Thess 2:1–12 im Horizont Apokalyptischen Denkens*. BZNW 135. Berlin: de Gruyter, 2005.

Michel, O. "οἰκουμένη." In *TDNT* 5:157–59.

Millar, Fergus. "The Emperor, the Senate, and the Provinces." *JRS* 56 (1966) 156–66.

Milligan, George. *St. Paul's Epistles to the Thessalonians: The Greek Text with Introduction and Notes*. Grand Rapids, MI: Eerdmans, 1908.

Moffatt, James. *Epistle to the Hebrews*. ICC. Edinburgh: T&T Clark, 1924. Reprint, 1948.

Moo, Douglas J. "The Christology of the Early Pauline Letters." In *Contours of Christology in the New Testament*, edited by R. N. Longenecker, 169–92. Grand Rapids, MI: Eerdmans, 2005.

———. *The Epistle to the Romans*. NICNT. Grand Rapids, MI: Eerdmans, 1996.

Moore, Carey A. *Judith*. AB 40. Garden City, NY: Doubleday, 1985.

Mordtmann, J. H. "Funde." *MDAI* 23 (1898) 164–65.

Morgan-Gillman, F. "Jason of Thessalonica (Acts 17:1–9)." In R. F. Collins, *Thessalonian Correspondence*, 39–49.

Morgenthaler, Robert. *Statistik des Neutestamentlichen Wortschatzes*. Zurich: Gotthelf-Verlag, 1982.

Morris, Leon. *The Apostolic Preaching of the Cross*. 3rd. ed. Grand Rapids, MI: Eerdmans, 1965.

———. *The Biblical Doctrine of Judgment*. Grand Rapids, MI: Eerdmans, 1960.

———. *The First and Second Epistles to the Thessalonians*. NICNT. Grand Rapids, MI: Eerdmans, 1991.

———. *The Gospel according to John*. NICNT. Rev. ed. Grand Rapids, MI: Eerdmans, 1995.

———. *The Gospel according to Matthew*. Grand Rapids, MI: Eerdmans, 1992.

Mosley, A. W. "Historical Reporting in the Ancient World." *NTS* 12 (1966) 10–26.

Moule, C. F. D. *An Idiom of the New Testament Greek*. 2nd ed. Cambridge: Cambridge University Press, 1959.

———. "Punishment and Retribution." *SEÅ* 30 (1965) 21–36.

Moulton, James H., and Wilbert F. Howard, eds. *Prolegomena*. Vol. 1 of *A Greek Grammar of the New Testament*, edited by J. H. Moulton. 3rd ed. Edinburgh: T&T Clark, 1908.

Moulton, James H., and George Milligan. *The Vocabulary of the Greek New Testament*. London: Hoddern & Stoughton, 1930. Reprint, Peabody, MA: Hendrickson, 1997.

Moulton, W. F., and A. S. Geden. *Concordance to the Greek New Testament*. Edited by I. Howard Marshall. 6th ed., revised. New York: T&T Clark, 2002.

Mounce, William D. *Pastoral Epistles*. WBC 46. Nashville: Thomas Nelson, 2000.

Müller, H. "ταράσσω." In *NIDNTT* 3:709–711.
Murphy-O'Connor, Jerome. "Lots of God-Fearers? *Theosebeis* in the Aphrodisias Inscription." *RB* 99 (1992) 418–24.
———. *Paul: A Critical Life*. Oxford: Clarendon, 1996.
———. *St. Paul's Corinth: Text and Archaeology*. Wilmington, DE: Michael Glazier, 1983.
Mussies, G. "Greek in Palestine and the Diaspora." In *The Jewish People in the First Century: Historical Geography, Political History, Social, Cultural, and Religious Life, and Institutions*, 1040–64. Vol. 2 of *Compendia Rerum Iudaicarum ad Novum Testamentum*, edited by W. J. Burgers and H. E. Gaylord. Assen: Van Gorcum, 1974.
Nanos, Mark D. *The Irony of Galatians: Paul's Letter in First-Century Context*. Minneapolis: Fortress, 2001.
———. *The Mystery of Romans*. Minneapolis: Fortress, 1996.
Naudé, Jackie A. "בוש." In *NIDOTTE* 1:532–37.
Neagoe, Alexandru. *The Trial of the Gospel: An Apologetic Reading of Luke's Trial Narratives*. SNTSMS 116. Cambridge: Cambridge University Press, 2002.
Neil, William. *The Epistle of Paul to the Thessalonians*. MNTC 12. New York: Harper, 1950.
Neufeld, Thomas R. *Put on the Armour of God: The Divine Warrior from Isaiah to Ephesians*. JSNTSup 140. Sheffield: Sheffield Academic Press, 1997.
Neusner, Jacob. *The Rabbinic Traditions about the Pharisees before 70*. 3 vols. Leiden: Brill, 1971.
Newman, Barclay M., and Eugene A. Nida. *A Handbook on the Acts of the Apostles*. New York: United Bible Societies, 1972.
Neyrey, Jerome H. "The Form and Background of the Polemic in 2 Peter: The Debate over Prophecy and Parousia." PhD diss., Yale University, 1977.
———. "The Symbolic Universe of Luke-Acts: 'They Turn the World Upside Down.'" In *The Social World of Luke-Acts: Models for Interpretation*, edited by J. Neyrey, 271–304. Peabody, MA: Hendrickson, 1991.
Nicholl, Colin R. *From Hope to Despair in Thessalonica*. SNTSMS 126. Cambridge: Cambridge University Press, 2004.
———. "Michael, the Restrainer Removed." *JTS* 51 (2000) 27–53.
Nickelsburg, George W. E. *Ancient Judaism and Christian Origins: Diversity, Continuity, and Transformation*. Minneapolis: Fortress, 2003.
Nickelsburg, George W. E., and Michael E. Stone. *Faith and Piety in Early Judaism: Texts and Documents*. Philadelphia: Fortress, 1983.
Nicole, J., P. Schubert, I. Jornot, and C. Wehrli. *Les Papyrus de Genève*. 3 vols. Amsterdam: Hakkert, 1967–96.
Niehaus, Jeffrey J. *God at Sinai: Covenant and Theophany in the Bible and Ancient Near East*. Grand Rapids, MI: Zondervan, 1995.
Ninow, Friedbert. *Indicators of Typology with the Old Testament: The Exodus Motif*. Frankfurt: Peter Lang, 2001.
Noack, B. "A Jewish Gospel in a Hellenistic World." *StudTheol* 32 (1978) 45–55.
Noack, Christian. *Gottesbewußtsein: Exegetische Studien zur Soteriologie und Mystik bei Philo von Alexandrien*. WUNT 116. Tübingen: Mohr Siebeck, 2000.

Nock, A. D. *St. Paul.* Vol. 186 of *The Home University Library of Modern Knowledge*, edited by G. N. Clark and G. R. De Beer. London: Oxford University Press, 1938. Reprint, 1948.

Nolland, John. *Luke: 18:35–24:53.* WBC 35c. Dallas: Word Books, 1993.

Noth, Martin. *Exodus: A Commentary.* Translated by J. S. Bowden. Philadelphia: Westminster, 1962.

O'Brien, Peter T. *Colossians, Philemon.* WBC 44. Waco, TX: Word Books, 1982.

———. *The Epistle to the Philippians.* NIGTC. Grand Rapids, MI: Eerdmans, 1991.

———. *Introductory Thanksgivings in the Letters Of Paul.* Leiden: Brill, 1977.

O'Sullivan, Firmin. *The Egnatian Way.* Newton Abbot: David & Charles, 1972.

Oropeza, B. J. "Apostasy in the Wilderness: Paul's Message to the Corinthians in a State of Eschatological Liminality." *JSNT* 75 (1999) 69–86.

———. *Paul and Apostasy: Eschatology, Perseverance, and Falling Away in the Corinthian Congregation.* WUNT 115. Tübingen: Mohr Siebeck, 2000.

Osborne, Grant R. *Revelation.* BECNT. Grand Rapids: Baker Academics, 2002.

Oxyrhynchus Papyri. 68 vols. London: Egypt Exploration Society in Graeco-Roman Memoirs, 1898–2003.

Papazoglou, Fanoula. "Macedonia under the Romans." In *Macedonia, 4000 years of Greek History and Civilization*, edited by M. B. Sakellariou, 192–207. Athens: Ekdotike Athenon, 1983.

Papyri graecae magicae: Die griechischen Zauberpapyri. Edited by K. Preisendanz. Stuttgart: Teubner, 1973–74.

Paul, Shalom M. "Unrecognized Biblical Legal Idioms in the Light of Comparative Akkadian Expressions." *RB* 86 (1979) 231–39.

Peels, H. G. L. *The Vengeance of God: The Meaning of the Root NQM and the Function of the NQM-Texts in the Context of Divine Revelation in the Old Testament.* OtSt 31. Leiden: Brill, 1995.

Perdue, Leo G. *Wisdom in Revolt: Metaphorical Theology in the book of Job.* JSOTSup 112. Sheffield: Sheffield Academic Press, 1991.

Perrin, N., and D. C. Duling. *The New Testament: An Introduction.* Edited by R. Ferm. 2nd ed. New York: Harcourt Brace Jovanovich, 1982.

Pervo, Richard I. *Profit with Delight: The Literary Genre of the Acts of the Apostles.* Philadelphia: Fortress, 1987.

Pesch, Rudolf. *Die Apostelgeschichte.* EKKNT 5.2. Neukirchen-Vluyn: Neukirchener Verlag, 1986.

Philo. Translated by F. H. Colson and G. H. Whitaker. 12 vols. Loeb Classical Library. Cambridge, MA: Harvard University Press, 1968–85.

Photius. *Ad Amphilochium Quaestio.* Edited by J. P. Migne. *Patrologia graeca 101.* 162 vols. Paris, 1857–86.

Plato. Translated by R. G. Bury, H. N. Fowler, and W. R. M. Lamb. 12 vols. Loeb Classical Library. Cambridge, MA: Harvard University, 1975–84.

Plevnik, Joseph. *Paul and the Parousia: An Exegetical and Theological Investigation.* Peabody, MA: Hendrickson, 1997.

Pobee, John S. *Persecution and Martyrdom in the Theology of Paul.* JSNTSup 6. Sheffield: JSOT Press, 1985.

Polhill, John B. *Acts.* NAC 26. Nashville: Broadman Press, 1992.

———. "Hope in the Lord: Introduction to 1–2 Thessalonians." *SBJT* 3 (1999) 22–44.

———. *Paul and His Letters.* Nashville: Broadman & Holman, 1999.

Polybius. Translated by W. R. Paton. 6 vols. Loeb Classical Library. Cambridge, MA: Harvard University, 1922–27.

Polycarp. *Letter to the Philippians.* In *The Apostolic Fathers,* translated by K. Lake. 2 vols. Loeb Classical Library. Cambridge, MA: Harvard University, 1912–13.

Pond, Eugene W. "The Background and the Timing of the Judgment of the Sheep and the Goats." *BSac* 159 (2002) 201–220.

Portefaix, Lilian. *Sisters Rejoice: Paul's Letter to the Philippians and Luke-Acts as Seen by First-Century Philippian Women.* ConBNT 20. Stockholm: Almqvist & Wiksell, 1988.

Porter, Stanley E. *Idioms of the Greek New Testament.* 2nd ed. Sheffield: Sheffield Academic Press, 1999.

———. *The Paul of Acts: Essays in Literary Criticism, Rhetoric, and Theology.* WUNT 115. Tübingen: Mohr Siebeck, 1999.

———. *Verbal Aspect in the Greek of the New Testament, with Reference to Tense and Mood.* Vol. 1 of *Studies in Biblical Greek,* edited by D. A. Carson. New York: Peter Lang, 1993.

Powell, Charles E. "The Identity of the 'Restrainer' in 2 Thessalonians 2:6–7." *BSac* 154 (1997) 320–32.

Powell, Mark A. "Reading Acts as History." *AsTJ* 46, no.1 (1991) 49–62.

Powery, Emerson B. *Jesus Reads Scripture: The Function of Jesus' Use of Scripture in the Synoptic Gospels,* edited by R. A. Culpepper and R. Rendtorff. BIS 63. Leiden: Brill, 2003.

Prat, Ferdinand. *The Theology of Saint Paul.* Translated by J. L. Stoddard. 2 vols. Westminster: Newman Bookshop, 1958.

Preisigke, Friedrich. *Wörterbuch der griechischen Papyrusurkunden.* Berlin: Selbstverlag der Erben, 1925–31.

Preuss, H. D. "The Coming Judgment." In *TDOT* 2:34–37.

Proctor, John. "Fire in God's House: Influence of Malachi 3 in the NT." *JETS* 36 (1993) 9–14.

Quarles, Charles L. "The ΑΠΟ of 2 Thessalonians 1:9 and the Nature of Eternal Punishment." *WTJ* (1997) 201–211.

Quell, G. "The Concept of Law in the OT." In *TDNT* 2:174–78.

Rabello, A. M. "The Legal Condition of the Jews in the Roman Empire." In *Aufstieg und Niedergang der Römischen Welt* 2.13, edited by H. Temporini and W. Haase. Berlin: de Gruyter, 1980.

Rahlfs, Alfred, ed. *Septuaginta.* Stuttgart: Deutsche Bibelgesellschaft, 1935. Reprint, 1979.

Räisänen, H. *Paul and the Law.* Tübingen: Mohr, 1983.

Raitt, Thomas M. *Theology of Exile: Judgment and Deliverance in Jeremiah and Ezekiel.* Philadelphia: Fortress, 1977.

Rajak, Tessa. "Jews and Christians and Groups in a Pagan World." In *To See Ourselves as Others See Us: Christians, Jews, "Others" in Late Antiquity,* edited by J. Neusner and E. S. Frerichs, 247–62. Chico, CA: Scholars Press, 1985.

———. "Was There a Roman Charter for the Jews?" *JRS* 74 (1984) 107–123.

Ramsay, William M. *The Cities of St. Paul: Their Influence on His Life and Thought.* London: Hodder & Stoughton, 1907. Reprint, Grand Rapids, MI: Baker Book House, 1979.

———. *St. Paul the Traveler and the Roman Citizen*. Grand Rapids, MI: Baker Book House, 1951.

Rapske, Brian. *The Book of Acts and Paul in Roman Custody*. Vol. 3 of *The Book of Acts in Its First Century Setting*, edited by Bruce W. Winter. Grand Rapids, MI: Eerdmans, 1994.

———. "Opposition to the Plan of God and Persecution." In *Witness to the Gospel: The Theology of Acts*, edited by I. H. Marshall and D. Peterson. Grand Rapids, MI: Eerdmans, 1998.

Read-Heimerdinger, Jenny. *The Bezan Text of Acts: A Contribution of Discourse Analysis to Textual Criticism*. JSNTSup 236. London: Sheffield Academic Press, 2002.

Reddit, Paul L. "Daniel 11 and the Sociohistorical Setting of the Book of Daniel." *CBQ* 60 (1998) 463–74.

Reed, Jeffery T. "Identifying Theme in the New Testament: Insights from Discourse Analysis." In *Discourse Analysis and Other Topics in Biblical Greek*, edited by S. E. Porter and D. A. Carson, 75–101. Sheffield: Sheffield Academic Press, 1995.

Reider, Joseph. *The Book of Wisdom*. New York: Harper, 1957.

Reimer, David J. "צדק." In *NIDOTTE* 3:744–69.

Reitzenstein, Richard. *Hellenistic Mystery-Religions: Their Basic Ideas and Significance*. Translated by J. Steely. Pittsburgh: Pickwick, 1978.

Richard, Earl J. *First and Second Thessalonians*. SP 11. Collegeville, MN: Liturgical Press, 1995.

Riddlebarger, Kim. *The Man of Sin: Uncovering the Truth about the Antichrist*. Grand Rapids, MI: Baker Books, 2006.

Rider, G. W. "An Investigation of the Granville Sharp Phenomenon and Plurals." ThM thesis, Grace Theological Seminary, 1980.

Riesenfeld, Ernst. "παρά with the Dative." In *TDNT* 5:731–33.

Riesner, Rainer. *Die Frühzeit des Apostels Paulus: Studien zur Chronologie, Missionsstrategie und Theologie*. WUNT 71. Tübingen: Mohr Siebeck, 1994.

Rigaux, Béda. *Saint Paul: Les Épîtres aux Thessaloniciens*. Paris: Gabalds, 1956.

Rissi, Mathias. "κρίσις." In *EDNT* 2:318–21.

Roberts, J. J. M. "Job's Summons to Yahweh: The Exploitation of a Legal Metaphor." *ResQ* 16 (1973) 159–65.

Robertson, A. T. *A Grammar of the Greek New Testament in the Light of Historical Research*. Nashville: Broadman, 1934.

Robinson, J. M., and Helmut Koester. *Trajectories through Early Christianity*. Philadelphia: Fortress, 1971.

Roetzel, Calvin J. "Election/Calling in Certain Pauline Letters: An Experimental Construction." *SBLSP* 29 (1990) 552–69.

———. *Paul: A Jew on the Margins*. Louisville: Westminster John Knox, 2003.

———. *Paul: The Man and the Myth*. Columbia: University of South Carolina, 1998.

Romaniuk, K. "Die 'Gottesfurchtigen' im Neuen Testament: Beitrag zur neutestamentlichen Theologie der Gottesfürcht." *Aeg* 44, no. 1–2 (1964) 66–91.

Rosenblatt, Marie-Eloise. "Under Interrogation: Paul as Witness in Juridical Contexts in Acts and the Implied Spirituality for Luke's Community." PhD diss., Graduate Theological Union, 1987.

Rowland, Christopher. *Christian Origins: The Setting and Character of the Most Important Messianic Sect of Judaism*. 2nd ed. London: SPCK, 2002.

Russell, Ronald. "The Idle in 2 Thess 3:6-12: An Eschatological or a Social Problem?" *NTS* 34 (Jan 1988) 105-119.

Saebø, M. "Theological Usage: בּוֹר׳." In *TDOT* 3:26-31.

Saldarini, Anthony J. *Pharisees, Scribes and Sadducees in Palestinian Society: A Sociological Approach.* Wilmington, DE: Michael Glazier, 1988.

Sand, A. "ἀνταπόδοσις." In *EDNT* 1:107-8.

Sanders, E. P. *Paul.* Oxford: Oxford University Press, 1991.

———. *Paul, the Law, and the Jewish People.* Philadelphia: Fortress, 1983.

Sanders, Jack T. "Christians and Jews in the Roman Empire: A Conversation with Rodney Stark." *SocAn* 53 (1992) 433-45.

Sauer, G. "גמל." In *TLOT* 1:320-21.

———. "נקם." In *TLOT* 2:767-69.

Savran, George W. *Encountering the Divine: Theophany in Biblical Narrative.* JSOTSup 420. London: T&T Clark, 2005.

Schaefer, Konrad R. "Zechariah 14: A Study in Allusion." *CBQ* 57 (1995) 66-91.

Schlatter, Adolf. *Der Evangelist Matthäus: Seine Sprache, sein Ziel, seine Selbständigkeit.* Stuttgart: Calwer Verlag, 1948.

———. *Gottes Gerechtigkeit: Ein Kommentar Zum Römerbrief.* Stuttgart: Calwer Verlag, 1935.

Schlier, H. "ἀποστασία." In *TDNT* 1:512-14.

Schmidt, Daryl. "The Syntactical Style of 2 Thessalonians: How Pauline Is It?" In R. F. Collins, *Thessalonian Correspondence*, 383-93.

Schmithals, Walter. "The Historical Situation of the Thessalonian Epistles." In *Paul and the Gnostics,* translated by J. E. Steely, 123-218. Nashville: Abingdon, 1972.

———. *Paulus und die Gnostiker: Untersuchungen zu den kleinen Paulusbriefen.* Hamburg: Herbert Reich Evangelischer Verlag, 1965.

Schnabel, Eckhard J. *Paul and the Early Church.* Vol. 2 of *Early Christian Mission.* Downers Grove, IL: InterVarsity Press, 2004.

Schneider, Gerhard. "ἀγοραῖος." In *EDNT* 1:23.

———. "ἀπό." In *EDNT* 1:124-25.

———. *Die Apostelgeschichte.* HTKNT 2. Freiburg: Herder, 1982.

———. "δικαίως." In *EDNT* 1:324-25.

———. "δίκη." In *EDNT* 1:336.

———. "παιδεύω." In *EDNT* 3:3-4.

———. "The Specific Uses of ἔρξομαι." In *EDNT* 2:666-84.

Schnelle, Udo. *Apostle Paul: His Life and Theology.* Translated by M. E. Boring. Grand Rapids, MI: Baker Academic, 2005.

Scholnick, Sylvia Huberman. "The Meaning of *Mišpāt* in the Book of Job." *JBL* 101 (1982) 521-29.

Schrage, W. "συναγωγή in the Septuagint." In *TDNT* 7:802-5.

Schreiner, Thomas. "Did Paul Believe in Justification by Works? Another Look at Romans 2." *BBR* 3 (1993) 131-58.

———. *Paul: Apostle of God's Glory in Christ.* Downers Grove, IL: InterVarsity Press, 2001.

———. *Romans.* BECNT 6. Grand Rapids, MI: Baker Books, 1998.

Schreiner, Thomas R., and Ardel B. Caneday. *The Race Set before Us: A Biblical Theology of Perseverance and Assurance.* Downers Grove, IL: InterVarsity Press, 2001.

Schrenk, G. "The Concept of Law in the OT." In *TDNT* 2:175.

———. "δίκαιος in the Greek and Hellenistic World." In *TDNT* 2:174–225.
———. "δίκη in the NT." In *TDNT* 2:181–82.
———. "ἐκδικέω, ἔκδικος, ἐκδίκησις." In *TDNT* 2:443–46.
Schroeder, Christoph O. *History, Justice, and the Agency of God: A Hermeneutical and Exegetical Investigation on Isaiah and Psalms.* Leiden: Brill, 2001.
Schuler, C. "The Macedonian Politarchs." *CP* 55 (1960) 90–100.
Schultz, Richard. "שׁפט." In NIDOTTE 4:213–220.
Schürer, Emil. *History of the Jewish People in the Age of Jesus Christ (175 B. C.–A. D. 135).* Revised and edited by Geza Vermes, Fergus Millar, Matthew Black, and Martin Goodman. 3 vols. Edinburgh: T&T Clark, 1973–86.
Schwartz, Earl. "The Trials of Jesus and Paul." *JLR* 9 (1991–92) 501–513.
Scott, J. Julius. *Jewish Backgrounds of the New Testament.* Grand Rapids, MI: Baker Books, 1995.
———. "Paul and Late Jewish Eschatology: A Case Study, 1 Thessalonians 4:13–18 and 2 Thessalonians 2:1–12." *JETS* 15 (1972) 133–43.
Seeligmann, I. L. "Zur Terminologie fürdas Gerichtsverfahren im Wortschatz des Biblischen Hebräisch." In *Hebräische Wortforschung.* VTSup 16. Leiden: Brill, 1967.
Seland, Torrey. *Establishment Violence in Philo and Luke: A Study of Non-Conformity to the Torah and Jewish Vigilante Reactions.* BIS 15. Leiden: Brill, 1995.
Seybold, K. "גמל." In *TDOT* 3:23–33.
Sharp, Granville. *Remarks on the Uses of the Definitive Article in the Greek New Testament: Containing Many New Proofs of the Divinity of Christ, from Passages Which Are Wrongly Translated in the Common English Version.* London: Vernor & Hood, 1803.
Shelton, Jo-Ann. *As the Romans Did: A Source Book in Roman Social History.* 2nd ed. New York: Oxford University Press, 1998.
Sherlock, Charles. *The God Who Fights: The War Tradition in Holy Scripture.* RSCT 6. Edinburgh: Mellen, 1993.
Sherwin-White, A. N. *Roman Society and Roman Law in the New Testament.* Oxford: Clarendon, 1963.
Shires, Henry M. *The Eschatology of Paul: In the Light of Modern Scholarship.* Philadelphia: Westminster, 1966.
Showerman, Grant. *Rome and the Romans: A Survey and Interpretation.* New York: Cooper Square, 1969.
Silva, Moisés. *Interpreting Galatians: Explorations in Exegetical Methods.* 2nd ed. Grand Rapids, MI: Baker Academic, 2001.
———. "The Pharisees in Modern Jewish Scholarship." *WTJ* 42 (1979–80) 395–405.
———. *Philippians.* 2nd ed. BECNT. Grand Rapids, MI: Baker Academic, 2005.
Sim, David C. *Apocalyptic Eschatology in the Gospel of Matthew.* SNTSMS 88. Cambridge: Cambridge University Press, 1996.
Simpson, John W. "The City of Thessalonica." In *DPL* 933–34.
———. "Thessalonians, Letters to the." In *DPL* 932–39.
Skeen, Judy. "Not as Enemies, but Kin: Discipline in the Family of God; 2 Thessalonians 3:6–10." *RevExp* 96 (1999) 287–94.
Skinner, Matthew L. *Locating Paul: Places of Custody as Narrative Settings in Acts 21–28.* Academia Biblica 13. Atlanta: Society of Biblical Literature, 2003.

Smallwood, E. Mary. *The Jews under Roman Rule from Pompey to Diocletian: A Study in Political Relations*. Vol. 20 of *Studies in Judaism in Late Antiquity*, edited by J. Neusner. Leiden: Brill, 1981.

Smith, Abraham. *Comfort One Another: Reconstructing the Rhetoric and Audience of 1 Thessalonians*. Louisville: Westminster John Knox, 1995.

Smith, Gary V. *The Prophets as Preachers: An Introduction to the Hebrew Prophets*. Nashville: Broadman & Holman, 1994.

Smith, John M. P. *The Day of Yahweh*. Chicago: University of Chicago Press, 1901.

Soards, Marion L. *The Speeches in Acts: Their Content, Context, and Concerns*. Louisville: Westminster John Knox, 1994.

Spicq, Ceslas. "ἀνατρέφω." In *TLNT* 1:115–16.

———. "δίκαιος." In *TLNT* 1:318–47.

———. "δίκη." In *TLNT* 1:318–20.

———. "ἱκανός." In *TLNT* 2:217–22.

———. "μάρτυς." In *TLNT* 2:447–52.

———. "ταράσσω." In *TLNT* 3:372–76.

———. *L'Épître aux Hébreux*. EBib. 2 vols. Paris: Librairie Lecoffre, 1953.

———. *Les Épîtres Pastorales*. Paris: Gabalda et Cie, 1947.

———. *Theological Lexicon of the New Testament*. Translated and edited by J. D. Ernest. 3 vols. Peabody, MA: Hendrickson, 1994.

Stacy, R. Wayne. "Introduction to the Thessalonian Correspondences." *RevExp* 96 (1999) 177.

Stambaugh, John, and David Balch. *The Social World of the First Christians*. London: SPCK, 1986.

Standhartinger, Angela. "The Origin of the Household Code in the Letter to the Colossians." *JSNT* 79 (2000) 117–30.

Stanley, Christopher D. *Arguing with Scripture: The Rhetoric of Quotations in the Letters of Paul*. New York: T&T Clark International, 2004.

———. "Who's Afraid of a Thief in the Night?" *NTS* 48 (2002) 468–86.

Stanton, Gerald B. *Kept from the Hour: Biblical Evidence for the Pretribulational Return of Christ*. 4th ed. Miami Springs, FL: Schoettle, 1991.

Staples, Peter. "Revelation 16:4–6 and Its Vindication Formula." *NovT* 14 (1972) 280–93.

Stec, D. M. "The Mantle Hidden by Achan." *VT* 41 (1991) 356–59.

Stegemann, Wolfgang. "War der Apostel Paulus ein römischer Bürger?" *ZNW* 78 (1987) 200–229.

———. *Zwischen Synagoge und Obrigkeit: Zur Historischen Situation der Lukanischen Christen*. Göttingen: Vandenhoeck & Ruprecht, 1991.

Steinmann, Andrew E. "Is the Antichrist in Daniel 11?" *BSac* 162 (2005) 195–209.

Stemberger, Günter. *Jewish Contemporaries of Jesus: Pharisees, Sadducees, Essenes*. Minneapolis: Fortress, 1995.

Stenschke, Christoph W. *Luke's Portrait of the Gentile's Prior to Their Coming to Faith*. WUNT 108. Tübingen: Mohr Siebeck, 1999.

Stern, Menahem. *Greek and Latin Authors on Jews and Judaism*. 2 vols. Jerusalem: Israel Academy of Sciences and Humanities, 1976–80.

Still, Todd D. *Conflict at Thessalonica: A Pauline Church and Its Neighbors*. JSNTSup 183. Sheffield: Sheffield Academic Press, 1999.

———. "Paul's Thessalonian Mission." *Southwestern Journal of Theology* 42 (Fall 1999) 4–16.
Stock, Augustine. *The Way in the Wilderness: Exodus, Wilderness, and Moses Themes in Old Testament and New*. Collegeville, MN: Liturgical Press, 1969.
Stott, John R. W., ed. *The Message of Acts: The Spirit, the Church and the World; The Bible Speaks Today*. Downers Grove, IL: InterVarsity Press, 1990.
Strabo. Translated by H. L. Jones. 8 vols. Loeb Classical Library. Cambridge, MA: Harvard University Press, 1967–83.
Strathmann, Hermann. "μάρτυς, μαρτυρέω, μαρτυρία, μαρτύριον." In *TDNT* 4:474–514.
———. "The Use of μαρτύριον." In *TDNT* 4:502–4.
Stuhlmacher, Peter. *Paul's Letter to the Romans*. Translated by S. J. Hafemann. Louisville: Westminster John Knox, 1994.
Stumpff, A. "ζῆλος, ζηλόω, ζηλωτής, παραζηλόω." In *TDNT* 2:877–92.
Suetonius. Translated by J. C. Rolfe. 2 vols. Loeb Classical Library. Cambridge, MA: Harvard University Press, 1979.
Supplementum epigraphicum graecum. 52 vols. Alphen aan den Rijn: Sijthoff & Noordhoff, 1923–2002.
Tacitus. Translated by C. H. Moore and J. Jackson. 5 vols. Loeb Classical Library. Cambridge: Harvard University Press, 1970–81.
Tajra, Harry W. *The Trial of St. Paul: A Juridical Exegesis of the Second Half of the Acts of the Apostles*. Tübingen: Mohr, 1989.
Talbert, Charles H. *Reading Acts: A Literary and Theological Commentary on the Acts of the Apostles*. New York: Crossroad, 1997.
Tate, Marvin E. *Psalms 51–100*. WBC 20. Dallas: Word Books, 1990.
Taylor, Justin. *Les Actes des Deux Apôtres: Commentaire Historique*. EBib 5. Paris: Gabalda et Cie, 1994.
The Tebtunis Papyri. 5 vols. London: Oxford University Press, 1902–2005.
Tertullian. *Against Marcion*. In vol. 3 of the *Ante-Nicene Fathers*, edited by A. Roberts and J. Donaldson. 10 vols. 1885–87. Reprint, Peabody, MA: Hendrickson, 1994.
———. *The Soul*. In vol. 3 of the *Ante-Nicene Fathers*, edited by A. Roberts and J. Donaldson. 10 vols. 1885–87. Reprint, Peabody, MA: Hendrickson, 1994.
———. *On the Resurrection of the Flesh*. In vol. 3 of the *Ante-Nicene Fathers*, edited by A. Roberts and J. Donaldson. 10 vols. 1885–87. Reprint, Peabody, MA: Hendrickson, 1994.
Thatcher, Tom. "The Plot of Gal 3:1–18." *JETS* 40 (1997) 401–410.
Theissen, Gerd. *The Social Setting of Pauline Christianity*. Translated by J. H. Schütz. Philadelphia: Fortress, 1982.
Theophrastus. *The Characters of Theophrastus*. Edited by J. M. Edmonds. Loeb Classical Library. Cambridge, MA: Harvard University Press, 1961.
Thielman, Frank. *Paul and the Law*. Downers Grove, IL: InterVarsity Press, 1994.
Thiselton, Anthony C. *The First Epistle to the Corinthians: A Commentary on the Greek Text*. NIGTC. Grand Rapids, MI: Eerdmans, 2000.
Thrall, Margaret E. *Greek Particles in the New Testament: Linguistics and Exegetical Studies*. NTTS 3. Grand Rapids, MI: Eerdmans, 1962.
Thucydides. Translated by C. Foster. 4 vols. Loeb Classical Library. Cambridge, MA: Harvard University Press, 1975–80.
Thurston, Bonnie. *Reading Colossians, Ephesians and 2 Thessalonians: A Literary and Theological Commentary*. New York: Crossroad, 1995.

Tiemeyer, Lena-Sofia. *Priestly Rites and Prophetic Rage: Post-Exilic Prophetic Critique of Priesthood.* FAT 19. Tübingen: Mohr Siebeck, 2006.
Tobin, Thomas H. *Paul's Rhetoric in Its Context: The Argument of Romans.* Peabody, MA: Hendrickson, 2004.
Tomlinson, Alan. "2 Thessalonians." Kansas City: Midwestern Baptist Theological Seminary, 2001. Photocopied.
Travis, Stephen H. *The Place of Divine Retribution in the Thought of Paul.* Cambridge: Cambridge University Press, 1970.
———. "The Problem of Judgment." *Them* 11 (1986) 52–57.
Trilling, Wolfgang. "ἡμέρα." In *EDNT* 2:119–21.
———. *Der zweite Brief an die Thessalonicher.* EKKNT 14. Neukirchen-Vluyn: Neukirchener Verlag, 1980.
———. *Untersuchungen zum zweiten Thessalonicherbrief.* Leipzig: St. Benno-Verlag, 1972.
Trites, Allison A. "The Importance of Legal Scenes and Language in the Book of Acts." *NovT* 16 (1974) 278–84.
Turner, Nigel. *Syntax.* Vol. 3 of *A Grammar of New Testament Greek*, edited by J. H. Moulton. Edinburgh: T&T Clark, 1963.
Vacalopoulos, Apostolos E. *A History of Thessaloniki.* Translated by T. F. Carney. Thessalonica: Institute for Balkan Studies, 1963.
Van der Lugt, Pieter. *Rhetorical Criticism and the Poetry of the Book of Job.* OtSt 32. Leiden: Brill, 1995.
Van der Minde, H. J. "δίκη." In *EDNT* 1:336.
VanGemeren, Willem A. *Interpreting the Prophetic Word.* Grand Rapids, MI: Academie Books, 1990.
———, ed. *New International Dictionary of Old Testament Theology and Exegesis.* 5 vols. Carlisle: Paternoster, 1997.
———. *The Progress of Redemption: The Story of Salvation from Creation to the New Jerusalem.* Grand Rapids, MI: Baker Books, 1988.
Van Leeuwen, C. "עד." In *TLOT* 2:838–46.
Van Minnen, Peter. "Paul the Roman Citizen." *JSNT* 56 (1994) 43–52.
Van Unnik, W. C. "Luke's Second Book and the Rules of Hellenistic Historiography." In *Les Actes des Apôtres: Traditions, rédaction, théologie*, edited by J. Kremer. Vol. 48 of BETL. Brussels: Duculot, 1979.
———. *Tarsus or Jerusalem: The City of Paul's Youth.* Translated by G. Ogg. London: Epworth, 1962.
Verhoef, Eduard. "The Delay of the Coming of the Lord Is Controlled by God." *BN* 100 (1999) 36–44.
Vermes Geza ed. *The Complete Dead Sea Scrolls in English.* New York: Penguin, 1997.
Vos, Geerhardus. *The Pauline Eschatology.* Grand Rapids, MI: Baker Book House, 1979.
Waddle, Sharon H. "Dubious Praise: The Form and Context of the Participial Hymns in Job 4–14." PhD diss., Vanderbilt University, 1987.
Wagner, J. Ross. "The Heralds of Isaiah and the Mission of Paul: An Investigation of Paul's Use of Isaiah 51–55 in Romans." In *Jesus and the Suffering Servant*, edited by W. H. Bellinger and W. R. Farmer, 193–222. Harrisburg, PA: Trinity, 1998.
Wallace, Daniel B. *The Article with Multiple Substantives Connected by Καί in the New Testament: Semantics and Significance.* Ann Arbor: UMI Dissertation Services, 1995.

———. *The Basics of New Testament Syntax*. Grand Rapids, MI: Zondervan, 2000.

———. *Greek Grammar beyond the Basics: An Exegetical Syntax of the New Testament*. Grand Rapids, MI: Zondervan, 1996.

———. "The Semantic Range of the Article-Noun-KAI'-Noun Plural Construction in the New Testament." *GTJ* (1983) 59–84.

Wanamaker, Charles. *The Epistles to the Thessalonians: A Commentary on the Greek Text*. NIGTC. Grand Rapids, MI: Eerdmans, 1990.

Ward, James M. "The Literary Form and Liturgical Background of Psalm 89." *VT* 11 (1961) 321–39.

Waterman, G. Henry. "The Sources of Paul's Teaching on the 2nd Coming of Christ in 1 and 2 Thessalonians." *JETS* 18 (1975) 105–113.

Watson, Duane F. *Invention, Arrangement, and Style: Rhetorical Criticism of Jude and 2 Peter*. SBLDS 104. Atlanta: Scholars Press, 1988.

Weaver, Dorothy J. "Luke 18:1–8." *Int* 56 (2002) 317–19.

Weber, Kathleen. "The Image of Sheep and Goats in Matthew 25:31–46." *CBQ* 59 (1997) 657–78.

Wedderburn, Alexander J. M. *A History of the First Christians*. London: T&T Clark International, 2004.

Weima, Jeffrey A. D. "The Slaying of Satan's Superman and the Sure Salvation of the Saints: Paul's Apocalyptic Word of Comfort (2 Thessalonians 2:1–17)." *CTJ* 41 (2006) 67–88.

Wells, Colin M. "Roman Empire." In *ABD* 5:801–6.

Wendland, Ernst R. "Can These Bones Live Again: A Rhetoric of the Gospel in Ezekiel 33–37, Part II." *AUSS* 39 (2001) 241–72.

Wenham, David. *The Rediscovery of Jesus' Eschatological Discourse*. Sheffield: JSOT Press, 1984.

Wenham, John W. "The Case for Conditional Immortality." In *Universalism and the Doctrine of Hell*, edited by N. M. de S. Cameron, 161–91. Carlisle: Paternoster, 1992.

Weitbrecht Stanton, H. U. "Turned the World Upside Down." *ExpTim* 44 (1932–33) 526–27.

Wessely, C., L. Mitteis, and R. Duttenhöfer, eds. *Griechische Urkunden der Papyrussammlung zu Leipzig*. Leipzig: Teubner, 1885–2002.

Westblade, Donald J. "Divine Election in Pauline Literature." In *Still Sovereign: Contemporary Perspectives on Election, Foreknowledge, and Grace*, edited by T. R. Schreiner and B. A. Ware, 63–87. Grand Rapids, MI: Baker Books, 2000.

Westermann, Claus. *Das Buch Jesaja: Kapitel 40–66*. ATD 19. Göttingen: Vandenhoeck & Ruprecht, 1966.

White, John L. "Saint Paul and the Apostolic Letter Tradition." *CBQ* 45 (1983) 433–44.

Whitehorne, John. "Antiochus IV Epiphanes." In *ABD* 1:270–71.

Whittaker, Molly. *Jews and Christians: Graeco Roman Views*. Vol. 6 of *Cambridge Commentaries on Writings of the Jewish and Christian World 200 BC to 200 AD*, edited by P. R. Ackroyd, A. R. C. Leaney, and J. W. Packer. Cambridge: Cambridge University Press, 1984.

Wiedemann, T. E. J. *Tiberius to Nero*. Vol. 10 of *The Cambridge Ancient History*, edited by A. Bowman, E. Champlin, and A. Lintott. 2nd ed. Cambridge: Cambridge University Press, 1996.

Wikenhauser, Alfred. *New Testament Introduction*. 4th ed. New York: Herder & Herder, 1963.

Wilder, Terry L. *Pseudonymity, the New Testament, and Deception: An Inquiry into Intention and Reception*. Lanham, MD: University of America Press, 2004.

William, David K. "Judgment and Community: Paul's Use of Apocalyptic and Judgment Language in 1 Corinthians 3:5–4:5." PhD diss., Yale University, 1989.

Williams, David J. *1 and 2 Thessalonians*. New International Biblical Commentary 12. Peabody, MA: Hendrickson, 1992.

———. *Acts*. San Francisco: Harper & Row, 1985.

———. *Paul's Metaphors: Their Context and Character*. Peabody, MA: Hendrickson, 1999.

Wilson, Alistair I. *When Will These Things Happen: A Study of Jesus as Judge in Matthew 21–25*. Cumbria: Paternoster, 2004.

Wilson, A. N. *Paul: The Mind of the Apostle*. New York: Norton, 1997.

Wilson, Todd A. "Wilderness Apostasy and Paul's Portrayal of the Crisis in Galatians." *NTS* 50 (2004) 550–71.

Winter, Bruce. W. *After Paul Left Corinth: The Influence of Secular Ethics and Social Change*. Grand Rapids, MI: Eerdmans, 2001.

———. "If a Man Does Not Wish to Work . . . A Cultural Historical Setting for 2 Thessalonians 3:6–16." *TynBul* 40 (1989) 303–315.

———. *Seek the Welfare of the City: Christians as Benefactors and Citizens*. Grand Rapids, MI: Eerdmans, 1994.

Witherington, Ben. *1 and 2 Thessalonians: A Socio-Rhetorical Commentary*. Grand Rapids, MI: Eerdmans, 2006.

———. *The Acts of the Apostles: A Socio-Rhetorical Commentary*. Grand Rapids, MI: Eerdmans, 1998.

———. *Conflict and Community in Corinth: A Socio-Rhetorical Commentary on 1 and 2 Corinthians*. Grand Rapids, MI: Eerdmans, 1995.

———. *The Paul Quest: The Renewed Search for the Jew of Tarsus*. Downers Grove, IL: InterVarsity Press, 1998.

———. *Women in the Earliest Church*. SNTSMS 59. Cambridge: Cambridge University Press, 1988.

Wodecki, P. Bernard. "*SLH* dans le Livre d'Isaïe." *VT* 34 (1984) 482–87.

Wood, C. T. *The Life, Letters and Religion of St. Paul*. Edinburgh: T&T Clark, 1925. Reprint, 1949.

Wrede, William. *Die Echtheit des zweiten Thessalonicherbriefs untersucht*. Leipzig: Henrichs, 1903.

Wright, J. S. "God." In *NIDNTT* 2:66–90.

Wright, N. T. "New Exodus, New Inheritance: The Narrative Structure of Romans 3–8." In *Romans and the People of God: Essays in Honor of Gordon D. Fee on the Occasion of His 65th Birthday*, edited by S. K. Soderlund and N. T. Wright, 26–35. Grand Rapids, MI: Eerdmans, 1999.

Xenophon. Translated by W. Miller, C. L. Brownson, E. C. Marchant, O. J. Todd, and G. W. Bowersock. 7 vols. Loeb Classical Library. Cambridge, MA: Harvard University Press, 1968–84.

Yinger, Kent L. "Romans 12:14–21 and Nonretaliation in Second Temple Judaism: Addressing Persecution within the Community." *CBQ* 60 (1998) 74–96.

Young, Norman H. "Who's Cursed and Why? (Galatians 3:10–14)." *JBL* 117 (1998) 79–92.

Zahn, Theodor. *Das Evangelium des Matthäus*. Leipzig: Deichert, 1905.

Zenon Papyri: Catalogue général des antiquités égyptiennes du Musée du Caire. Edited by C. C. Edgar. 5 vols. Le Caire: Imprimerie de l'Institut Francais d'Archeologie Orientale, 1925–1940.

Zerwick, Maximilian. *Biblical Greek*. Rome: Pontificii Instituti Biblici, 1963.

Zimmerli, Walther. *Ezekiel 1: A Commentary on the Book of the Prophet Ezekiel, Chapters 1–24*. Translated by R. E. Clements. Philadelphia: Fortress, 1979.

Author Index

A

Abasciano, Brian J., 155, 183
Achtemeier, Elizabeth., 163, 183
Ahn, Yong-Sik Joseph., 94, 95, 96, 162, 164, 167, 183
Aland, Kurt & Barbra., 135, 183
Alexander, Desmond., viii, 183
Alexander, Loveday., 48, 183
Allison, D.C., 84, 152, 188
Appian, 2, 3, 90, 183
Applebaum, Shimon., 27, 183
Archer, G.L., xiii, 191, 193
Arichea, Daniel C., 79, 183
Aristophanes, 57, 183
Auld, A. Graeme., 75, 183
Aus, Roger D., 12, 80, 81, 94, 121, 129, 131, 132
Avishur, Yitshak., 99, 184

B

Bailey, John A., 8, 9, 12, 15, 17, 18, 120, 184
Baker, David., viii, 183
Balch, David., 59, 198, 207
Balz, H., ix, 32, 54, 59, 153, 184
Banker, John, 72, 184
Barclay, John M.G., 11, 34, 35, 184
Barram, Michael., 101, 184
Barrett, C.K., 46, 47, 52, 53, 54, 55, 56, 60, 64, 83, 104, 184
Barton, John., 103, 184
Bassler, Jouette., 77, 78, 92, 127, 128, 129, 184, 195, 196
Bauckham, Richard., 29, 74, 89, 98, 168, 184, 199

Bauer, Walter., vii, 184
Bauman, R.A., 64, 184
Baur, F.C., 6, 184
Beale, Gregory K., 43, 107, 158, 160, 164, 184
Beare, Francis W., 72, 184
Beasley-Murray, George., 158, 159, 185
Beker, Johan C., 8, 17, 43, 185
Becker, Jürgen., 24, 37, 185
Beckwith, Roger., 41, 185
Benoit, P., 35, 185
Bertram, G., 33, 185
Best, Ernest., 16, 50, 76, 83, 97, 100, 110, 117, 119, 124, 126, 137, 150, 153, 155, 156, 157, 170, 185
Betz, Hans D., 77, 185
Beutler, Johannes., 110, 185
Bicknell, E.J., 117, 134, 185
Birch, Bruce C., 127, 185
Black, Mark., 29, 185
Blass, F., vii, 185
Blenkinsopp, Joseph., 163, 185
Bloesch, Donald G., 95, 185
Blomberg, Craig., 7, 185
Bock, Darrell L., 102, 185
Boecker, Hans J., 85, 105, 185
Boeckh, A., vii, 185
Boers, Hendrikus., 116, 117, 185
Bornemann, Wilhelm., 6, 185
Bornkam, Günther., 24, 26, 185
Botterweck, G.J., xii, 185
Bovati, Pietro., 99, 102, 103, 105, 186
Bovon-Thurneysen, A., 82, 186
Bratcher, Robert G., 143, 186
Briggs, C.A., vii, 186
Brin, Gershon., 105, 186
Brindle, Wayne A., 149, 186
Brocke, Christoph von., 2, 186

Brooks, James A., 130, 186
Brown, Colin., x, 85, 186,
Brown, F.S.R., vii, 186
Brown, Raymond E., 162, 186
Brown, Stephen G., 162, 186
Bruce, F.F., 2, 16, 24, 25, 26, 34, 50, 51, 53, 54, 56, 57, 58, 59, 61, 62, 64, 76, 82, 91, 108, 113, 120, 137, 138, 140, 143, 146, 150, 155, 156, 160, 169, 170, 186
Brug, John F., 173, 186
Büchsel, Friedrich., 78, 167, 186
Bultmann, Rudolf., 7, 37, 38, 186
Burkeen, W.H., 152, 170, 186
Burton, E.D., 60, 187
Burtt, Edwin A., 37, 187

C

Cadbury, H.J., 26, 28, 46, 187, 197
Campbell, William S., 31, 35, 155, 187
Cambier, J.M., 76, 77, 187
Caneday, Ardel B., 155, 206
Carpenter, E., 74, 187
Carroll, John T., 79, 187
Carson, D.A., 43, 50, 79, 92, 162, 184, 187, 192, 203, 204
Cassidy, Richard J., 55, 60, 61, 62, 64, 102, 187
Černy, Ladislav., 107, 187
Chae, Young S., 84, 187
Charles, J. Daryl., 74, 98, 99, 187
Charles, R.H., 166, 187
Charlesworth, James H., 40, 187
Childs, Brevard S., 105, 187
Chilton, Bruce., 40, 187
Chilton, David., 107, 187
Chisholm, Robert B., 112, 187
Clement, 7, 12, 86, 99, 188
Clements, R.E., 75, 188, 212
Clines, David J., 90, 188
Coats, George, W., 112, 196
Collange, Jean Francois., 72, 188
Collins, Adela Y., 161, 188
Collins, Raymond., 8, 9, 13, 120, 192, 193, 196, 199, 200, 205

Coppes, L.J., 74, 188
Court, J.M., 84, 188
Cranfield, C.E.B., 58, 188
Culy, Martin M., 53, 188
Curkpatrick, Stephen., 102, 188
Curtius, E., viii, 185

D

Dana, H.E., 72, 188
Danby, H., 188
Davis, James, F., 92, 188
Davies, W.D., 31, 42, 61, 84, 128, 144, 152, 155, 188
Day, John N., 101, 188
Day Peggy L., 102, 188
de Boer, Martinus C., 15, 188
de Villiers, Pieter G.R., 170, 189
Debrunner, A., vii, 185
Deissmann, Adolf., 29, 188
Delling, Gerhard., 107, 188
Demosthenes., 75, 82, 103, 113, 189
den Heyer, C.J., 24, 189
Denney, James., 154, 189
Denton, D.R., 128, 189
deSilva, David., 113, 124, 189
Dewailly, L.M., 169, 189,
Dibelius, Martin., 30, 144, 189
Dio Cassius., 5, 26, 56, 189
Diodorus Siculus., 57, 189
Diogenes., 106, 189
Dionysius. , 2, 47, 189
Dittenberger, W., ix, xi, xii, 35, 189
Dixon, Paul S., 162, 189
Dobschütz, Ernst von., 126, 127, 157, 189
Dodd, C.H., 43, 189
Donahue, John R., 161, 189
Donfried, Karl P., 51, 52, 59, 62, 63, 64, 117, 129, 160, 189
Doukhan, Jacques B., 165, 189
Dunham, Duane A., 116, 189
Dunn, James D.G., 43, 60, 64, 66, 77, 88, 91, 107, 190
Duttenhöfer, R., xi, 210
Dyer, Keith D., 161, 190

E

Eadie, John., 156, 190
Edson, Charles., 2, 190
Ehrenberg, Victor., 63, 190
Ehrensperger, Kathy., xv, 31, 190
Ellicott, Charles J., 126, 190
Ellingworth, Paul., 103, 109, 120, 130, 131, 190
Ellis, E. Earle., 41, 190
Engberg-Pedersen, T., 38, 190
Eusebius., 6, 190
Evans, Craig A., viii, 128, 186, 188, 190

F

Farrow, Douglas., 162, 190
Fee, Gordon D., 72, 73, 98, 132, 149, 190
Feinberg, Paul D., 149, 151, 191
Fekkes, Jan., 107, 191
Feldman, L.H., 54, 191
Ferguson, Everett., 4, 5, 191, 194, 198
Ferguson, William D., 60, 191
Field, D.H., 57, 191,
Fields, Weston W., 99, 191
Findlay, G.G., 100, 191
Fiore, Benjamin., 98, 191
Fitzmyer, Joseph A., 35, 78, 191
Fletcher-Louis, Crispin., 95, 191
Ford, Desmond., 160, 191
Ford, J.M., 77, 191
Forester, W., 54, 191
Frame, James E., 10, 50, 83, 91, 101, 103, 104, 110, 120, 122, 124, 126, 133, 135, 137, 153, 156, 157, 160, 170, 191
France, R.T., 41, 161, 191
Franz, J., viii, 185
Freed Edwin D., 23, 191
Freedman, David N., vii, 191
Freiherr, F., ix, 189
Friedrich, G., xiii, 196
Fudge, Edward., 80, 138, 139, 191
Fuhs, H.F., 74, 191
Fuks, G., 29, 191

Fung, Ronald Y.K., 88, 191
Fürst, D., 33, 192

G

Gaertringen, H. Von., ix, 189
Gager, John G., 15, 192
Gane, R.E., 74, 192
Garlington, Don., 88, 192
Gasque, W. Ward., 25, 192
Gaventa, Beverly H., 8, 192
Geddert, Timothy J., 161, 192
Gempf, Conrad., 192, 194
Giblin, Charles., 70, 82, 91, 149, 153, 160, 192
Gill, David W.J., 192, 194
Gillman-Morgan, F., 58, 192, 200
Glasson T. Francis., 94, 95, 96, 192
Goguel, Maurice., 14, 192
Goldingay, John E., 165, 192
Goldstein, Horst., 100, 192
Goulder, Michael D., 19, 165, 192
Grech, P., 38, 192
Green, Gene L., xviii, 5, 6, 7, 15, 16, 17, 20, 50, 76, 82, 83, 86, 87, 91, 97, 100, 101, 103, 104, 106, 107, 114, 117, 118, 122, 124, 125, 127, 129, 130, 131, 132, 133, 134, 136, 137, 140, 141, 142, 143, 146, 150, 153, 155, 160, 162, 167, 170, 171, 173, 192
Green Michael., 139, 192
Greenberg, Moshe., 102, 192
Greenlee, J. Harold., 135, 192
Greeven, H., 173, 192
Grenfell, B.P., xi, 192
Gschnitzer, Fritz., 60, 192
Gundry Volf, Judith M., 155, 156, 192
Gunther, John J., 88, 192
Günther, W., 54, 192

H

Haacker, Klaus., 50, 193
Habel, Norman C., 90, 192
Haenchen, Ernst., 34, 56, 60, 192

Hafemann, Scott J., 128, 193, 208
Hahn, H.C., 55, 193
Hamilton, Victor P., 99, 193
Hammond, Nicholas G., 2, 193
Hamp, Vinzenz., 99, 193
Hannah, Darrell D., 162, 165, 166, 193
Hanton, Howard A., 79, 183
Harder, Günther., 121, 193
Harding, M., x, 195
Harrington, Daniel J., 74, 113, 161, 189, 193
Harnack, Adolf von., 29, 193
Harris, Murray J., 52, 87, 89, 91, 106, 133, 139, 141, 168, 193
Harris, R.L., xiii, 193
Harrison, R.K., 112, 193
Hartman, Lars., 158, 160, 193
Hastings, James., ix, 193
Hatzopoulos, M.B., 60, 193
Hawthorne, Gerald F., viii, 72, 193
Hays, Richard B., 41, 43, 88, 193
Heil John P., 84, 193
Hemer, Colin J., 25, 46, 47, 48, 64, 194
Hendrix, Holland L., 3, 4, 194
Hengel, Martin., 23, 24, 25, 26, 28, 29, 31, 34, 35, 46, 49, 194
Herbert, A.S., 163, 194
Herodotus., 57, 90, 93, 194
Hester, James D., 144, 194
Hickling, C.J.A., 105, 194
Hiebert, D. Edmond., 148, 194
Hill, David., 85, 86, 194
Hill, Judith L., 2, 16, 55, 194
Hock, Ronald F., 25, 26, 194
Holland, Glenn., 13, 18, 94, 158, 194
Holland, Tom., xv, 39, 40, 41, 42, 43, 194
Holley, George H., 37, 38, 194
Hornblower, S., xi, 194
Horsley, G.H.R., x, 59, 60, 194
Howard, D.M., 139, 194
Hubbard, D.A., 43, 194
Hubbard, Robert L., 85, 195
Hughes, Frank W., 17, 129, 149, 195
Hunt, A.S., xi, xii, 192, 195

I

Ignatius., 99, 195
Irenaeus., 6, 7, 195
Isocrates., 75, 195

J

Jackson, F.J.F, 46, 187, 197
Jenni, Ernst., xiii, 109, 195
Jerome., 29, 195
Jervell, Jacob., 46, 195, 198
Jewett, Robert., 4, 6, 7, 8, 10, 46, 50, 58, 88, 116, 124, 171, 173, 174, 195
Johnson, J. de M., xii, 195
Johnson, Luke T., 61, 64, 73, 195
Johnson, S. Lewis., 78, 92, 195
Johnson, Sherman E., 2, 195
Jones, A.H.M., 57, 190, 195
Jornot, I., xi, 202
Josephus., 12, 27, 28, 32, 40, 48, 54, 56, 57, 59, 86, 90, 93, 99, 102, 106, 110, 195
Joubert, Stephan J., 98, 195
Judge, E.A. , 59, 61, 62, 63, 64, 195

K

Kaiser, Otto., 134, 195
Kaiser, W., 74, 195
Kapelrud, Arvid S., 109, 196
Käsemann, Ernst., 58. 196
Katz, Peter., 136, 196
Kaye, B.N., 53, 196
Kearsley, R.A., x, 194
Kennedy, H.A.A., 75, 154, 159, 196
Keener, Craig S., 84, 196
Keesmaat, Sylvia C., 127, 128, 139, 140, 196
Kilgallen, John J., 111, 196
Kim, Johann D., 155, 196
King, Greg A., 109, 196
Kirchhoff, A., viii, 185
Kittel, Gerhard., xiii, 134, 196
Klassen, William., 101, 196
Klein, Ralph W., 139, 196

Klein, Robert, W., 107, 196
Klein, William W., 156, 196
Klingbeil, M.G., 139, 196
Knierim, Rolf P., 112, 196
Knight, George W., 73, 111, 196
Knight, Jonathon., 74, 196
Koester, Craig., 108, 197
Koester, Helmut., xviii, 8, 17, 45, 46, 158, 170, 197
Köhler, Wilhem., 87, 196
Konkel, A.H., 74, 196
Krentz, Edgar., 129, 138, 168, 196
Krodel, Gerhard., 129, 162, 164, 197
Kühlewein, J., 74, 75, 197
Kurze, Georg., 134, 135, 197

L

Lake, Kirsopp., 46, 54, 183, 187, 188, 190, 195, 197, 203
Lambrecht, Jan., 170, 197
Lamp, Jeffrey S., 77, 78, 197
Lampe, Peter., 172, 197
Lang, F., 97, 98, 99, 197
Lanier, David E., 110, 197
LaRondelle, Hans K., 144, 154, 197
Le Tellier, Robert I., 99, 197
Lebram, J.C.H., 158, 197
Leclerc, Thomas L., 80, 197
Lenger, M.T., xi, 192
Lenski, R.C.H., 130, 197
Levinskaya, Irina., 54, 197
Levinsohn, Stephen H., 55, 197
Lewis, J.P., 74, 197
Liddell, Henry George., x, 197
Lightfoot, J.B., 62, 154, 197
Lillie, William., 91, 198
Lindars, Barnabas., 38, 95, 198
Lindsey, F. Duane., 127, 198
Lipinvski, E. , 105, 198
Livy., 3, 198
Llewelyn, S.R., x, 194
Loh, I-Jin., 72, 198
Longenecker, Richard., 19, 23, 198, 200
Longman, Tremper., 80, 81, 198
Louw, J.P., x, 61, 198

Lowery, David K., 118, 198
Lucian., 47, 198
Lührman, Dieter., 52, 198
Lünemann, Gottlieb., 137, 198
Lyall, Francis., 61, 198
Lysias., 75, 82, 198

M

Maccoby, Hyam., xviii, 30, 31, 37, 198
Magdalene, F. Rachel., 90, 198
Malherbe, Abraham., 6, 8, 12, 50, 51, 52, 58, 76, 78, 86, 87, 91, 97, 101, 103, 104, 120, 122, 124, 130, 134, 135, 137, 138, 140, 141, 142, 143, 144, 153, 155, 160, 161, 170, 199
Malul, Meir., 102, 199
Manson, Thomas W., 84, 199
Mantey, J.R., 72, 188
Manus, C.U., 62, 199
Marguerat, Daniel., 46, 47, 48, 92, 199
Marshall, I. Howard., 8, 13, 14, 19, 46, 47, 48, 49, 51, 73, 95, 111, 117, 120, 130, 133, 136, 137, 143, 145, 146, 151, 153, 154, 156, 160, 167, 170, 189, 199, 201, 204
Martin, George., 127, 199
Martin, R.P., viii, 193
Martin, V., xii, 195
Marxsen, Willi., 7, 199
McClain, T. Van., 149, 199
McDonald, Lee M., 7, 199
McGaughy, Lane C., 53, 199
McKay, John., 24, 27, 199
McKay, Kenneth L. , 143, 199
McRay, J.P., 2, 25, 42, 199
Meadowcroft, Tim., 165, 199
Mealy, J. Webb., 107, 199
Mearns, C.L., 95, 170, 199
Meeks, Wayne A., 2, 58, 124, 198, 200
Menken, Maarten J.J., 10, 14, 118, 119, 138, 141, 143, 145, 146, 153, 155, 157, 160, 170, 171, 200
Metzger, Bruce M., 53, 54, 89, 103, 119, 157, 200

Metzger, Paul., 162, 200
Michel, O., 61, 200
Millar, Fergus., 64, 200, 206
Milligan, George., x, 7, 137, 153, 162, 170, 200, 201
Mitteis, L., xi, 210
Moffatt, James., x, 109, 200
Moo, Douglas J., 50, 58, 76, 77, 88, 152, 187, 200
Moore, Carey A., 82, 200, 209
Mordtmann, J.H., 3, 200
Morgan-Gillman, F., 58, 200
Morgenthaler, Robert., 10, 200
Morris, Leon., 50, 51, 76, 79, 83, 84, 85, 91, 97, 103, 104, 107, 113, 117, 119, 120, 121, 122, 123, 126, 142, 145, 150, 152, 153, 157, 187, 200
Mosley, A.W., 46, 200
Moule, C.F.D., 73, 139, 200
Moulton, James H., x, 64, 200
Mounce, William D., 73, 111, 201
Muddiman, John., 103, 184
Müller, H., 66, 201
Murphy-O'Connor, J., 24, 25, 30, 32, 52, 56, 58, 201
Mussies, G., 35, 201

N

Nanos, Mark D., 43, 88, 201
Naudé, Jackie A., 99, 201
Neagoe, Alexandru., 59, 60, 201
Neil, William., 51, 114, 135, 141, 156, 201
Neufeld, Thomas R., 93, 201
Neusner, Jacob., 27, 40, 187, 201, 203, 207
Newman, Barclay M., 51, 64, 201
Neyrey, Jerome H., 61, 74, 202
Nicholl, Colin R., 116, 133, 162, 165, 166, 202
Nickelsburg, George., 27, 41, 201
Nicole, J., xi, 201
Nida, Eugene A., x, 51, 61, 64, 72, 103, 120, 130, 131, 190, 198, 201

Niehaus, Jeffrey., 136, 201
Ninow, Friedbert., 136, 144, 201,
Noack, B., 43, 202,
Noack, Christian., 34, 202
Nock, A.D., 26, 27, 202
Nolland, John., 151, 202
Noth, Martin., 105, 202

O

O'Brien, Peter T., 70, 72, 91, 119, 145, 187, 202
Oepke, A., 94, 202
Oropeza, B.J., 154, 155, 202
Osborne, Grant R., 77, 202
Otto, Kaiser., ix, 134, 189, 196

P

Papazoglou, Fanoula., 4, 202
Parsons, Mikeal C., 53, 188
Paul, Shalom M., 89, 202
Peels, H.G.L., 93, 202
Perdue, Leo G., 89, 202
Perrin, N., 15, 16, 202
Pervo, Richard I., 46, 202
Pesch, Rudolf., 52, 58, 202
Philo., 12, 28, 29, 33, 34, 35, 75, 86, 99, 106, 112, 202
Photius., 29, 202
Plato., 57, 75, 82, 202
Plevnik, Joseph., 92, 93, 94, 202
Pobee, John S., 131, 202
Polhill, John B., 23, 24, 25, 28, 56, 203
Polybius., 128, 203
Polycarp., 7, 82, 203
Pond, Eugene W., 84, 203
Portefaix, Lilian., 55, 203
Porter, Stanley E., viii, 7, 12, 32, 76, 79, 87, 105, 122, 125, 140, 142, 143, 150, 151, 152, 190, 196, 199, 203, 204
Powell, Charles E., 162, 164, 203
Powell, Mark A., 47, 48, 49, 203
Powery, Emerson B., 41, 203
Prat, Ferdinand., 114, 203

Preisigke, Friedrich., 113, 203
Preuss, H.D., 142, 203
Proctor, John., 98, 203

Q

Quarles, Charles L., 139, 140, 203
Quell, G., 105, 203

R

Rabello, A.M., 26, 203
Rahlfs, Alfred., 103, 203
Räisänen, H., 87, 203
Raitt, Thomas M., 139, 203
Rajak, Tessa., 26, 203
Ramsay, William M., 25, 26, 27, 52, 204
Rapske, Brian., 25, 56, 204
Read-Heimerdinger, J., 53, 204
Reddit, Paul L., 158, 188, 204
Reed, Jeffrey T., 70, 204
Reid, D.G., viii, 80, 81, 113, 193, 198
Reider, Joseph., 113, 204
Reimer, David J., 85, 204
Reitzenstein, Richard., 30, 204
Reyburn, William D., 143, 186
Richard, Earl J., 8, 45, 46, 204
Riddlebarger, Kim., 158, 204
Rider, G.W., 151, 204
Riesenfeld, Ernst., 87, 204
Riesner, Rainer., 49, 204
Rigaux, Béda., 6, 7, 10, 127, 138, 167, 204
Ringgren, H., xiii, 185
Rissi, Mathias., 78, 167, 204
Roberts, C.H., xii, 195
Roberts, J.J.M., 89, 90, 204
Robertson, A.T., 72, 76, 151, 204
Robinson, J.M., 8, 204
Roehl, H., viii, 185
Roetzel, Calvin J., 32, 37, 156, 204
Romaniuk, K., 54, 204
Rosenblatt, Marie-Eloise., 104, 105, 204
Rowland, Christopher., 127, 205
Russell, Ronald., 170, 171, 172, 205

S

Saebø, M., 109, 205
Saldarini, Anthony J., 27, 205
Sand, A., 91, 205
Sanders, E.P., 87, 205
Sanders, Jack T., 45, 46, 205
Sauer, G., 74, 105, 205
Savran, George W., 136, 205
Schaefer, Konrad R., 134, 205
Schlatter, Adolf., 78, 92, 205
Schlier, H., 153, 205
Schmidt, Daryl., 13, 205
Schmithals, Walter., 50, 170, 205
Schnabel, Eckhard J., 25, 26, 29, 34, 205
Schneider, Gerhard., ix, 33, 57, 58, 83, 103, 139, 141, 142, 184, 205
Schnelle, Udo., xviii, 205
Scholnick, Sylvia H., 90, 205
Schrage, W., 152, 205
Schreiner, Thomas., 58, 77, 88, 155, 205, 211
Schrenk, G., 83, 86, 100, 102, 103, 104, 205, 206
Schroeder, Christoph O., 85, 206
Schubert, P., xi, 201
Schuler, C., 60, 206
Schultz, Richard., 80, 81, 206
Schürer, Emil., 19, 28, 206
Schwartz, Earl., 105, 206
Schwemer, Maria., 23, 194
Scott, J. Julius., 27, 40, 154, 206
Seeligmann, I.L., 99, 206
Seland, Torrey., 56, 206
Seybold, K., 74, 206
Sharp, Granville., 150, 151, 206
Shelton, Jo-Ann, 4, 206
Sherlock, Charles., 80, 206
Sherwin-White, A.N., 57, 60, 62, 206
Shires, Henry M., 94, 206
Showerman, Grant., 57, 206
Silva, Moisés., 27, 72, 88, 206
Sim, David C., 84, 152, 206
Simpson, John W., 2, 4, 206
Skeen, Judy., 170, 173, 206
Skinner, Matthew L., 104, 207
Smallwood, E. Mary., 26, 63, 207

Smith, Abraham., 121, 207
Smith, Gary V., 80, 207
Smith, John M.P., 107, 207
Soards, Marion L., 105, 111, 207
Spawforth, A., xi, 194
Spicq, Ceslas., xiii, 32, 64, 66, 73, 83, 103, 108, 110, 207
Stacy, R. Wayne., 19, 207
Stambaugh, John., 59, 207
Standhartinger, Angela., 91, 207
Stanley, Christopher D., 41, 108, 207
Stanton, Gerald B., 149, 207
Staples, Peter., 77, 207
Stec, D.M., 75, 207
Stegemann, Wolfgang., 25, 28, 62, 207
Steinmann, Andrew E., 158, 207
Stemberger, Günter., 27, 207
Stenschke, Christoph W., 15, 207
Stern, Menahem., 28, 207
Still, Todd D., 16, 46, 47, 52, 57, 59, 60, 70, 91, 101, 107, 124, 125, 208
Stock, Augustine., 144, 208
Stone, Michael E., 27, 201
Stott, John R.W., 51, 208
Strabo., 2, 3, 24, 208
Strathmann, Hermann., 110, 208
Stuhlmacher, Peter., 88, 208
Stumpff, A., 55, 208
Suetonius., 4, 5, 208

T

Tacitus., 5, 208
Tajra, Harry W., 26, 59, 60, 62, 63, 64, 65, 104, 105, 208
Talbert, Charles H., 60, 208
Tate, Marvin E., 143, 208
Taylor, Justin., 56, 208
Tertullian., 6, 7, 208
Thatcher, Tom., 88, 208
Theissen, Gerd., 58, 208
Theophrastus., 57, 208
Thielman, Frank., 88, 208
Thiselton, Anthony., 98, 208
Thrall, Margaret E., 55, 208
Thucydides., 90, 93, 208

Thurston, Bonnie., 8, 9, 17, 209
Tiemeyer, Lena-Sofia., 163, 209
Tobin, Thomas H., 88, 209
Tomlinson, Alan., xv, 117, 209
Travis, Stephen H., 78, 114, 129, 131, 209
Trilling, Wolfgang., 8, 10, 13, 14, 17, 107, 119, 120, 209
Trites, Allison A., 111, 112, 209
Turner, E.G., xi, 195
Turner, G., xi, 192
Turner, Nigel., 51, 87, 122, 142, 151, 209

V

Vacalopoulos, A.E., 4, 5, 209
Van der Lugt, Pieter., 90, 209,
Van der Minde, H.J., 83, 209
VanGemeren, Willem A., xi, 43, 109, 158, 209
Van Leeuwen, C., 112, 209
Van Minnen, Peter., 25, 29, 209
Van Unnik, W.C., 31, 32, 34, 35, 47, 209
Verhoef, Eduard., 165, 209
Vermes, Geza., 40, 89, 206, 209
Vos, Geerhardus., 94, 209

W

Waddle, Sharon H., 90, 209
Wagner, J. Ross., 128, 209
Wallace, Daniel B., 12, 32, 53, 72, 76, 78, 79, 87, 122, 130, 139, 142, 150, 151, 152, 156, 210
Wanamaker, Charles., 6, 7, 8, 11, 13, 16, 51, 76, 78, 82, 83, 87, 97, 100, 101, 107, 110, 113, 119, 120, 124, 125, 126, 127, 129, 130, 133, 134, 135, 136, 137, 140, 141, 142, 143, 144, 153, 154, 160, 162, 171, 210
Ward, James M., 143, 210
Waterman, G. Henry., 158, 159, 210
Watson, Duane F., 98, 210
Weaver, Dorothy J., 102, 210
Weber, Kathleen., 84, 210

Wedderburn, Alexander., 34, 210
Wehrli, C., xi, 201
Weima, Jeffrey A.D., 158, 159, 160, 210
Wells, Colin M., 4, 210
Wendland, Ernst R., 139, 210
Wenham, David., 158, 159, 161, 210
Wenham, John W., 139, 210
Weitbrecht, Stanton., 61, 210
Wessely, J.C., xi, 210
Westblade, Donald J., 156, 210
Westermann, Claus., xiii, 163, 195, 210
White, John L., 70, 210
Whitehorne, John., 161, 210
Whittaker, Molly., 28, 210
Wibery, Carlton L., 130, 186
Wiedemann, T.E.J., 4, 5, 211
Wikenhauser, Alfred., 7, 211
Wilder, Terry L., 16, 73, 211
William, David K., 97, 98, 211
Williams, David J., 83, 100, 101, 103, 110, 111, 113, 134, 138, 142, 143, 149, 150, 156, 157, 158, 160, 166, 211
Wilson, Alistair I., 84, 211
Wilson, A.N., 25, 211
Wilson, Todd A., 154, 211
Winter, Bruce W., 42, 55, 58, 170, 171, 172, 184, 192, 211
Witherington, Ben., 7, 27, 42, 54, 55, 59, 60, 62, 91, 96, 97, 98, 101, 134, 137, 156, 211
Wodecki, P. Bernard., 163, 211
Wood, C.T., 24, 211
Wrede, William., 7, 211
Wright, J.S., 54, 211
Wright, N.T., 128, 211

X

Xenophon., 57, 103, 113, 211

Y

Yinger, Kent L., 101, 212
Young, Norman H., 88, 212

Z

Zahn, Theodor., 159, 212
Zerwick, Maximilian., 72, 212
Zimmerli, Walther., 102, 212

Scripture Index

OLD TESTAMENT

Genesis

3:17–19	171
15:6	88
16:5	79
18:28	131
19:23–24	99

Exodus

3:2	134, 136
14:23–31	136
14:24	99
19:13	134
19:16	134
19:19	134
20:12	91
20:16	112
21	105
21:20	105
23:7	85
24:14	79
33	127

Leviticus

5:1	112
26:25	105
26:28	33
28	33

Numbers

1:20	59
1:22	59
5:11–31	112
5:12–31	75,
5:13	112
14	127
16:46	106, 140
25:5	79, 80

Deuteronomy

4:36	33
5:16	91
8:5	33
17:6	111
19:15	111
21:18	33
22:14	112
32:6	74, 91
32:33	97
32:35	83, 85, 91, 101, 131
32:41–43	105

Joshua

6:15–21	99
7:14–18	74
22:22	153

Judges

5:5	106, 140
13:2	59

1 Kings

8:31–32	131
8:32	79, 85

2 Kings

17:37	41

1 Chronicles

28:12	161
29:2	161

2 Chronicles

3:3	161
4:11	161
5:14	161
6:22–23	131
29:19	153

Ezra

1:14	161

Job

1–20	90, 188
4–14	210
8	89
9–10	89
9:2	89
9:15	80
9:20–22	90

Psalms

7:1–17	85
7:8–9	131
7:11	131
9:4	131
9:8	131
9:19	80
19:9	127
27:4–5	93
28:7	135
34:16	106, 140
35:25	131
37:9	91
44	127
54	85
59	85
62:12	73, 92
67:36	142
79:6	137
88:8	142, 143
96:13	106, 140
98:2	95
103:6	85
109	85
119:37	127
137:8	74

Proverbs

3:11	33
13:24	33
15:32–33	33
19:18	33
20:22	104
24:12	93
27:12	104

Isaiah

2:10	106, 107, 139, 140
2:19	107
2:21	107
3:11	74
8:15	74
13	134
13:1–10	109, 142
13:2–16	95
14:13–14	158
28:13	74

Isaiah - continued

29:6	97, 99, 135
34:8	78, 131
35:4	131
41:21–29	85
43:26	80
49:4	89
51–55	127
51:3	144, 146
52:12	152
54:17	91
56:8	152
59	93
61:2	93
63:1–6	93, 93
63:4	93
66	80, 81, 131, 136, 162, 163
66:4	137
66:4–6	131
66:6	93, 131
66:7	81
66:9	80
66:15	94, 135, 136
66:15–16	99, 100
66:15–18	135, 136
66:16	80, 136
66:18–24	132, 152, 165
66:19	163
66:24	97

Jeremiah

1:14–19	167
2:19	153
4:4	99
4:22	137
5:14	99
6:11	74
9:3	137
10:25	137
11:20	102
15:10–11	127
15:15	127
21:12	99
24:4–7	144, 146
25:30	93
25:31	80, 139
31:31–34	144, 146
46–51	139
51:6	93

Lamentations

1:15	93
3:64	131

Ezekiel

11:23	165
13:5	109, 142
16:38–41	102
16:41	102
17:20	80
20:18	173
21:36	99
25–32	139
25:17	102
28:8–9	158
34	84
37	139
37:10	152

Daniel

5:3	161
7:9	135
8:24	59
9:16	59
10–12	165
10:13–21	165
11	161
11:31	158
11:36–37	158
11:36–45	158
12:1	166

Hosea

4:1	167
5:4	137
6:5	78
7:8	173
7:12	33
8:12	41
9:7	102
10:10	33

Joel

1:15	109, 142
3–4	19
3:12	78
3:13	93

Amos

5:18–20	95, 109, 142

Micah

7:4	102

Habakkuk

2:4	88, 88

Zephaniah

1	109
1:12	109
1:18	99
3:5	99

Haggai

2:22	139

Zechariah

9:12	152
14:5	134

Malachi

3	98

NEW TESTAMENT

Matthew

3:11	98
5:12	98
5:17–18	41
7:13	72
7:22	108
10:15	78, 79
10:18	111
11:20–24	79
12:36	73
13:24	53
13:31	53
16:16	156
16:24–26	92
16:27	92
24:3	133
24:4–15	159
24:9	xvii, 153
24:14	165
24:15	161
24:31	15
24:36	152
25:31–46	83
25:37	32
25:41	138
25:42	98

Mark

4:11	162
7:34	52
13	19
13:5–27	159
13:9	111
13:14–27	161
14:21	41
14:63	111
15:15	64

Luke

2:1	61
2:23	52
3:16	98
4:16	32
8:13	154
10:12	108
12:8	134
14:12–14	92
17:22–37	95
17:30	94
18:1–8	101
18:7	101
21:10–19	123
21:12	151
21:22	101
22:37	41
23:2	64
23:16	33
23:22	33
23:29	32
23:55–24:35	55
24:27	41
24:31	52
24:32	52
24:44–45	41
24:45	52

John

3:18–21	79
5:27–28	79
5:29	79

Acts

1:8	165
2:19	97
4:18	113
5:1–11	55
5:17	55
6:7	137
6:13	111
7	112
7:2–50	111
7:9	55
7:20	32
7:20–21	32
7:20–22	33
7:21	32
7:22	33
7:24	101
7:58	111
9:32–42	55
13:14	54
13:16	15
13:45	55
14:1	15
16:8–13	66
16:13–34	55
16:14	52, 54
16:37–39	25
17	30, 69, 115, 177
17:1–2	15, 51
17:1–9	v, 45, 46, 49, 50, 51, 66, 71
17:3	52
17:4	15, 55
17:6–9	60
17:7	146
17:9	64
17:10–13	50
17:12	15
17:14–15	50
17:17	15
17:31	77, 78
18:4	15
18:5	15, 50
18:6–7	58
18:12	50, 57
19:23	66
19:38	57
20	50
21:20	55
21:38	61
21:39	25
22	30
22:3	24, 25, 31, 32, 33

	34, 36, 55	5:3–5	123, 155
22:25–29	25	5:5	170
22:25–30	25	5:9	78
22:28	29	5:12	38
23:6	27	5:19	83
23:27	25	6:13	83
24:2	113	6:16	83
24:5	61	7:15–18	38
24:27	104	7:24	37
25	104	8:9	131
25:1–3	104	8:14–17	128
25:6–12	25	8:18	94
25:8	104	8:23	37
25:15	104	8:39	170
28:4	104	9–11	155
28:23	53	9:3–4	155
		9:22	72
		11:1–10	91
		11:25	162

Romans

1–3	76, 78	11:30–32	137
1:2	24, 41	11:35	91
1:3	121	12:9–21	101
1:7	117, 119, 143, 168	12:14–21	101
1:17	83	12:19	91, 100, 101
1:24	78	12:20	97
2	92	15:21	165
2:1–11	78	15:31	56
2:5	76, 94	16:21	58
2:6	92	16:25	94, 133
2:6–8	73	16:25–26	41
2:8	78		
2:11	87, 137		
2:13	83, 87, 88		

1 Corinthians

2:15	72	1:2	143
3:4	83	1:3	117, 119, 168
3:5	78	1:7	94
3:20	83, 88	1:7–8	133
3:21–22	83	1:8	80, 108, 133
3:23	137	1:10	121
3:24	83	1:18	72, 163
3:24–26	88	3	97, 98
3:26	76	3:13	94, 133
3:28	88	3:13–15	97, 98
4:7	121	3:15	78

1 Corinthians - continued

3:19	87
4:1	162
4:4	83
5:5	80
6:11	83
10:11	94
11:23–26	15
11:32	33
15	11
15:3–7	15
15:15	110
15:24	167
15:26	167

2 Corinthians

1:2	119, 168
1:3–7	14
1:8	121
1:14	80
2:15	163
3:18	146
4:16	37
5:10	167
5:21	83
6:1–10	123
6:3–13	169
7:5	132
7:11	101
7:14	123
8:8–13	132
8:24	123
9:3	123
9:9–10	83
10:6	101
11:24	56
13:13	170

Galatians

1:1	168
1:3	119
1:3–4	117
1:6–7	88
1:12	133
1:13–24	31
2:16	83
3:1–18	88
3:8	41
3:11	87, 88
6:11–13	88

Ephesians

1:2	119, 168
1:17	133
1:20–23	80
3:4–7	162
5:6	78, 142
5:9	83
6:2–3	91

Philippians

1:1–7	122
1:2	119
1:6	80, 108
1:21–24	72
1:22–23	72
1:26	133
1:27–28	129
1:28	72
1:29	128
2:1	82
2:6–11	15
2:10	80
3:4–7	31
3:9	83
3:14	128
3:20–21	128
4:16	51, 173

Colossians

1:1–12	122
1:2	119
1:9–10	80

3:6	78, 142	5:8–9	72
3:18–4:1	91	5:9	78
3:22–25	91	5:12–14	173
3:24	91, 128		

2 Thessalonians

1 Thessalonians

		1	v, xvii, xviii, 20, 21, 22
1:1	6, 71		24, 44, 68, 69, 70, 71, 76
1:2	9, 12, 117		79, 81, 86, 87, 93, 94, 96
1:2–3	67		98, 100, 103, 110, 113, 114
1:2–10	66, 156		116, 137, 148, 162, 163
1:3	9, 120, 122		168, 175, 176, 177, 178,
1:3–10	155		179, 180
1:4	65, 121	1:1	71
1:6	124	1:1–2	116, 146
1:8	65, 123	1:1–12	v, 146, 178
1:9–10	65	1:2	9, 168
1:10	19, 78	1:3	9
2:1	121	1:3–4	66
2:1–6	65	1:3–10	116, 116
2:7–8	51	1:3–12	14
2:9	51, 52	1:4	12, 70, 156
2:10	65	1:4–5	18
2:13	9, 12	1:4–7	14, 65
2:13–16	66	1:4–10	71
2:14	82, 124, 125	1:5	76, 78, 82, 86
2:14–16	55, 56, 65, 66, 70	1:5–8	80
3:1–3	124	1:5–10	114, 123, 178, 195
3:2	50	1:6	83, 90
3:2–3	65	1:6–7	70
3:3–5	124	1:7	12
3:6–13	156	1:8	97, 100
3:10	120, 122	1:9	104, 106, 140
3:13	143	1:10	53, 65, 113
4:2	142	1:11	113, 156
4:5	137	1:11–12	116
4:6	100, 101, 110	2	130, 152, 160, 179
4:11–12	172, 173	2:1	121, 149, 150, 151, 152
4:13–18	14	2:1–2	130
4:13–5:13	11	2:1–7	165
4:16	133, 134, 166	2:1–12	11, 18
4:17	156	2:1–15	133
5:2	17, 66, 108, 142	2:2	16, 18
5:3	138		

2 Thessalonians - continued

2:3–4	17, 159
2:5	19, 66, 115, 149, 157, 164
2:6	164
2:6–7	166
2:8–12	155, 164
2:9–12	166
2:13	9, 65, 72, 121
2:13–14	156
2:13–15	66
2:15	12, 121
3	174
3:1	12, 121
3:7–9	52
3:8–9	172
3:17	7

Hebrews

1:1	94
3:12	154
10:25	108
10:27	98
10:30	91, 92, 101
10:38	83
12:6	33
12:7	33
12:10	33
12:23	78

James

1:2–4	123, 128
1:27	89
5:5	32

1 Peter

1:5–7	128, 133
1:7	94
1:13	94
2:3	131
2:14	101
2:20	89
2:23	77
3:6	91
4:13	94
4:17–19	127

2 Peter

2:1	72
2:4–10	74
2:6–9	74
2:11	89
3:7	98
3:8	89

Jude

1–7	98
4–8	104
6	78, 79
7	74, 98, 138
9	166

Revelation

6:16	106, 140
6:17	108
9:17–18	97
12:6	32
12:7–9	166, 166
12:14	32
14:7	79
14:19	93
16	77
16:4–6	77
16:5	83
16:7	77
18:6–7	131
19:1–2	131
19:15	93
20:11	106, 107, 140
20:11–15	91, 167
22:12	73, 92

www.ingramcontent.com/pod-product-compliance
Lightning Source LLC
Chambersburg PA
CBHW071941240426
43669CB00048B/2554